MIMESIS
INTERNATIONAL

SOCIOLOGY
n. 16

AF580692

FRANCESCO BAGNARDI

MANUFACTURING INFORMALITY

Global Production Networks and Informalized Labour Regimes in Europe's Peripheries

This research was financially supported by a PhD grant funded by the Italian Ministry of Foreign Affairs and the European University Institute. Part of the volume was finalised within the SHARE project, which has received funding from the European Research Council (ERC) under the European Union's Horizon 2020 research and innovation programme (Grant agreement No. 715950).

The research for this manuscript started as a PhD dissertation project I undertook at the European University Institute in Fiesole a few years ago. As in any long-term research, there is a long list of people who were crucial for its completion whom I am grateful to. In particular, the guidance of Prof. Dorothee Bohle and the support of Prof. Annalisa Murgia were fundamental to convince me I could write a PhD dissertation first, and even a book later. I am grateful to colleagues, friends and family who provided support, critical feedback, love and happiness in the making of this work. I am particularly indebted to my wife Tika and my parents Rosanna and Enzo. Finally, I am grateful to the gate-keepers and workers who shared their stories and a piece of their struggles with me. My debt with them is the heaviest and remains unpaid.

© 2024 – Mimesis International
www.mimesisinternational.com
e-mail: info@mimesisinternational.com

Book series: *Sociology*, n. 16

Isbn: 9788869774874

© MIM Edizioni Srl
P.I. C.F. 0241937030

TABLE OF CONTENTS

LIST OF TABLES

LIST OF FIGURES

LIST OF ABBREVIATIONS

AIDA	Albanian Investment and Development Agency
BAT	Barletta-Andria-Trani
BSPSH	Bashkimi I Sindikatave të Pavarura të Shqipërisë (Union of the Independent Trade Unions of Albania)
CGIL	Confederazione Generale Italiana del Lavoro (Italian General Confederation of Labour)
CISL	Confederazione Italiana Sindacati Lavoratori (Italian Confederation of Workers' Trade Unions)
CLES	Committees for Formalization of Irregular Labour
CMT	Cut, make and trim
EMU	European Monetary Union
EQI	European Quality of Government Index
EU	European Union
FDI	Foreign direct investment
FIAA	Foreign Investors Association of Albania
GDC	General Directorate of Customs
GDP	Gross Domestic Product
GDT	General Directorate of Taxation
GIZ	Deutsche Gesellschaft für Internationale Zusammenarbeit (German Society for International Cooperation)
GPN	Global production network
GVC	Global value chain
HRM	Human resource management
ILO	International Labour Organization
IMF	International Monetary Fund
INAIL	Istituto nazionale Assicurazione Infortuni sul Lavoro (National Institute for Insurance against Accidents at Work)
INPS	Istituto Nazionale della Previdenza Sociale (National Social Security Institute)
INSTAT	Instituti Shqiptar I Statistikës (Albanian Institute of Statistics)

ISTAT	Italian National Institute of Statistics
IOE	International Organization of Employers
KSSh	Konfederata e Sindikatave të Shqipërisë (Confederation of Trade Unions of Albania)
LPT	Labour process theory
MFA	Multifiber Arrangement
OPT	Outward Processing Trade
OSH	Occupational safety and health
SMEs	Small and medium enterprises
UIL	Unione Italiana del Lavoro (Italian Union of Labour)
WGI	Worldwide Governance Indicators
WTO	World Trade Organization

INTRODUCTION

Fieldwork glimpses

When I began my fieldwork in the late spring 2018, I first reached out to an old university colleague of mine. Like many in our region, Apulia, he had left right after getting his BA degree. We had both graduated in Political Science and International Relations, which is of little use in finding a job in a province where the unemployment rate for those under 30 was roughly 30% and where the most important sectors remain tourism, low-skilled services, and garment-footwear manufacturing. Thanks to social networks, we kept track of each other's lives and exchanged sporadic greetings and communications. I knew his hometown was the centre of the garment-footwear district that I was planning to investigate, and I figured he might be able to introduce me to leads who could help me with the fieldwork. I explained my project to him, and he took on the role of gatekeeper, referring me to his aunt, Paola. She agreed to meet me at her apartment not far from the centre of an industrial city in the South of Italy.

Paola was 53 when we met in 2018. The day we met, she had a free afternoon from work and she was at home with her young son, who spent the whole time of our chat in his room. Paola prepared the coffee, offered me biscuits, listened with interest to my project and the purpose of the interview, and readily responded to my questions. At the end of the interview, she shared some of her thoughts that were not strictly linked to the interview protocol. She was concerned for her thirteen-year-old son, who did not like school and was on track to fail the year. The bad news had triggered long discussions in the family. On the one hand, Paola argued, nowadays everyone needs a degree. On the other, what can parents do if a child does not want to study? They had finally decided to persuade him to enrol in a vocational training school, possibly one specialized in tourism and food service. Jobs are fairly easy to come by in that sector in the South of Italy, Paola explained. At the same time, she had doubts: 'Can you really raise a family on a waiter's salary?' She maintained that such a thing might have been possible when she was young, but certainly not nowadays. I blabbered some words about the importance of finding something that really motivates you, especially when you are a teenager. Paola nodded in agreement. Although she was not particularly impressed by my comment, she did not expect much more.

Paola had started working at the age of 12. She grew up in a conservative family, constantly on the edge of poverty. There were no professional high schools in her city, and her parents did not want to let her take the bus every day with all the other youngsters to reach the closest school which was in a neighbouring town, a fifteen-minute ride away. Moreover, the school entailed costs that the family could not afford or was unwilling to pay. Yet, Paola could not just stay idle at home. Her sister was already in charge of home chores and care work, so Paola had to find another job. Her mother helped her find work in a sweatshop close to the family home. The city centre was full of basements turned into sweatshops back then and Paola had always dreamt to be a tailor. She started working on a sewing machine for what she thought would be a temporary arrangement and ended up staying in the sector for about 30 years, moving on only a few years before we met.

Paola had changed employers and workshops and dealt with many different tasks—sewing, cutting, and even working as a garment-quality inspector for some time. She never really became the tailor she wanted to, but she could work alongside fashion designers and sample-makers when her employers asked her to. She had worked in cramped garages and big warehouses. She told me she preferred small workshops because 'you get to talk with the other girls while you work'. Even today, around 70% of the garment industry's workforce in the district is made up of women, and female unemployment is locally much higher than the national average. In other words, the local garment industry remains a common occupation, almost a destined route, for many women without a high level of formal education.

Paola spent much of her career without a formal contract. In some periods she had one, but her actual employment relationship was regulated through a verbal agreement that consistently circumvented the terms of the written contract. She did not complain, 'the important thing is to get your pay at the end of the day', she argued back then. And she mentioned there was always 'some kind of contract anyway', even if it was just there on paper and never really complied with. Also, informality in employment relations was so widespread that it seemed silly to ask for something different and especially women had to settle with what the local labour market seemed to offer. 'It was the same everywhere', Paola revealed to me. 'If you told them you wanted your social insurance contribution paid, and this and that, they would just reply, 'You need to look for work at the cement plant. There you can get those things, not here [in the garment sector]'.

When a first demand crisis hit the sector in the 1990s, for Paola work turned into an ordeal. She changed many employers, suffered long idle periods, was seldom able to secure another formal contract, and found herself being regularly cheated and paid less than what she was entitled to. Yet, she did not feel too strongly about it. Many of the employers she worked for were subcontractors. Many of their clients—themselves middlemen in a much longer production chain—were apparently going bankrupt as well. Subcontractors were the first to be hit when demand slumped, were left unpaid when clients went bankrupt and faced cut-throat competition to secure declining orders from the few other clients still standing. Even amidst the crisis, 'there was mutual respect with the employer', she reported. Also, she liked the work, had gotten to know all the tricks as she had grown older and more self-confident in her tasks, and was often a guide for newcomers and was a reliable resource for the managers. Yet, Paola also told me about rampant cheating and wage theft, the days she went to work with high fever, and the late-night overtime she endured to complete the orders on time for deliveries.

Paola had left the garment sector a few years before we met. She had come to realize that the industry was now just 'scraping the bottom of the barrel'. Since then, Paola had done several other jobs, all of them informal—cleaning, homecare, elderly care. Then she got a job in a small cleaning company thanks to her brother who was already working there. Paola is officially a janitor now—she has a contract, and her pension and social contributions have so far been regularly paid.

I asked her if she ever thought about her labour rights or her pension while working in the garment industry with bogus part-time contracts or without a contract at all. She revealed she never thought about it because that was how things worked, repeating that 'it was the same everywhere'. She has just recently begun to give it some thought because her contribution records amount to a very tight pension, and she has a long way to go before she can retire with a decent allowance. I asked if she felt betrayed or cheated. She replied: 'No...well, I mean, that was just how things worked'. Has she ever felt responsible for accepting to work informally? After all, I argued, somebody could say that she was not only avoiding paying her own contributions but also her taxes, so she was *cheating the system* as well. She responded that you cannot do much if they tell you, 'Either take the job like this or get lost'. The employers are the cheaters, she asserted. Or even more so, their consultants who know all the tricks of the profession to circumvent laws and contracts and never get caught. She added that the shopkeepers who never give you an invoice of your purchase just to avoid paying taxes are also cheaters. For Paola, it is clear that employment informalization and tax avoidance are wrong. The problem for her is that there was never really a choice.

The puzzling worldwide persistence of informality

Paola's testimony is far from exceptional. The literature on the garment sector reports similar experiences across time and space. Hammer and Plugor (2019, p. 8) report excerpts of interviews with workers in the fast-fashion industry in the East Midlands, in England, that closely recall Paola's daily experience at work: 'The job is as and when required'; 'There is no such thing [as an employment contract] in the garment sector. This is very unusual'; 'We never asked and were never given one'; 'I have been working for a long time and have never been given a contract. I thought this is normal'.

In their study on Bulgarian factories, Medarov, Tsoneva, and Nikolova (2019) report unilateral payment systems, erratic working hours and despotic management below any labour law standards. Other past and recent studies show that informal workers and entrepreneurs in small retail, restaurant and clothing businesses in the UK share many of the working experiences that Paola reported (Rainnie, 1985; Rainnie et al., 2013; Ram et al., 2019). A paternalistic and, at times, benevolent employment relationship alternates with despotic and highly exploitative forms of informalization.

Informal employment is not a matter concerning mature sectors or marginal and shrinking groups of workers. The majority of the global working population is employed in the informal economy (Dibben and Williams, 2012; ILO, 2018). In many regions of the world, informal employment is growing faster than formal work (Williams, 2015). In developing countries, more than half of the non-agricultural workforce is employed in the informal economy, and in all advanced economies, new forms of casual, atypical and precarious employment that would be considered informal in developing countries are on the rise (Vanek et al., 2014). In post-socialist countries, informality persists despite economic growth and institutional change (Williams, 2015), while in advanced economies work de-standardization and insecurity have become the 'new normal', blurring the boundaries between informality and formalized but precarious employment (Siegmann and Schiphorst, 2016; Smith, 2016). In the European Union (EU), for example, Williams et al. (2017, p. 1) estimate that '11.6% of total labour input in the private sector [...] is undeclared, and undeclared work constitutes on average 16.4% of gross value added (GVA)'. Estimates also confirm that '61.8% of all undeclared work is work conducted in the context of an employment relationship, 37.3% is self-employment, and 0.3% is family work' (Williams et al., 2017, p. 1).

Empirical research shows that workers in informal employment generally face worse and more precarious conditions and experience obstacles to exercising their rights or accessing justice when rights are not respected (ILO, 2018; McKay et al., 2012; Williams and Horodnic, 2019). Even using very conservative estimates of the phenomenon—such as those based on the Eurobarometer survey[1]—workers without contracts are consistently more likely than formal employees to face a poor physical work environment, have fewer possibilities of using cognitive skills at work, have fewer training opportunities and career prospects, and perceive lower job security (Williams and Horodnic, 2019; OECD/ILO, 2019). Informal employment, indeed, often coincides with precariousness, lack of access to social rights and employment protections, employment instability and managerial power to unilaterally vary working tasks and arrangements (McKay et al., 2012). Undeclared work in formal firms is concentrated in labour-intensive production (agriculture, construction, and certain manufacturing sectors) and low-end services (cleaning, care, hospitality) (McKay et al., 2012), and it is linked to low workforce commitment and low enterprise-specific qualifications and training. Informal work is more

1 Surveys data about informal work shall be considered conservative proxy because are based on direct questions about highly sensitive issues. The same Eurobarometer calls for caution and suggests that survey data on such sensitive issues can provide no more than a *very conservative assessment* of the phenomenon (EC, 2020a; EU and OECD, 2015). Consider, for example, that 95% of those surveyed in the 2019 Eurobarometer report having not undertaken any form of undeclared work in the previous year, and only 3% of all dependent employees reported receiving part or all their salary informally, with Italian and Greek respondents scoring lower than Dutch, Danish and Swedish ones (3% against 10%, 8% and 7%, respectively). Yet a third of all those surveyed reported knowing somebody who has engaged in economic activity without declaring it (EC, 2020a) and evidence derived from alternative estimation methods shows that informal labour inputs are usually higher than what participants self-report in surveys (Williams et al., 2017).

precarious and fluctuates much more than formal one (Pfau-Effinger, 2017; Williams and Windebank, 1998).

Additionally, informal employment generally correlates with poverty and one reinforce the other (Berdiev et al. 2020)—poor workers are more likely to engage in informal employment and informal employment is typically associated with low remuneration and unfavourable working conditions. In other words, informal employment reinforces the marginality of those workers and households that rely more heavily on it (Williams, 2014). The 2019 Eurobarometer shows that those who report having worked informally are more likely than others to struggle to pay household bills (8% of informals against 3% of non-informals) (EC, 2020). To put it simply, informal employment is a consistent feature of our economic system, concerns certain sectors more than others, and generally impairs workers' income, rights, and social protection.

This is not the only negative consequence of economic informality. Informal economic practices represent unfair competition and increase the overall tax burden for those companies that work according to the rules, while it also reduce (both formal and informal) firms' productivity (Packard et al., 2012) and capacity for innovation and upgrading. Firms operating informally are free riders that overburden regular firms by escaping tax and regulations (Beltrán, 2020; EU and OECD, 2015) and generally specialize in low-quality, low-productivity production processes (La Porta and Shleifer, 2014).

Finally, informal employment curtails tax revenues and reduces state legitimacy. Having reliable data on tax gap levels—namely, the revenues lost because of tax evasion—is not an easy endeavour. Not all states provide such estimates in a comparable fashion, even within the EU. Murphy (2019) estimates that the tax gap due to informal economic activities in the EU as a whole ranges from €750–900 billion per year, or, put differently, around 5.5% of the EU's entire GDP (based on 2015 data). According to Murphy's calculations, in Italy alone in 2015, the gap reached €165.5 billion—that is, around 12% of the national GDP. Other estimates of Italy's tax gap register lower but still impressive numbers. According to national estimates, Italy's general tax gap was €109 billion on average between 2012 and 2016. Of this amount, €11.4 billion was unpaid/evaded social security contributions and €97.6 billion related to direct and indirect taxes (but mainly personal income taxes of self-employed and small businesses and VAT) (Prometeia, 2019).

The diffuse damages that different groups incur due to informal employment make its persistence a puzzling feature of our time. Why does it persist despite the widespread costs and the formal opposition of public authorities?

Informality's persistence remains a puzzling empirical reality also because it keeps challenging theoretical predictions. Rather than proving a remnant of disappearing traditional societies, as *dualist* analytical perspectives have posited, or the product of burdensome regulations, red-tape and taxation, as *neoliberal* approaches have argued, it seems that informality might be a more or less permanent feature of our societies. As Morris and Polese (2015, p. 1) have put it, 'informality is here to stay'. Therefore, investigating the conditions and drivers that foster it remains both analytically and politically crucial.

Dealing with a double puzzle

What causes informality then, and what makes it so persistent? How can we account for the role of the actors involved in it? And how can we identify and disentangle macro-structural drivers, locally specific factors and micro-dynamics that enable the reproduction of informality while avoiding the drawbacks and blind spots of the existing literature?

If dualist and neoliberal analytical perspectives, as I will contend in the book, have not withstood the test of time and empirical validation, *structuralist* and *new institutionalist* approaches offer alternative readings on the matter. Structuralist approaches posit that the persistence of informality must be explained in light of economic and productive structures—namely, that the ways capitalism works reproduces either large sectors or small interstices of the economy where the informality thrives and intertwines with formal economic activities. New institutionalist frameworks, instead, explain informality as the result of a clash between formal institutions and informal norms. The correlation is as follows. The more citizens' morality clashes with the formal script of institutions, the more people are inclined to go informal and the larger the informal economy grows. When citizens believe that laws, taxation, and formal rules are unfair or illegitimate—namely, when formal regulations clash with informal ways of ordering their lives—they go informal.

Going back to my first glimpse of the fieldwork, Paola, the garment worker, was not so fond of formal rules. She certainly thought ill of high taxes and poor welfare services, and she worked informally, beyond the law, for a good part of her career. Her story would surely fit the institutional clash thesis. She did not really trust public institutions, telling me how she and other workers managed to evade the labour inspectors' visits at work and still laugh about it. However, at odds with certain new institutionalist ideal-type of informal, she also thought that employers and their consultants were cheaters and unfair. As I interpret her account, she meant that it is bad to avoid taxes if you have a choice. Her experience revealed one crucial question new institutionalists approaches often risk overlooking: do economic structures and power relations matter in the decisions of those who go informal? If that's the case, how are economic structures and institutional misalignment connected? And whose interests does informality's persistence serve?

As the World Bank (Perry et al., 2007) reports in a highly cited analysis of informal economic activities in Latin America, informalization is heterogeneous in its practices, consequences and motivations, and it is deeply rooted in the institutional and historical developments of different locales. However, if entrepreneurs usually *exit* the formal economy out of a rational examination of costs, risks and benefits, informal dependent workers are much more likely to be *excluded* from the formal economy and end up being informals because of a lack of better alternatives. Therefore, it is crucial to understand whether informalization promotes *control and domination* or rather *emancipation and positive flexibility*. Or better, we need to understand under which conditions informalization resembles one situation or the other.

The new institutionalist approach emphasizes the social embeddedness of informal practices—namely, the relationship between actors and locally-specific formal and informal rules and institutions. Yet, it offers limited analytical clout to analyse the multifarious dynamics of informal employment revealed by my fieldwork and the copious existing literature. To start, the new institutionalist approach has little to say about the sectoral dynamics of informality. While the garment sector was an almost undisputed informalized industry in Paola's account, other sectors in the same region and city offered standard, formalized employment. As she mentions in the interview, the big cement factory was a recognized example of such male-dominated, regular employment practices in the city. Arguably more important is the fact that there are—and were back when Paola started working—garment factories that work in full compliance with labour laws and collective contracts. Not only is a sectoral dynamic at play in shaping informalization processes, but also certain firm-level dynamics are crucial in determining informalized employment relations.

New institutionalist approaches, however, generally neglect the crucial role of these micro-level factors. If what matters is the institutional clash between citizen and state morality, why are certain sectors consistently more informalized than others even though they are embedded in the same institutional context? And why do certain firms go informal while others do not, even when they work in the same sector, are embedded in the same institutional contexts, and arguably face the same opportunities and constraints to go informal?

The new institutionalist model reveals to be of limited use in explaining the lived experience of workers like Paola. Understanding her story and the trajectory of the local garment sector required an analysis of history and classes, production processes and power relations. Paola started working when she was very young. She was not able to achieve a formal education nor challenge the lack of a formalized employment relations—even had she wanted to—because the family pressured her to find a job and employers would not offer anything different than informal work to young women. She grew in the sector, and while she changed many employers, full formalization was never a possibility for her, so that she ended up accepting it as a structural feature of the kind of employment she could get. Nonetheless, she learnt to seek professional growth and satisfaction at work. She never really thought about the harmful sides of informality until well into her working life when the crisis hit, hard times came, and it was too late to bargain. Perhaps banking on informal employment was a choice for her employers, though. It is, therefore, crucial to distinguish her from them because of the different positions they hold within the employment relationship. If, for employers, navigating informality was a business strategy and the level of institutional clash might have been an important driver of their choices, for workers like Paola, the spaces for agency were more heavily constrained. As such, their bargaining power vis-à-vis employers, their access to justice and workers organizations' support, and alternative employment opportunities certainly came before their potential misalignment with formal laws and institutions.

It is crucial, therefore, also to analyse the power that different classes have in the processes of informalization. In other words, to investigate informals' patterns of agency and their power relations, we need to investigate local institutional contexts *together with—and not at the expense of*—the analysis of economic processes and structures. Can the structuralist approach, then, fully explain the fortunes of informal entrepreneurs and the misfortunes of precarious, low-paid, 'downgraded labour' (Williams, 2010, p. 18; for the original use of the term, see: Castells and Portes, 1989, p. 26)? With its emphasis on the transformation of capitalism, can such an approach also elucidate the role of institutions, culture, and social norms that new institutionalists find to be a crucial driver of informality? And most of all, can structuralist approaches account sufficiently for the role of actors' agency in shaping and reproducing informal employment relations?

Informal employment: Structures, contexts, and agency

In this book I contend that the structuralist perspective is a good starting point for studying the persistence of informal employment but it clearly needs revision. On the one hand, structuralist approaches overlook the role of socio-institutional contexts in informalization processes. On the other, they neglect the ways in which actors can actively reproduce or disrupt informal employment relations. I aim, therefore, to develop an *extended structuralist framework* that can explain the persistence of informalized employment relations by looking at its structural economic drivers, the role of local socio-institutional contexts, and the agency of the actors involved.

I first analyse the role of the state and policies that tackle informal employment. While informality has detrimental effects on revenues and legitimacy, it cannot be assumed that state actors will consistently attempt to curb informal economic practices and that the persistence of informality is necessarily a sign of institutional failure. By analysing existing sets of policies against informal employment in two different countries, I investigate the *politics of informalization* behind its persistence. Fighting informality is often a costly endeavour for political actors in government. While new institutionalist literature – with the exception of public choice approaches - generally overlook the political dynamics in anti-informality policy-making, a structuralist perspective allows us to account for its distributional effects. It can therefore provide a glimpse on the political processes of its reproduction without assuming that state actors' preference would always be a world without informal employment. Curbing informality has economic and political costs, and not all political actors are able or willing to fully commit to formalizing or eradicating agendas. Instead, other forms of *low-compliance equilibrium* might prevail. In such cases, a certain persistence of partial informal employment ends up being tolerated if it rewards certain crucial voter groups or if it is crucial to maintain the competitiveness of important sectors of the economy. Moreover, by focusing on anti-informality policies, I show that informal employment is resilient vis-à-vis attempts at curbing it. Firms and workers can reshape and change patterns of informalization in response to changes in formal regulations and enforcement.

Besides public policies, I posit that informalization dynamics are better understood as the result of multiple relationships negotiated in the workplace. This implies that, within specific social contexts and formal regulations and enforcements, workers and firms are the main actors that ultimately shape informalization and determine its persistence. By drawing on the conceptual toolbox of *Labour Process Theory* (LPT), I redefine informalization as a tool for, among other things, labour control. Thus, I read employment informalization as a process through which the employment relation moves away from formal regulations and gets crucially reshaped by customs, informal rules, and unfettered power relations. The characteristics, persistence, and disruption of informal employment result from the continuous negotiations of informalized employment relations that unfold at the workplace level between employers and employees.

The agency of these two sets of actors, therefore, becomes the focus of my analysis. At the same time, actors' bargaining power is shaped by the position a firm holds in broader production networks and the local socio-institutional context in which it operates. By combining labour process analysis and the study of *Global Production Networks* (GPNs), I tease out the drivers that determine and reproduce the different types of informalized labour regimes emerging along complex production chains. Through such a framework, I reconstruct the coexistence of a differentiated landscape of informalized and formalized employment relations within the chain and across the regions analysed. I explain such variation by looking both at managers' and workers' agency in negotiating the terms of informalization. I find that where workers' associational power solidifies in effective trade union organization and local infrastructures, non-compliance is generally prevented. In contrast, where workers lack associational power, informalization can acquire hegemonic and negotiated or despotic and unilateral features according to workers' individual levels of market bargaining power. Both workers' and firms' space for manoeuvre in negotiating employment relations, however, are understood in light of the firm's position within GPNs and its embeddedness within a specific local context.

Extending the structural reading of informality

To combine LPT and GPNs approaches in the study of informal employment, I build an extended structuralist approach. I draw on the extended case method, to bring the missing analysis of actors' agency (their negotiation of informalization within the workplace) and institutional contexts (which, together with the governance and structures of the production chain, shape firms' and workers' negotiating power) into the study of informalized employment relationships.

I apply this framework to the analysis of the garment-footwear production networks in the Apulia region of Southern Italy, and in Albania. The analysis seeks to unveil the mechanisms underlying the persistence of informal employment. I have selected this sector as a *typical case study*: the predominance of informal employment relations and the highly globalized and fragmented production in the garment-footwear sector means it offers a good arena to expand upon existing structuralist theories.

I carried out in-depth qualitative fieldwork based on interviews, focus groups and non-participant observation in Italy and Albania. Besides hosting the production networks of interest, these two countries represent optimal subunits for the GPNs typical case study design because of the persistence of informality despite multiple policies attempting to reduce it. The case and research design, overall, offers the possibility to analyse how common structural pressures derived from the same production networks are received by different local institutional contexts and how structural, institutional and workplace dynamics interact in shaping informalization patterns.

Structure of the book

The next chapter will evaluate the analytical purchase of existing approaches that explain informality and set the stage to advance an alternative theoretical framework. In Chapter 2, I will tease out the elements of the extended structuralist framework combining LPT and GPNs perspectives. Chapter 3 will then describe the methodology used, explain the rationale of case selection and inquiry techniques adopted and clarify how fieldwork challenges were addressed during the research.

The remaining chapters present the results of my empirical investigation. Chapter 4 explains why competing theoretical approaches seem ill-equipped to investigate the mechanisms of the persistence of informal employment in the two countries of interest. A general discussion of the shortcomings of alternative perspectives applied to the cases of Albania and Italy lays the ground to introduce the extended structuralist approach. In the same chapter, I advance a political-economic analysis of anti-informality policy-making, showing how political and economic costs of eradicating informality lead political actors in power to either reverse or only partially implement effective policies. I show that state institutions settle for partial formalization rather than eradication, while firms and workers can keep circumventing institutional rigidities and monitoring by engaging in partially informalized employment practices. The result is the emergence of a *low-compliance equilibrium* that curbs most of the extreme forms of full informalization while tolerating alternative forms of partial informalization. Chapter 4 also sets the formal institutional contexts in which the agency of firms and workers unfolds.

Chapter 5 details the development of the garment-footwear sector, focusing closely on how it 'lands' and develops in the regions under investigation. Chapter 6 teases out the agency of firms within global production networks and in the specific locales examined and shows how firms' strategies reproduce and enhance the pressures for labour flexibility and cost compression. Chapter 7 illustrates how differentiated informalization processes emerge along the chain and respond to firms' need for labour's flexibility, discipline, and cost compression. Through this analysis, I show that informalization is better understood as a tool of labour control in the workplace rather than a mere cost-cutting device or an institutional failure. The chapter goes on to show how local labour markets and workforce segmentation contribute to shape and favour informalization dynamics and how workers mobilize the elements of their local contexts and their (market and associational) bargaining power to reject, negotiate, cope with, or exit employment informalization. Finally, Chapter 8 provides an analytical typology of the formalized and informalized, negotiated and hegemonic, or unilateral and despotic, labour regimes that emerge in the production networks analysed. The typology explains the persistence of variegated informalized employment regimes throughout the chains and across institutional contexts by factoring in actor's bargaining powers and agency as embedded in the social context and economic structures. The conclusions reflect upon the relevance of the theoretical innovations and findings of this work.

1.
REVISITING INFORMALITY
The shortcomings and insights of existing approaches

1.1. *Defining economic informality*

At the most general level, informal economic activities can be defined as the sum of all 'activities and entrepreneurships that are not registered in accordance with the prescribed laws, are not in compliance with labour legislations, escape monitoring by the state officials, lack appropriate conditions at work, and are mostly temporary and casual in nature' (Routh 2011, p. 208). Beyond the apparent clarity of the concept, a certain definitional ambiguity remains (Godfrey, 2011; Williams and Windebank, 1998).

The first attempt to define economic activities occurring outside of the registered, formalized economy dates to the early 1970s, Hart's (1973) study on the urban economy of Accra, Ghana. Hart's seminal article distinguishes between formal and informal *income-earning opportunities* and stresses how the great bulk of Accra's urban population relied on informal means to increase its income. This first conceptualization posits a sectoral division of income-earning activities between those undertaken in organized public and private institutions and organizations (the formal sector) and those in unregistered petty trade, small-scale production and services (the informal sector). While the term 'informal sector' is still widely adopted, more nuanced approaches attempted to point out the underlying bias of such a definition. As Routh (2011, p. 220) puts it, the sector-based definition is 'essentially targeted at measuring the informal entrepreneurship' and aimed to ascertain its contribution to the overall economy. It emphasizes informal *self-employment* and leaves aside informal *dependent employment*. It also assumes a clear-cut distinction between the formal and informal economies, and it implies a certain homogeneity of activities within the informal sector. Such an approach fails to make sense of the heterogeneity of informal economic activities, the existence of different employment statuses within the informal economy, and the increasing blending of formal and informal economic activities (Godfrey, 2011; Routh, 2011; Hussmans, 2004; Williams and Windebank, 1998).

The term *informal employment* was specifically conceived to address these shortcomings and was adopted by the International Labour Organization (ILO) at the 17th International Conference of Labour Statisticians in 2003 (Hussmans, 2004). This definition focuses on the *nature of the employment* in which the economic activities occur rather than the *status of the enterprise* (registered or unregistered). This conceptualization recognizes that formal and informal economic activities are not necessarily separated and distinct since even registered firms in the formal sector might employ unregistered workers. As suggested by Chen (2016, p. 413), such a definition allows observers to identify informal employment sub-categories, such as informal self-employment and informal wage employment—the latter being defined as 'hired without social protection contributions by formal or informal enterprises or as paid domestic workers by households'. These categories can be further distinguished in sub-groups as illustrated in Table 1.1 (which, for the sake of simplicity, excludes unpaid work and favours).

Table 1.1. Different forms of informal employment

Self-employment	Wage/dependent employment
• Employers in informal enterprises; • own-account workers in informal enterprises; • contributing family workers (in informal and formal enterprises); • members of informal producers' cooperatives.	• Employees of informal enterprises; • casual or day labourers; • temporary or part-time workers; • contract workers; • unregistered or undeclared workers; • industrial outworkers (homeworkers); • paid domestic workers.

Source: Adapted from Chen (2016).

The term *informal economy* is also widely adopted. This definition refers to all the economic activities and outputs produced by unregistered firms (i.e., those operating in the informal sector) as well as by workers employed informally in formally registered firms (Chen, 2016). These specifications underscore that the boundary between compliance and non-compliance with formal rules is less dichotomous than a sector-based definition would suggest since firms might comply with certain regulations while violating others (Godfrey, 2011, p. 253).

Defining economic informality is not a neutral exercise but rather a *classification struggle.* While economists and statisticians are primarily interested in accounting for the contribution of informal economic practices to economic growth, labour sociologists generally focus more on the living standards, employment relations, and working conditions of informal workers. The former are inclined to adopt the sectoral definition while the latter adopt the definition more sensitive to employment statuses (Routh, 2011). As La Hovary (2016, p. 99) explains, classification has become a matter of political controversy even in international arena such as the ILO. The International Employers' Organization (IOE), which represents employers within the ILO, in fact, includes in the definition of informality only fully unregistered firms, thus excluding the partially registered activities within formal firms. It also expresses 'great concern at the conflation of non-standard forms of employment and the informal economy' (La Hovary, 2016, p. 100). The main concern for employers' associations is to level the playing field and curb informality as a source of unfair competition rather than impeding it as a tool to expand flexible (and precarious) working conditions. Other perspectives, instead, might want to focus exactly on the effects of informality on workers.

Furthermore, for analytical purposes, it is crucial to avoid 'defining informal employment in a negative and residual manner' (Williams and Windebank, 1998, p. 4) as the mere ensemble of all the activities that are not formal (see also: Connolly, 1985, p. 64) while drawing a definition that can encompass a range of distinct phenomena. To address these ambiguities, Williams and Windebank (1998, p. 4) define informal employment as the:

> paid production and sale of goods and services that are unregistered by, or hidden from, the state for tax social security, and/or labour law purposes, but which are legal in all other respects.

The authors continue, noting that:

> ...informal employment is composed of three types of activity: evasion of both direct (i.e. income tax) and indirect (e.g. VAT, excise duties) taxes; social security fraud where the officially unemployed are working whilst claiming benefit; and avoidance of labour legislation, such as employers' insurance contributions, minimum wage agreements or certain safety and other standards in the workplace, such as through hiring labour off the books or sub-contracting work to small firms and the self-employed asked to work for below-minimum wages.

This definition includes both dependent informal employment and informal self-employment and it is the working definition adopted in this research. Its strength lies on its focus on the nature of employment rather than on the mere status of the firms where employment occurs. Further, like previous definitions (see: Castells and Portes 1989, p. 12), it stresses the *unregistered* rather than the *unregulated* nature of informal employment. Informal economic activities, in fact, are not informal because of their inherent spontaneity and lack of regulation, but rather because they are unregistered and develop beyond formal regulations. At the same time, they remain heavily regulated by social, cultural and economic (informal) rules and indirectly by formal institutions that set the boundaries of what has to be considered formal.

Finally, *informal* activities are distinguished from *illegal* ones because the process that produces a specific product or service violates laws and regulations while the final product or service itself does not. Other scholars (Webb et al., 2013; 2009) distinguish informality from illegality because the former refers to activities that are *illegal* but *socially legitimate*. According to this distinction, however, the production of goods and services that are illegal but still socially acceptable or legitimate should be considered within the realm of informal economy. The problem with that definition is the need to detail, bound and measure the social legitimacy of certain practices, goods and services (see: Darbi et al., 2018). Whose perspective should be considered to assess the legitimacy of certain goods and activities to determine whether they are informal or illegal? What is the minimum threshold of social acceptability of such goods or activities before they would shift from illegal to informal? The definition I adopt avoids the risk of conceptual confusion and provides clear boundaries for the activities, practices, and relationships being investigated under the label of informal employment or work.

In the remainder of the chapter, I engage with the main theoretical approaches addressing the persistence of informalized employment.

1.2. *Dualist and neoliberal approaches: analytical shortcomings and empirical counterevidence*

The dualist approach is highly influenced by the *modernization theory* of developmental studies. It emerged in the 1970s as a way of analysing the predominance of the informal sector in Third World countries. Dualist accounts treat informal employment as any work outside the formal economy and frame it as the remnant of a pre-modern, traditional approach to economic organization (Williams, 2015; Hart 1973; Lewis, 1954; for a review, see: Gërxhani, 2004a). In his seminal study on informal income-generating activities in Accra, Ghana, Hart (1973) shows that informal employment is both a secondary source of income for workers with formal but low-paid jobs and a full-time occupation for workers in the informal sector. He associates informality with informal self-employment and entrepreneurship and contends that 'the distinction between formal and informal income opportunities is based essentially on that between wage-earning and self-employment' (Hart, 1973, p. 68). *Informals* are mainly petty-entrepreneurs who find ready access to the informal sector thanks to the low entry capital required and by leveraging their social networks and family and kinship ties. The dualist perspective posits the detachment and mutual exclusion of formal and informal economic activities, with the modern *capitalist* sector on one side and the *subsistence*, *traditional*, *informalized* sector on the other (Lewis, 1954). Informality implies backwardness and low productivity. Where a large informal sector exists, this is the result of an uncompleted process of economic and institutional modernization and informals are those yet to be incorporated into still developing formal labour markets. In this view, informality is inherently temporary. Once a modern nation-state and a well-functioning capitalist economy are established, workers in subsistence-level economic activities will be absorbed by the formal sector.

The persistence of informal employment in the developing economies even after decades of stable growth, general income increases, and rising quality of institutions—together with the emergence of new forms of informal activities in advanced capitalist economies (Vanek et al., 2014)—challenges the main predictions of the dualist perspective. And while quantitative research has found that nations with higher levels of wealth and human development have generally lower levels of informality (La Porta and Shleifer, 2014; Williams, 2015), the dualist perspective still presents crucial blind spots. Indeed, it fails to problematize the relationship between formal and informal activities which are seen as mutually exclusive, and it draws on the assumption that the mode of production and social regulation of the post-Second World War advanced economies—with growing levels of stable, formalized full-time employment and expanding institutionalized welfare systems—is the inevitable end-point of every national developmental path (Williams and Windebank, 1998). The crisis of the Fordist model of development and social regulation and the pervasiveness of new forms of employment informalization in advanced economies thus call for a rebuttal or a critical revision of the dualist approach (Breman and van der Linden, 2014).

Alternatively, the neoliberal perspective argues that economic actors deliberately decide to engage in informal economic activities to escape high taxes, inefficient public regulatory burdens, state interference and public officials' corruption (de Soto, 1989; Loayza et al., 2005; Maloney, 2003; Snyder, 2004). Informality is, in this view, framed as a matter of free choice and economic rationality that emerges where over-burdening or corrupt institutions increase the cost of formal market transactions. Thus, the informal sector is a place of unfettered competition, informals are unregistered entrepreneurs devoted to enhancing market efficiency, and informality can even be a driver of growth, development, and emancipation. In the neoliberal perspective, economic informality is not the sign of backwardness but rather the result of the inherent dynamism of economic forces and a welcomed violation of *bad rules* that impair the efficiency of free markets and the freedom of economic actors. The remedy to tackle informality is deregulation. Reducing tax burdens, regulatory constraints, social security schemes and state interference is thought to curb entry barriers in the formal sector, increasing its efficiency and reducing the incentives to engage in informal activities.

Critiques stress how the neoliberal approach fails to make sense of informality's persistence where neoliberal market-enhancing institutions are fully established (Aliyev, 2016; 2015; 2014; Rekhviashvili, 2016; Williams, 2015). Moreover, empirical cross-national analyses do not find a clear association between state intervention in the economy (with the level of public spending used as a proxy measure) or the taxation and the size of the national informal economy (Williams, 2017; Williams and Martinez, 2016). Further, the neoliberal perspective emphasizes the role of the entrepreneurial spirits within society but overlooks the cases in which informalization become a tool to enforce exploitative and flexible practices of production (Portes and Sassen-Koob, 1987) or even a strategy to resist and domesticate, rather than embrace, market competition and hierarchies within firms (White and Williams 2016; Rekhviashvili, 2016; Morris and Polese, 2015; 2014; Morris, 2012; Morrison et al., 2012; Polese and Rodgers, 2011; Gibson-Graham, 2008; Smith and Rochovská 2007).

1.3. *Structural theories: Informalization and downgraded labour*

Unlike for the other two perspectives, one of the crucial tenets of the structuralist approach is to consider formal and informal economies as intertwined and overlapping rather than discrete and separate. Informal employment is embedded in, rather than detached from, the formal world economy, and it is a persistent feature of the post-Fordist, flexible mode of accumulation. It is not an escape from over-regulation and institutional inefficiency but the by-product of a deregulated, flexible, and interdependent global economy. The informals are not merely marginal actors unable to be absorbed in the formal and protected employment but rather over-exploited, precarious workers (i.e., downgraded labour) and their employers maximize profits by circumventing labour laws remaining well entangled in the workings of the formal economy (Slavnic, 2010; Woolfson, 2007; Harvey, 1990; Portes et al., 1989; Portes and Walton, 1981; Portes, 1978).

Drawing on the conceptual frameworks of critical political economy, the structuralist perspective contends with the neoliberal shift of the 1970s, macro-structural changes of globalized capitalism, increased worldwide competition, and retrenching welfare states and deregulation led to increasingly precarious employment relations. This approach considers economic actors as neither inherently entrepreneurial and dynamic nor backward and marginalized. Instead, structuralist scholars maintain that a global process of economic restructuring along fragmented subcontracting chains and new global dynamics of competition offer economic actors in core economies increased opportunities to go informal (Slavnic, 2010; Leonard, 2000; Castells and Portes, 1989; Harvey 1990; Portes and Sassen-Koob, 1987) and lead firms in economic peripheries to engage in informality to guarantee the flexibility and responsiveness needed to be integrated into the global economy (Slavnic, 2010; Theron, 2010; Hudson, 2005; Gallin, 2001).

A recent strand within the structuralist literature looks at the relationship between the integration of firms located in late-industrialized economies in GPNs and the recurrence of informal forms of employment. This perspective investigates 'how the workings of GPNs create and reinforce a dynamic process of informalization' (Phillips, 2011, p. 382). Informalization is not considered to be the result of exclusion from the modern economy, but rather as the mechanism that guarantees the incorporation of firms from peripheral regions into wider processes of capital accumulation (Selwyn, 2019; Beladi et al., 2016; Baez, 2014; Roberts, 2013; Phillips, 2011). This strand of scholarship, in facts, asserts that economic and social development, working conditions, and profits increasingly depend on the position that firms and regions hold in global and regional networks of production (Barrientos, 2013; Barrientos et al., 2011; Lakhani et al., 2013). Firms located in peripheral economies, lacking other institutional and economic comparative advantages, specialize in labour-intensive and low-added-value activities. For them, informality becomes a strategy to maintain the workforce enough cheap and flexible to cope with the economic requirements of being integrated into production networks. Thus, the crucial driver of informalization is not exclusion from, but rather the *adverse incorporation* into broader GPNs within the formal economy (Roberts, 2013; Phillips, 2011).

Drawing on the concept of *peripheral accumulation* (Portes and Walton, 1981; Portes, 1978), the structuralist account finds that the informal economy of peripheral regions subsidizes the formal one by providing cheap labour, enabling profits and ensuring labour reproduction through the thick informal networks that peripheral societies provide. At the same time, as Phillips (2011) argues, the dynamics of informalization in the peripheral firms within GPNs reinforce the power relations that constitute the pre-conditions of adverse incorporation itself. Indeed, informal employment hinders the possibility of firms' industrial upgrading (which requires a loyal and committed workforce) and undermines the capacity for labour mobilization (which is an essential impetus to formalization processes). This implies that peripheral firms will be unable to upgrade to higher added-value segments of production, and they will keep relying on informalization to maintain their competitiveness.

While the structuralist perspective sheds new light on the relationship between informal employment and the formal economy, it overlooks a series of important facets. For instance, it ignores the possibility that informal activities may arise as a form of resistance to neoliberal economic processes rather than as a necessary, inevitable managerial strategy to cope with harsh market competition (Stenning et al., 2011; Smith and Rochovská, 2007; Scott, 1998). It also neglects the possibility that the participation of certain social groups in economic processes, although exploitative, might still represent an emancipatory push against oppressive social relations. Moreover, it offers no tools to investigate the post-socialist space, in which informality was not a result of the integration into the market economy but rather a consolidated feature of socialist systems and a crucial driver in the post-socialist transformation (Polese and Rodgers 2011; Greskovits, 1998; Stark 1996; 1986; Szelenyi, 1988). And finally, it provides little space for an analysis of actors' choices within given economic structures. Indeed, structuralist accounts do not sufficiently problematize how agency, even when highly constrained, remains crucial in hindering or reproducing given structural constraints. Put more simply, structuralist accounts seem to posit that informal employment will be reproduced as long as the overall structural constraints remain intact.

1.4. *A post-structural perspective: challenging market-centric approaches in the study of informal employment*

These three main approaches have been challenged more recently by post-structuralist and institutionalist accounts because they fail to problematize the multiple motivations of informals' engagement with the informal economy and the rationales regulating informal work. These approaches consider informality as either a survival strategy, a tool for enhanced exploitation, or a form of unleashed entrepreneurial freedom. Yet, they all portray informality as based solely on the need for profit or income maximization.

The marginals of the urban markets in yet-to-develop economies struggle to make an income outside the formal sector. The informal self-employed workers analysed by the neoliberal approach are mainly driven by the opportunity to increase the wealth produced, exchanged, and appropriated beyond formal regulations. The precarious workers of the structuralist approach engage with informalization because they have no alternative and are exploited by profit-maximizing entrepreneurs in complex, competition-driven economic structures. These approaches all see informality as the epitome of the market, even though a large number of studies shows that informalisation can be rooted in complex systems of social relations and values that escape profit-seeking rationales and market-based regulating mechanisms (Rekhviashvili, 2016; Morris and Polese, 2015; 2014; Polese and Rodgers, 2011; Stenning et al., 2011; Ghezzi, 2010; Smith and Rochovská, 2007; Burawoy et al., 2000; Verdery and Burawoy, 1999). Networks of reciprocity, loyalties to kinship, and community ties can shape informal economic activities and displace market-like logics of action. Actors might decide to engage in informal work to re-build spaces of sociality and autonomy (Morris 2013; 2012) or even to resist imposed state-led marketization (Rekhviashvili, 2016). Moreover, informality might persist because of its social and cultural embeddedness even when it becomes economically unprofitable (Ghezzi, 2003).

Other accounts highlight how consolidated perspectives emphasize specific factors of informalization at the expense of others. For example, the dualist perspective focuses on marginality and underdevelopment, structuralist views focus on the economic drivers of informalization, and neoliberal approaches point to burdensome regulations. Instead, critical readings of informality argue that the varying configurations of informal economies depend on *multifarious cocktails* (Williams and Windebank, 1998) of economic, social, institutional and environmental conditions rather than on a mono-casual logic of explanation. As Williams and Marcelli (2010, pp. 229-30) note,

> only by re-embedding this economic practice in its social, cultural, and geographical context [can it] be more fully understood. The economic, therefore, cannot be simply conjectured to be separated from the society in which it takes place; this [informal] economic practice is a subset of the society in which it occurs.

1.5. *Re-embedding informal employment: The new institutionalist turn*

Taking these critiques seriously, the new institutionalist approach (Williams et al., 2015; Pejovich, 2012; Lekovic, 2011; Gërxhani, 2004b; Feige, 1997; 1990; Assaad, 1993) focuses precisely on the mechanisms through which the embeddedness in specific social, institutional, and cultural contexts affect informal economic practices. Drawing on new institutional economics and economic sociology, this framework defines institutions as the 'rules of the game' that constrain human actions and reduce the uncertainty and complexity of human interactions (North, 1990). Institutions can be distinguished as either formal or informal. The former are the codified laws and regulations established and enforced by the state and by other public authorities; the latter are the norms, values and beliefs of citizens and communities.[1]

The emergence of informal economic activities is seen as the result of the interactions between formal and informal institutions. Specifically, the *institutional asymmetry thesis* posits that the emergence and endurance of informal economic practices result from a lack of alignment between formal institutions' prescriptions and the set of citizens' social and cultural norms. The greater the clash between the state's and the citizens' morality, the thesis goes, the greater the informal economy. The clash is usually measured through survey questions that reconstructs respondents' tax morale, their perceived acceptability of non-compliance with specific formal rules, and often their satisfaction of how institutions spend taxpayers' money.

Data on the magnitude of informality are also collected through direct surveys that ask the respondents to report whether they engaged with

1 As Feige (1990, p. 991) puts it 'the critical criterion for distinguishing between above-ground or formal activity on the one hand, and underground or informal activity on the other, is whether the activity adheres to the established, prevailing institutional rules of the game'.

undeclared economic activities. These studies find a strong cross-national association between the two measures (the formal–informal institutional clash and the magnitude of informality), and these same two measures also co-vary across different economies. This correlation is usually valid at both the individual and societal levels and applies to informal dependent employment (Williams and Franic, 2017; Williams and Horodnic, 2017; 2015; Williams, 2015), informal entrepreneurship (Williams and Shahid 2016), or even undeclared work for private households (Williams et al., 2015). For Webb and Ireland (2015, p. 23):

> when formal institutions fail to structure and govern economic activity, informal institutions can serve as an alternative guiding framework. In this way, informal institutions provide a complementary framework to formal institutions, at times overlapping with and supporting formal institutions while at other times providing a different framework that can guide and facilitate activities within society when formal institutions for whatever reason fail to do so.

Informality, therefore, emerges because of a mismatch between formal and informal realms or a failure of formal institutions—that is, when they fall short in promoting economic transactions, smoothing exchanges and facilitating economic activities. Following Williams and Horodnic (2019, p. 4), three stylized *waves* of new institutionalist arguments can be recognized:

> [I]n the first wave [...] the focus was upon formal institutional failures and imperfections (e.g. misallocation and misuse of public resources). The second wave of thought started to recognise the role of informal institutions, acknowledging that even in the situations where formal institutional failings are identified, this would not necessarily lead to participation in undeclared work unless it would be acceptable by the informal institutions. As such, participation in undeclared work is attributed to the asymmetry between the codified laws and regulations of a society's formal institutions (state morale) and the socially shared unwritten rules of its informal institutions (civic morale). The third wave of thought has then brought together the first two waves and argued that formal institutional failings and imperfections produce the asymmetry between the formal institutions (state morale) and informal institutions (civic morale), which, in turn, leads to a greater participation in undeclared work.

The causal chain unpacks as follows: formal institutions fail, this leads to institutional asymmetry and increases the social acceptability of engaging in undeclared work. Alternatively, some scholars do not directly infer institutional misalignment from a failure of public institutions. Their approach, on the contrary, stresses the resilience of misaligned informal norms besides the appropriateness or the failure of formal institutions. In this perspective, the institutional misalignment causing informality is not the result of illegitimate formal regulations or ineffective enforcement, but it is rather the result of a deep-rooted mismatch of these institutions with deviant informal norms that comes from past and sticky ways of organizing socio-economic relations. In these approaches, the persistence of misaligned informal norms is usually taken as a starting point of the analysis. Misaligned informal norms are the legacy of past regulative systems that survive after abrupt transformation of those same systems, such as in the case of the transition from a planned to a market economy in post-socialist countries (see among others: Feige, 1997; Gërxhani, 2004b), or the passage from a traditional to a modern capitalist society under colonial rule in developing economies (see among others: Assaad, 1993). While the presence of clashing social norms is self-evident in these specific cases, the mechanisms that guarantee the reproduction and persistence of such informal norms are generally not completely clear. Historical institutionalist contributions (for example, see: Steinmo, 2018) instead have developed case-by-case, historically thick analyses of the making and persistence of such resilient and deviant informal norms. These historical analyses, however, rarely problematize specific structural factors that can shape formal and informal institutions making such as the economic developmental path of specific locales and their position in broader production systems.

All in all, while the new institutionalist perspective presents an over-encompassing and replicable approach, it retains at least three crucial, intertwined, and mutually influencing shortcomings. First, it remains ambiguous on the direction of causality of its correlation; second, it overlooks the different positions of individuals that engage in informal activities and the relational nature of certain forms of informality (such as informal wage employment); finally, it relies–with the exception of the public choice literature–a simplified reading of institutions that tends to downplay the political dynamics that underpin the making and enforcing of formal rules vis-à-vis informality.

An uncertain direction of causality

While the institutional clash thesis identifies a correlation, it is unable to define a clear direction of causality. The association between the institutional clash and the magnitude of informality found in numerous studies does not necessarily imply that informality is driven only by this clash. Instead, it could be argued that the position of certain individuals in the economic structure and their likelihood of engaging in informal work (due to a lack of formal jobs, for example) shapes their morality such that it collides with the formal one. As new institutionalist scholars recognize in a study on envelope wage practices[2] in Southern Europe:

> There is strong evidence that envelope wages are more prevalent among those who have difficulties most of the time in paying their household bills. This reveals that this illegitimate wage practice is largely concentrated amongst weaker and more vulnerable employees who are not only easier to persuade to accept employment contracts based on unwritten verbal agreements but also less inclined to adhere to the formal rules, doubtless because they view them as made for others rather than them (Williams and Horodnic, 2015, pp. 215-18).

Having no alternatives than engaging in informal employment might lead individuals to perceive formal rules as unjust and disadvantageous. While the existing new institutionalist literature generally finds out that economic conditions might shape individuals' perception of and trust in formal institutions, it does not investigate the mechanisms through which such relationship unfolds. The emphasis on the interplay between formal and informal institutions moves the investigation away from the dynamics between structural factors and the formation and reproduction of these same institutions. It remains unclear, therefore, whether and to what extent the emergence and persistence of discordant social norms triggers the making of informal economic activities or, on the contrary, a vast informal economy resulting from the structural lack of adequate formal employment, leads informals to develop norms and beliefs that reframe formal institutions and laws as unfair and unjust. The literature I now turn to has found that perceptions of state enforcement and informality depend greatly on one's position in the economic structure.

---

2 Envelope wage refers to the employers' practice of 'paying their employees two salaries, an official declared salary that is declared to the authorities for tax and social security purposes, and an unofficial ('envelope') wage that is not declared' (Williams and Horodnic, 2015, pp. 204-5).

Not all informals are the same

As a World Bank extensive report on Latin America (Perry et al., 2007; see also: Packard et al., 2012) shows, while informal entrepreneurs decide to *exit* the informal economy out of an evaluation of costs, risks and benefits, informal dependent employees are rather *excluded* form formal labour markets. Workers would generally 'prefer an equivalent job in the formal sector', or, as my own fieldwork reveals, would generally prefer their employment relations to be fully formalized. Workers' informality, in other words, might often be the result of their employers' choices (see: Williams, Horodnic and Windebank, 2017). By the same token, the level of institutional misalignment resulting from individual and group attitudes towards institutions is heavily shaped by the position that each holds within the broad economic structure.

In her in-depth investigation of street-vending and squatting practices (both informal activities) in three Latin American capitals (Santiago, Bogotà, and Lima), Holland (2017) shows that the enforcement of laws against informal practices can have socially *progressive* or *regressive* effects, that is, enforcement can target informal practices that generally advantage poorer or richer societal groups. On these premises, Holland finds that the poor are far more supportive of state tolerance of informal activities than the rich when these are progressive and substitute for absent welfare measures. The poor tolerate the informal practices they engage in often out of necessity, but resist other kinds adopted by the rich, such as, for example, using legal loopholes to evade taxes, escape industrial electricity bills, and circumvent building regulations. In other words, one's class and direct engagement with informal activities shape her perception of informality. If one belongs to those social groups that are generally exposed to informal practices, she is more likely to justify them, even though this does not generally imply a distrust of formal rules and state morality or a general acceptance of all informal practices, as institutionalists assume.

Furthermore, one's inclination toward the tolerance of informality is not just a matter of direct material interest but also of group belonging. As Holland (2017, p. 90) finds, 'even poor individuals who do not violate the law support forbearance [of informal activities] based on their group affinity (or their concern that they too might need to violate the law one day)'. Similarly, as survey data across the Balkans showed, working informally is usually linked to exposure to others that engage in informality. This can shape individual's perception of formal institutions, making them appear unfair or illegitimate (SELDI, 2016). The 2019 Eurobarometer also brings data that call for a cautious analysis of the relationship between economic structural factors and citizens' morale. In the survey, Europeans experiencing economic uncertainty trust institutions such as the labour inspectorate or social security authorities less than those who do not experience such uncertainty, regardless of their direct participation in informal employment (EC, 2020a).

Other contributions within the new institutionalist perspective that focus on informal entrepreneurship (Darbi et al., 2018; De Castro et al., 2014; Webb et al., 2014; 2013; 2009) share the emphasis on institutional dynamics and overlooks the role of actors' position within broader economic structures. These works analyse in detail the agency of entrepreneurs in the informal economy but neglect the analysis of employees altogether. This signals not just a matter of focus but rather a confirmation of a theoretical blind spot. New institutionalist approaches see informal economic activities as the result of an individual's choice to seize business opportunities in the informal economy. Such approaches—which draw on business and entrepreneurship studies—are ill-equipped to investigate informal employment dynamics thoroughly. In fact, engaging in informal employment takes at least two parties, employer and employee, and within such a relationship, informality is continuously negotiated and reshaped.

To sum up, different strands of new institutionalism neglect the differentiated roles of individuals engaging in the informal economy and the fundamentally relational nature of informal employment. Different aims and returns move different actors, and given the power asymmetries between employers and employees, informalization choices might be crucially shaped by such differential. Moreover, since employment remains a continuously negotiated process, the forms and shapes of employment informalization will also depend on the actors' preferences and bargaining power rather than merely on their alignment with a formal institutional morality.

The missing politics of formal and informal institutions

Most studies within the new institutionalist perspective consider institutions as the rules of the game that regulate economic behaviours—their main function is to coordinate economic activities. When informal rules and formal institutions clash, they fail to maintain citizens' trust and compliance, and informal activities emerge as a socially acceptable alternative. The failure of formal institutions to change informal institutions (or to align with them) leads to the emergence of informal ones through the mechanism of institutional mismatch and distrust. This mismatch, therefore, is not merely a matter of formal rules per se, but it can also be the result of insufficient state capacities or ineffective enforcement.

A crucial limitation of such an approach is that it does not sufficiently problematize the multiple political dynamics that continuously shape formal and informal institutions. By assuming that the primary goal of formal institutions is to make economic transactions possible and that informal institutions prevail as a consequence of formal institutions' failure to deliver on this objective, it overlooks the possibility that the actors shaping formal institutions might actually be willing to tolerate—or even support—the persistence of informal economic activities.

There is conspicuous evidence, though, that political actors shaping formal rules can benefit from informal activities or might simply come to terms with their persistence. The literature stresses that enforcement policies (and therefore the level of indirect tolerance of informal activities) are often a matter of political competition (Feierherd, 2020; López-Cariboni, 2019; Holland, 2017; Amengual, 2016), that informality can be deliberately fostered by political authorities to enhance local firms' competitiveness (Mezzadri, 2010; Fernandez-Kelly and Garcia, 1989; Standing, 1989), and that forbearance might be purposely promoted as an instrument of *social policy by other means* (Dewey and Di Carlo, 2021; Afonso 2019; Dorlach 2019; Seelkopf and Starke, 2019). Informality, in fact, has distributive consequences and often favours certain groups at the expense of others. It is, therefore, crucial to take seriously the political dynamics that shape formal regulation and enforcement, without assuming that formal rules are necessarily designed to minimize informalization and without positing that the presence of informal activities is automatically a sign of low enforcement capacity and failing institutions.

A strand of the new institutionalist literature has focussed on the political dynamics of partial enforcement by mobilizing *public choice theory* and clientelism (for a comprehensive review of the literature, see: Gërxhani, 2004a; see also: Gërxhani and Wintrobe, 2021; Imami et al., 2024). These approaches, however, focussed on tax evasion rather than employment informalization and therefore generally overlook the differential role of employees and employers in shaping the political dynamics behind enforcement and forbearance. Moreover, public choice approaches do not explicitly problematize the structural-developmental logics (cf. Dewey and Di Carlo 2021) that contribute to shape, together with electoral drivers, the politics of forbearance and eradication. As Hadjimichalis and Vaiou (1990, pp. 97-98) put it in relation to the Southern European experience:

> While observations about the inefficiency of Southern European states to control informal activities do hold, their explanatory power is rather weak, since the politics involved are far more complicated and incorporate regional differences in at least two major ways. Support (or simply tolerance) of informal activities on the one hand helps regional economies compete in international markets, which would be difficult if 'regular' work relations were enforced; on the other hand it helps individuals and families raise adequate incomes, which would have been otherwise impossible in places where welfare services and employment opportunities are minimal.

In other words, informality is a matter of *political contention* that depends on both electoral variables and economic structural constraints of each locale. By focussing on the interplay between formal and informal institutions, the new institutionalist perspective risks overlooking the crucial dynamics through which economic structures influence the dynamics behind the emergence and reproduction of the formal and informal institutions that end up shaping informality.

As it will be shown in Chapter 4, informalization (and its forbearance) has winners and losers with different power resources, it benefits certain groups and disadvantages others. Thus, it is crucial to equip ourselves with tools that can analyse the relations of political actors and the preference of their constituents and support coalitions when we investigate the presence and effectiveness of state policies against informal employment. Any approach that focuses merely on the relationship between individuals' and the state' moralities remains ill-equipped to explain the political dynamics that shape state action vis-à-vis informal employment.

Finally, puzzling empirical aspects remain unanswered by the new institutionalist perspective. For example, a focus on institutional mismatch cannot explain why firms or even entire sectors and industries embedded in the same formal and informal institutional contexts engage differently with informal employment (Ram et al., 2019; see also: van der Linden and Breman, 2020; Mezzadri, 2020). As employment relations scholars consistently find, firms' non-compliance with labour laws and collective contracts is often associated with specific sectors across institutional contexts (Jaehrling and Méhaut, 2013; Bernhardt et al., 2013; 2007).

Besides sector-specific drivers, other factors such as gender have been found crucial in determining individuals' inclination to engage in informal economic practices. From a new institutionalist perspective, for example,

Gërxhani (2007) shows that a consistent gender gap exists in Albanians' tax morale and their inclination to evade taxes that can be explained only by referring to structural factors, such as the concentration of women in the state sector (where tax evasion is unlikely) and the concentration of men in self-employment (where circumventing tax regulation is rather more common).

In the next chapter, I justify the boundaries of the specific set of informal practices that will be the subject of the book and I present a novel theoretical framework to investigate them by revisiting and extending the structuralist approach.

Table 1.2. Existing theoretical approaches to informality

Theoretical approach	Main categories of *informals* considered	Causal explanations	Shortcomings of the approach
Dualist approach	*Marginal economic actors* excluded from formal labour markets (both informal self-employed and informal wage employees).	Informality is the result of backwardness, uncompleted institutional modernization and economic underdevelopment; *Informality as a survival strategy*.	Formal and informal economy are considered as detached and distinct; Despite predictions, informality persists and appears in new forms in advanced economies.
Neoliberal approach	*Free-market spirits (informal self-employed)*.	Informality is a rational response of economic actors to red-tape, over-regulation, high taxes and corruption; *Informality as emancipation from a burdensome state.*	Overlooks dependent informal employment and exploitation; Despite predictions, informality persists where regulation and tax burden are minimal.
Structuralist approach	*Downgraded labour* (informal wage employees and dependent informal self-employed, such as homeworkers).	Informality is the by-product of a deregulated, flexible, hyper-competitive globalized economy, and a response to the crisis of welfare state and public regulations; *Informality as an exploitative mechanism.*	Lack of analysis of patterns of agency; Despite predictions, informality existed where deregulated free-mar did not (see the shadow economy in Communist countries).
New institutionalist approach	*All the categories above.*	Informality is the result of a clash between public institutions (state's morality) and informal norms (citizens' morality); *Informality as a misalignment of citizens' and state's morality.*	Uncertain direction of causality (does the institutional clash cause informality or the other way around?); Treats informal employment and entrepreneurship as undifferentiated phenomena; Overlooks how formal and informal economy interact; Treats informal employment as an individual choice rather than a (contested) relationship of actors with competing interests; Does not explain why actors embedded in the same formal/informal context engage differently with informal activities.

2.
INFORMAL EMPLOYMENT AS LABOUR CONTROL
Economic Structures, Socio-institutional Contexts, and Informals' Agency

2.1. *One piece at a time: Focusing on informal wage employment and dependent self-employment*

Despite a lively debate, no single theoretical perspective seems to wholly grasp the heterogeneous reality of informal employment and the broader informal economy (Williams and Onoshchenko, 2015; Williams et al., 2012; Williams and Round, 2008; see Table 1.2). Informality is a multifaceted and heterogeneous reality and the theories that develop mono-casual explanations of the persistence of informality (underdevelopment, a burdensome state, or neoliberal capitalism) risk seeing only a part of the broader picture.

The new institutionalist perspective, on the contrary, offers a comprehensive *explicans* (a formal–informal institutional clash) for the emergence of any type of informal economic practices. Yet, as I argued, even this perspective does not address the fact that not all *informals* are equal, and they may be induced into informality for different reasons, through different mechanisms, and under different pressures. As such, it overlooks the internal variety of informal employment. The persistence of informal employment, therefore, means different things to the different people involved in it, and each theoretical approach refers to a subset of the really-existing informal activities even when it seeks to provide overarching explanations (Pfau-Effinger, 2009). One way to address this shortcoming is to *bridge multiple perspectives*. For example, drawing on empirical enquiries of informal economic practices, some scholars propose to apply different theoretical approaches simultaneously to make sense of the different informal realities observed (Williams et al., 2012; Williams and Round, 2008).

Alternatively, one can focus on specific forms of informalization to avoid undue generalizations. Given the complexity of the informality phenomenon and the critical analysis of the literature, the purpose of this research is not to explain all forms of informality present in a specific region or economy. On the contrary, I contend that we need to treat different forms of informality and diverse process of informalization as distinct social phenomena. Moreover, focusing on some specific informalization processes can bear more fruits than seeking all-encompassing generalizations over multiple and diverse realities. Thus, this research focuses on *partial or total informal wage employment* and *dependent self-employment* (i.e., home-based work) incorporated into formal production networks.

2.2. *Informal employment: Negotiated, socially embedded, and economically constrained*

Any analysis of employment informalization processes clearly needs to consider the role of formal and informal institutions. At the same time, informal employment also responds to economic drivers and motives, however deeply embedded it is in social, political, and cultural institutions. Moreover, different actors engaging in informality have different power and positions that inevitably shape informalization dynamics. Informals are generally divided into those who *exit* and those who are *excluded* from formal economic activities. At the same time, any process of employment informalization needs to be understood, as with all employment dynamics, as a relationship continuously mediated by employers and employees. Framing informalization decisions as a matter of more or less constrained choice vis-à-vis institutions is, in fact, problematic exactly because informalized employment relations are the result of a negotiation (albeit an asymmetrical one) between employers and workers. Thus, informal work cannot be analysed merely as an individual decision (however based on bounded rationality and embedded in a social and institutional context it may be) to either evade or clash with formal rules. Quite the contrary, employment informalization is determined not by the unilateral action of one individual vis-à-vis formal institutions and informal scripts and morality, but by her preferences, the preferences of her counterpart in the employment relation, and the bargaining power of both. Formal and informal norms remain crucial because they contribute to shape employment relationships and dynamics, but they are not the sole nor the central drivers of employment informalization.

Moreover, neither institutions nor the political actors shaping them can be assumed to automatically reject informal employment. Informality has distributional effects; it rewards certain groups rather than others, has progressive and regressive effects, and cannot be considered merely as a deviation from formal rules or a failure of formal institutions. On the contrary, the actors shaping formal rules and institutions might tolerate, refrain from tackling, or deliberately ignore, informality because this fits their own preferences or the preferences of their constituency. Therefore, we need to consider the really-existing institutions that shape informality as drafted, driven and implemented by really-existing political actors with their specific interests and preferences.

Finally, while institutional, social, and cultural factors do shape informality, employment informalization is ultimately negotiated in the workplace and mediated within the employer–employee relationship. This implies that any account of informality cannot avoid seriously investigating the economic power relations of the actors that shape informalized employment. Departing from this premise, it is possible to propose a framework capable of analysing the dynamics of informalization as a negotiated process by accounting for local contexts and the economic structures and power relations that constrain employers and employees. At the same time, within the same analytical lens, it is possible to enquire into the political preferences and agendas of political actors that shape the realm of formal institutions within which informal employment develops and persists.

Firstly, I use LPT and the concept of *labour control* and *labour/factory regimes* to redefine informalization as *a tool of labour control* in employment relations. Secondly, building on the GPNs literature, I develop an alternative analytical perspective that is comprehensive enough to analyse how economic, institutional, and social factors shape the informalization process and how the agency of the main actors of employment informalization, that is, employees, employers and the state, actively contribute to steer, reproduce, or disrupt informalization.

2.3. *Toward an extended structural perspective on informal employment: Labour process theory and the global production networks approach*

This section clarifies the pieces of a theoretical framework that situate the analysis of employee–employer relations—and therefore employment informalization—within the broader economic, structural, and institutional contexts in which these processes are embedded. The aim is to address the shortcomings of previous structuralist approaches. Furthermore, by combining LPT and the GPNs approach, I *extend* the structuralist approach by incorporating a serious analysis of local contexts and actors' patterns of agency.

Labour process analysis: Core theory and central problems

Labour process analyses investigate the mechanisms, dynamics and relations through which labour power (the potential to work) is transformed into actual work-effort and how the value produced in this transformation is distributed (Thompson and Vincent, 2010, pp. 47-8; for a review of the literature see: Bagnardi and Maccarrone, 2023). Such a transformation is an inherently contentious process because of the indeterminacy of the exchange. As Smith (2006, p. 390) notes,

> [w]orkers generally know in advance of starting a job the wages they will be paid for their time at work, but not the exact quantity of labour-effort that is required for the particular job. Labour power, what the employer hires and the worker exchanges, is indeterminate because the precise amount of effort to be extracted cannot be 'fixed' before the engagement of workers, machinery and products for purposeful (profitable within capitalism) action in the labour process.

The indeterminacy of the commodity exchanged—labour power—is a matter of continuous negotiation. Employment relations are, therefore, continuously contested because they are based on the potentially conflicting interests of workers and employers. While managers need to secure control over workers to maximize their work-effort, workers arguably aim to maximize remuneration, satisfaction, and fulfilment at work. Work intensification and the strive for efficiency clash with workers' search for higher wages, control over work organization, and increased autonomy in the workplace. Any production process is a rather open-ended relationship in which managers need to set in motion labour power by continuously *convincing* or *coercing* workers to take part and put effort into the labour process while accepting both the technical organization of work and the given distribution of the value produced with their effort.

The core theory of the labour process can be organized into a few central tenets (Taylor, 2010; Thompson and Vincent, 2010; Thompson and Smith, 2000; Thompson, 1990). Workplace dynamics are the core concern of labour process analyses because at the workplace labour needs to be controlled for value to be extracted, and workers' resistance towards managerial control emerges. The labour process, therefore, is regulated by a *structured antagonism* between actors with structurally different interests. Furthermore, even though workplace dynamics never escape this antagonism and are therefore *relatively autonomous* from the contexts in which they are embedded, the ways in which managerial control is obtained and resisted depends on different factors originating within and beyond the workplace (Baglioni et al., 2022). The technical aspects of the production process itself, the level of technology, the competition and cooperation with other firms, the features of end markets, the uneven resistance of different groups of workers (see: Friedman, 1977), the local labour supply and labour mobility, laws, institutions, and informal norms, all contribute to shaping managerial strategies to maximize the labour-effort in different firms and workers' resistance to enhance pay, fulfilment and autonomy. In some cases, the maximisation of the value extracted from labour relies on tight and coercive control, in others it might need to ensure a certain level of workers' creativity and commitment. Every strategy will face some form of resistance or accommodation from workers and any temporary arrangement is destined to be challenged. The resulting employment relationships, therefore, are a continuously contested mix of consent, coercion, hegemony, and control dynamics.

The relative autonomy and the embeddedness of the labour process

The core LPT posits that developments and changes within the workplace are the result of internal patterns of struggle and cooperation and remain relatively autonomous from the broader environment. At the same time, *labour control regimes*—namely, the ensemble of rules that managers mobilize to control labour and ensure the maximization of work-effort maximization—are still shaped by the resistance of workers and their strength vis-à-vis managers, as well as by sectoral structures, competitive pressures of the firm, local labour markets, and the institutions regulating employment relations. Relative autonomy, therefore, should not be overemphasized. If labour process analyses focus merely on workplace dynamics, they risk neglecting the ways in which formal and informal institutions, local norms and practices, broader production networks, and the mechanisms that ensure the reproduction of labour shape workplace relationships. Such a risk is labelled as the LPT *connectivity gap* (for a critical overview of the theoretical attempts to address the gap, see: Thompson and Vincent, 2010). To address it, we need to read workplace dynamics in their interaction with 'other loci of social relations' (Taylor 2010, p. 51). As

Thompson and Smith (2009, p. 917) put it, a 'conceptual and empirical focus on the labour process only becomes a problem if privileging those social relations becomes a means of denying the significance of others'.

In fact, even the early contributions of labour process theorists recognized that 'the degree of competition among capitalists, the size of corporations, the extent of trade union organization, the level of class consciousness among workers, the impact of governmental policies, the speed of technological change' (Edwards, 1979, p. 15), local customs, and the residual institutional protections that workers had won with past struggles (Friedman, 1977) are all crucial and necessarily context-specific factors that shape the prevailing forms of labour control. Burawoy (1985; 1979), for example, investigates how state regulations profoundly affect workplace dynamics. He finds that protective legislation against despotic managerial practices, and the presence of a social wage that partially disentangles labour reproduction from work, modifies the way labour control is achieved in production processes. Welfare states and labour laws, indeed, weaken managers' coercive power, introduce new apparatuses to organize relations within production (*the internal state* —namely, trade unions' rights at work, co-decision councils, protection against unfair dismissals and the like) and push management to shift from despotic to hegemonic forms of control, seeking workers' consent rather than their subordination.

More recently, Smith (2006) has investigated how labour markets and new job opportunities shape work organization and mechanisms of labour control. Quitting, or just threatening to do so, is a part and parcel of the antagonistic relationship between workers and managers. Retention and exit strategies can be a source of continuous conflict and influence the way workers and managers shape the work organization. Workers can, in certain cases, use the threat of exit as a tool of negotiation. An abundant supply of labour, on the contrary, weakens the bargaining power of employees. Thus, the features of labour markets crucially shape how employees and employers negotiate working conditions and employment relations.

The relative autonomy of the workplace, therefore, is better understood as a way to select and bound a specific arena in which the actors and processes of interest are analysed rather than a way to rule out the influence of other factors on employment dynamics (Edwards 2010, p. 32). Any production process is regulated by a rather complex mix of economic as well as intertwined societal, cultural, ideological, and political factors. Following Burawoy (1985, p. 122, emphasis in the original),

> the process of production contains political and ideological elements as well as purely economic moments. That is, the process of production is not confined to the *labour process* – to the social relations into which men and women enter as they transform raw materials into useful products with [the] instrument of production. It also includes *political apparatuses* which reproduce those relations of the labour process through the regulation of struggles.

In other words, if controlling labour to maximize work-effort is imperative in any economic enterprise, how to secure this control is a multidimensional phenomenon. The combination of managers' strategies, workers' resistance, and temporary settlements between the two, shapes the specific factory/labour regimes. Structured antagonism does not necessarily entail open conflict, and labour control relies on a mix of *coercion* and *consent*. Yet, the factors determining such a mix depend on the agency of managers and workers as well as on local contexts, non-economic axes of social differentiation and locally specific, formal and informal regulations. Contextual factors serve as resources and constraints for both managers to secure labour control and workers to negotiate work organization, resist managerial control (Baglioni et al., 2022; Castree et al., 2004, chap. 2) and shape labour control regimes. Consequently, 'understanding the labour process requires understanding that what occurs on the shop floor is shaped by what goes on outside the factory or office gates' (Rainnie et al., 2010, p. 299). This does not mean that every workplace is singular and unrepeatable, but rather that each workplace mediates differently the same economic processes and might lead to different labour regimes (Pattenden, 2016; Jonas, 1996; Peck 1996).

The connectivity gap and political economy: labour processes within production networks

LPT's emphasis on workplace dynamics requires a cautious problematization of how to factor external dynamics into labour process analyses. In fact, by focusing on firm-level dynamics of control and resistance, earlier LPT accounts overlooked the ongoing seismic shift in production organization (Hauptmeier and Vidal, 2014; Bagnardi and Maccarrone, 2023). Earlier labour process analysis predicted the general affirmation of hegemonic labour regimes within vertically integrated firms with monopoly power (Burawoy, 1985; Edwards, 1979; Friedman, 1977) while, in fact, production processes were already restructuring in fragmented chains of production. Through subcontracting and outsourcing practices, lead firms can retain all the higher-added-value production activities while outsourcing to other firms many activities once carried out in-house. Extensive subcontracting relations thus allow companies to maintain control over the labour process through a firm-to-firm supply relationship while offloading the responsibility of employing labour directly to subcontracting firms.

The growth of outsourcing practices and the de-verticalization of companies do not imply the diffusion of monopoly power but rather its transformation (Harrison, 1994; Murray, 1983). Investing in high return production phases while outsourcing phases with lower returns and high costs and rigidities became a common managerial strategy (Crouch, 2019; Drahokoupil and Fabo, 2019; Schwartz, 2019; Greco, 2016; Weil, 2014; Wills, 2008). Through subcontracting, firms can go beyond coercion and consent and pursue labour control through outsourcing. Harrison (1994) labelled this process *concentration without centralization:* lead firms can *concentrate* control over the organization of production without having to *centralize* the production process in one firm, avoiding the strings, rigidities, and costs that the direct control of the workforce implies (Taplin, 1996). A focus on labour–capital relations within the workplace led earlier LPT approaches to neglect how relations between firms were already profoundly reshaping the future of the labour control regimes. For example, keeping control of the production process through firm-to-firm subcontracting relations—and avoiding the direct responsibility of employing workers—became a new generalized control strategy that earlier labour process analyses could not predict.

Within the GPNs debate, a growing number of scholars have fruitfully analysed the change of employment relations brought about by global production reorganization (López, 2021; Naz and Bögenhold, 2020; Baglioni, 2018; Hammer and Plugor, 2019; 2016; Flecker et al., 2013; Flecker and Meil, 2010; Lakhani et al., 2013; Newsome et al., 2015). GPNs analysis represents a relatively recent development within a strand of international political economy that has focused on the dynamics and effects of global trade and the restructuring of production processes.[1] The GPNs literature studies the role of organized labour and collective actions in

1 GPN perspectives emerged explicitly as a sympathetic critique of the previous firm-centric global value chain (GVC) approach. However, I consider both as part of a continuum in the analytical efforts to understand the dynamics of global fragmentation and re-organization of production. I therefore use the terms 'networks' and 'chains' interchangeably. For a reconstruction of the two

shaping the development trajectories of firms and territories (Anner, 2015a; Cumbers et al., 2008) and analyses how even informal and individualized forms of worker agency are shaped by and contribute to shape broader production structures (Mezzadri and Fan, 2018; De Neve, 2014; Carswell and De Neve, 2013; Rogaly, 2009). Workers are considered active agents who contribute to influence GPNs (Coe, 2012; Coe and Jordhus-Lier, 2011; Newsome et al., 2015) and the ways labour gets integrated and disciplined within global production is crucial to understand firms' strategies and the governance of production chains (Taylor et al., 2015; Rainnie et al. 2013; Cumbers et al., 2008).

The GPNs perspective enquires into the role of social and institutional contexts as well. Social and cultural differences, including gender and race, are part and parcel of global processes of accumulation, and GPNs often build upon and reinforce social differences and the social segmentations of the workforce in order to amplify workers' vulnerability and extract higher rates of surplus (Werner, 2016; Bair and Werner, 2011; Huws, 2011; Bair, 2010; Tsing, 2009).

A recent strand within this literature explicitly analyses labour control regimes in firms integrated into broader chains of production by looking at the local institutional and social context in which each labour process is embedded and the governance of the chain in which the firm is integrated. These GPN analyses investigate the emergence of specific managerial control strategies and the patterns of workers' resistance to account for the diverse factory regimes that compose the production chains (Newsome et al., 2015). The study of GPN governance and labour regimes reinforces both approaches and integrates the GPNs perspective's sensitivity to firm-to-firm relations and local contexts with a focus on the agency of managers and employees within each firm (Newsome et al., 2015, p. 14; see also: Flecker and Meil, 2010; Flecker et al., 2013; on the garment industry: Hammer and Plugor, 2016; 2019; López, 2021).

In sum, the GPNs perspective offers an appropriate meso-level approach to fill the connectivity gap of earlier labour process studies. The combination of LPT and GPNs analysis fruitfully links employment dynamics at the workplace level with the broader structural, sectoral, and contextual drivers shaping them.

---

approaches and an analysis of their differences and commonalities see Bair (2009), and Henderson et al. (2002).

2.4. *Reframing informal employment through the labour process perspective: Informality as a tool of labour control*

The LPT focus on the continuous negotiations shaping employment provides fundamental insights for the study of employment informalization. In line with the perspective suggested by Ram et al. (2019, p. 2, see also: Ram et al., 2017, p. 370), when analysing informal employment, it is important to pay attention to

> dynamics within firms at the micro level that create and sustain informal practices, including the social relations between owners, workers and other relevant actors (that is, the 'labour process'). [...]. As such, 'informality' [can be defined] as a process of workforce engagement, collective and/or individual, based mainly on unwritten customs and the tacit understandings that arise out of the interaction of the parties at work. As such, informality is a dynamic rather than a fixed characteristic, and is highly context-specific.

By mobilizing the conceptual toolbox provided by the LPT, we can consider employment informalization as one of the possible strategies available to managers to ensure labour participation in the production process. *Employment informalization, therefore, moves the labour control regime away from formal and institutionalized regulations toward the realm of social norm and informal practices.*

One might argue that every labour process has a crucial informal component even under full compliance with formal regulations. In fact, not all aspects of the labour process can be codified, and many work activities are based on rules of behaviour and organization that are not officially regulated or written in employment contracts (Godfrey and Schulze, 2015). Yet, the informalization of employment I refer to is *non-compliant informality*—namely, that set of behaviours and practices in breach of formal laws and regulations (see: Ram et al., 2019). Such process entails an informalized privatization of the employment regulatory space (see: MacKenzie and Martínez Lucio, 2005; Martínez Lucio and MacKenzie, 2017; Bagnardi, 2023a) through which the role and influence of formal institutional regulations shrinks, while informal norms, practices and regulation become more crucial (Harriss-White, 2003; Mezzadri, 2016; 2017).

Informalized labour regimes thus rely on specific control apparatuses that differ from the apparatuses regulating formal employment relations. Informalization significantly impinges on the legal instruments available to workers to negotiate the terms of their employment and the organization of production with management, but also the protection of their rights and their access to justice when these are violated (see: Vosko et al., 2017). Moreover, informalization individualizes the employment relationship, moving it away from collective agreements and labour laws negotiated by collective actors and through institutionalized processes. Informalized employment relations, in fact, very often rely on *ad hominem*, verbal agreements between employers and employees. As such, informalization needs to be actively sought by employers, and it needs to be accepted (or not sufficiently resisted) by workers in a process of imposition, refusal, adaptation and continuous contestation as in the formation of any labour control regime. It does not necessarily come at the expense of the workers but it individualizes employment relations and deprives them of the existing context-specific legal protections and constraints. This entails a more overt exercise of power relations in which the specific individual bargaining power of workers and managers becomes even more crucial than in formalized work.

Stressing the active role of the actors involved in the informal employment relationship does not mean that such actors are free from the constraints set by economic structures, historical legacies, and specific institutional and social contexts. It instead offers a perspective to analyse how such structural constraints and opportunities shape actors' agency and sets the arena within which the actors involved in the informalization process act This allows me to address two main blind spots of the new institutionalist perspectives. Firstly, it allows analysis of how different actors with different economic powers and positions impose or receive, resist or sustain informalization processes and rebuts the mono-causal logic of informalization as an institutional clash. Secondly, it enables the problematization of how formal and informal economic activities influence each other.

At the same time, this approach remains rooted in the structuralist perspective and aims to extend it to overcome its main shortcomings. It considers the multiple linkages between the formal economy and informalization and offers a new perspective to analyse how changes in the organization of the formal economy influence the persistence of informal work. Yet, in contrast to the great bulk of structuralist accounts that assume informality will persist as long as the given structural constraints do, this approach traces the patterns of *informals'* agency within structural constraints and socio-institutional contexts and sheds new light on how local actors navigate informality, and whether and how their agency contributes to reproduce, transform, or disrupt it.

To avoid the connectivity gap problem, it is crucial to account for the embeddedness of the informalized labour process within both economic and institutional structures of opportunities and constraints. A combination of GPN analysis and LPT can investigate how outsourcing becomes a way to displace the rigidities of direct employment and control and value chains turn into '*insecurity-and-risks transfer chains*' (Frade and Darmon, 2005)—namely, mechanisms through which firms externalize production and employment relations in order to escape the resistance, overhead costs and responsibilities of standard, regulated and direct employment (Crouch, 2019; Wills, 2008; Grimshaw and Rubery, 2005). By combining GPN analysis and LPT, I reframe production networks as webs of 'embodied labour' (Cumbers et al., 2008) and analyse how labour regimes change at each node in the chain in mutually dependent ways. By factoring in the pressures that the chains governance poses for each firm, the opportunities and constraints offered by the local institutional context (in terms of labour legislation or monitoring institutions, for example), and the agency of the actors (such as the presence or absence of an effective labour movement) I can map and analytically explain the emergence of multiple, diverse, interlinked labour processes in the chain.

Among the different control strategies within chains, informalization characterizes certain labour regimes and not others that can take different paths and forms. To explain this variation, I look to local contexts, the firm's position in the GPN, and the agency and bargaining powers of the actors in the workplace. This perspective not only provides a more comprehensive picture of a sector and of the informalization processes within it but also explains how the nodes of the production chains are interdependent and interlinked and how the emergence of one specific (more or less informalized) labour regime in one firm depends on and in turn shapes the labour regimes that emerge in the other nodes of that same chain.

At the same time, an analysis that focuses on the institutional context is needed. By framing informal labour as a process through which employment relations escape formal and collective regulations, I consider the informalization a de-facto deregulation of employment relations and a mechanism that enhances employers' discretion vis-à-vis institutions and workers' rights. Within such a perspective, I can identify the social groups with a stake in promoting or opposing informal employment and I can reconstruct the political dynamics and socio-economic blocs that favour policies of eradication or forbearance. This allows me to broadly identify the electoral and structural constraints that shape political actors' success in eradicating informal employment.

Figure 2.1. A theoretical framework to study informal employment

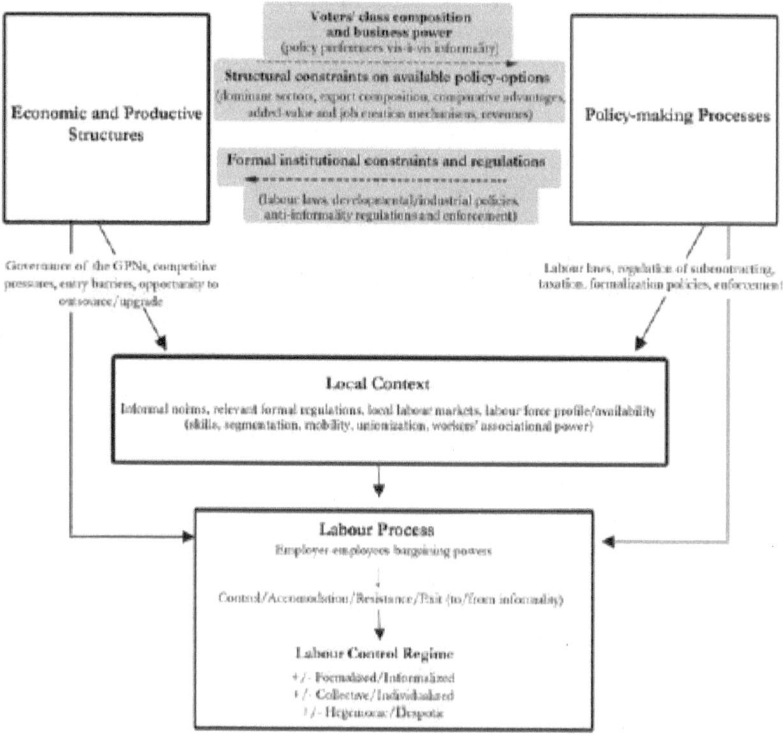

Source: Author's own elaboration

My approach offers a variant of Ram and colleagues' (2019; 2017) proposal to combine different theoretical lenses to analyse informality. Here, the GPNs perspective can account for policy and law formations, localities' history, the role of institutions and institutionalized actors such as trade unions, labour inspectors and enforcement agencies, while LPT provides the tools to analyse worker and employer agency and to understand informal employment as the result of a contested workplace relationship that is deeply embedded in both production networks and local contexts. In other words, my approach takes seriously the invitation to analyse informal work by paying due attention to both broader structures and social contexts as well as the agency of actors in the workplace.

Figure 2.1 offers a stylized representation of the theoretical framework I develop. On the top of the scheme, economic and productive structures and policy-making processes are linked and mutually influencing.

On the one hand, the specific economic structures of a given locality shape the policy-making that targets informalization dynamics. Such influence unfolds through economic and political mechanisms. Economic structures determine the class composition of voters and, therefore, their interests vis-à-vis informality. At the same time, economic structures shape the power of specific sectoral business groups and the material constraints on available policies in terms of revenues, employment, export, crucial economic sectors, and local firms' competitive advantages. To put it simply, a national or regional economy dominated by sectors that rely on massive informalization to stay competitive will face specific economic consequences in terms of loss of competitiveness, employment, exports, and even revenues, if a political agenda to eradicate informality is pursued. On the other hand, the policies enacted constrain the behaviour of economic actors by setting specific regulations, taxation, incentives and through the enforcement of such rules.

This first bloc of the theoretical framework—represented figuratively by the shaded background behind the mechanisms at play—is not the main focus of the book. Nonetheless, these mechanisms are briefly analysed in Chapter 4 and offer the background for the rest of the study. In Chapter 4, I show how specific economic structures entail economic and political costs for those actors in government that pursue anti-informality policies. This results in policy reversals or enforcement sabotage and a *low-compliance equilibrium* whenever informalization processes have become a crucial feature of a locality's economy.

The second part of the framework shows that both economic structures and policy-making processes shape local contexts and firms' labour processes. Economic structures are the sectors and the kind of GPNs in which local firms are embedded, with their governance, their opportunities for upgrading, their competitive pressures and constraints. Policy-making output represents the institutional frame within which local actors move. Such factors interact with the local context and shape local labour markets, local industrial legacies, the history of workers' organization, and labour force segmentation. Structures and institutions are received and transformed by local contexts and crucially influence the labour regime emerging in each local firm. The position of firms within GPNs shape managers' opportunities to upgrade and outsource and tie them to specific productive activities. Institutional frameworks, trade union legacies, and local labour markets determine workers' collective and individual power. As shaped by their power relations, the continuous contestation of employment relations between workers and managers determines the prevailing labour regime, whether informal or not.

The second bloc of the theoretical framework guides the rest of the book. In Chapter 5, I detail the functioning and history of the specific sector and regions under analysis. Chapter 6 and Chapter 7 are dedicated to the analysis of managers' and workers' agency, and Chapter 8 brings structures, contexts and agency together to explain the varieties of informalized labour regimes identified.

3.
STUDYING INFORMALITY PERSISTENCE IN EUROPE'S PERIPHERIES
Research Goals, Methods, and Empirical Strategies

3.1. *Research questions and goals*

Why does informal employment persist despite the widespread costs and the hostility of public authorities? How do actors in regions with significant levels of informal employment cope with, use, or resist informalization processes? And how does their agency contribute to reproduce or disrupt informality?

The core concern of this research is to analyse the *mechanisms* that make informal employment endure. Concerning states, I research why public policies fail to eradicate informal employment. With respect to firms, I question the conditions under which, and the mechanisms through which, firms impose and rely on informal employment. Finally, regarding workers, I investigate whether they accept, cope with, or resist informalization and how their agency contributes to the variegation and persistence of informality.

The book has, therefore, two main goals. On the one hand, it proposes a novel understanding of informalization as a tool of labour control. In the following chapters, I will show how such a reframing provides a fine-grained understanding of the varieties of informalization processes and offers a theoretical perspective to investigates how informalization persists in different shapes and forms. On the other hand, the book unveils the mechanisms underlying the persistence of informality by focusing on the agency of the major actors involved.

3.2. *Same sector, different regions*

The research focuses on the garment-footwear production networks that have developed in Apulia, a region of Southern Italy, and Albania. In Apulia, I focus on the industrial districts of the provinces of Bari and Barletta-Andria-Trani (BAT) which have seen an historical presence of *both* the garment *and* the footwear sectors (ARTI, 2020; 2021). They also present various specializations in both industries, with relatively high levels of exports and production. In the first steps of the fieldwork, focusing on a rather limited number of cities made the search for gatekeepers and access to the initial informants easier. For Albania, instead, I investigated the whole national industry, which is concentrated around the cities of Tirana, Durres, Korca, Shkoder, Elbasan, Berat and Vlora (Shehi, 2017).

The garment-footwear industry represents a *typical case study* (Hancké, 2009; Seawright and Gerring, 2008) to analyse the persistence of informality with a structuralist approach. On the one hand, it epitomizes a globalized, highly volatile and fragmented industry (Dicken, 2015; Gereffi and Frederick, 2010). On the other, it maintains high levels of informality. This facilitates the access to usually *hard-to-reach workplaces* (see: Clark et al., 2020) such as those that generally involve workers and firms engaging in informal practices. It also makes informal practices generally easier to approach exactly because of their spread and sets the stage for an in-depth analysis of the mechanisms of informal employment reproduction.

The literature on garment-footwear has reported similar forms of informalization across different institutional contexts, from the UK (Hammer and Plugor, 2019; 2016; Ram et al., 2017), to Italy (Ceccagno, 2017; Toffanin, 2016; Burroni et al., 2008), to a great part of Eastern Europe (Medarov et al., 2019; Pickles and Smith, 2016; Clean Clothes Campaign, 2014) as well as the developing regions of Asia (Anner 2020; Mezzadri and Fan, 2018; Mezzadri, 2017; De Neve, 2014) and Africa (Gifawosen, 2019; Tilly et al., 2013). This makes this sector apt for a critical analysis of the mechanisms through which similar structural economic pressures interact with different socio-institutional contexts.

The research design is also rooted in the GPNs methodological traditions that focuses on commodity fluxes to reconstruct the relations among actors within the chain (see: Barrientos, 2002). In line with such an approach, I started my inquiry looking at Southern Italian firms and retraced their supply chains by analysing reports, statistical data on trade, and conducting interviews with experts, managers, workers, and stakeholders. This work led me to Albania, where suppliers and competitors for Apulian firms emerged. In Albania, I repeated the same inquiry I had carried out in Italy. The case study design takes the chain as its main unit of analysis but develops a multi-level analysis of public policies, firms, and workers considering the emerging workplace regimes as *analytical embedded subunits of analysis* (Yin, 2003).

3.3. *Extending the structuralist perspective*

Methodologically, this research draws on the *extended case study method* as developed in Burawoy et al. (1991; see also: Burawoy, 1998). Such a method identifies a theory to test, reconstruct, or reinforce, and through fieldwork and qualitative research—usually participant observation or interviews—looks at actors' everyday practices in order to find anomalies or shortcomings in the given theory. Then, it analyses these anomalies in light of the macro conditions and pressures that shape them. Such anomalies might be deviant cases, unpredicted patterns of behaviour, empirical puzzles or 'theoretical gaps or silences' (Burawoy, 1991:10). The extended case method looks at such gaps and blind spots to reconstruct the existing theory through a new, more comprehensive perspective that includes studying the interaction between macro-structural forces and micro-patterns of action. Leaving the core postulates of the given theory intact, the method aims to explain the empirical anomalies and deepen the empirical investigation to reinforce the initial theory (Burawoy, 1998).

The point of departure of this research is the structuralist perspective of informality. The *theoretical silence* of classic structuralist perspectives is their lack of attention to the role of agency and their neglect of the role of institutions in the informalization process. The *anomaly* is represented by the presence of actors' patterns of conflict and adaptation that matter for the reproduction of informality, which the structuralist approach usually ignores. By unveiling the mechanisms of conflict and adaptation adopted by the actors involved, I link macro-structural constraints and micro-patterns of agency. Thus, I reconstruct and reinforce the structuralist theories of informality by offering an approach that unpacks how structural constraints, institutional contexts, workers' and employers' bargaining power and agency shape informalization in the employment relationship. In line with the extended case method, I followed an iterative and abductive approach to link the theories I started my research with and field data. This led me to reconceptualize informalization as a tool of labour control to better grasp the mechanisms of its persistence.

3.4. *Fieldwork, research techniques, and data*

The research developed as a multi-sited qualitative fieldwork study (Marcus, 1995; Mazzucato and Wagner, 2018) carried out in the summer of 2018 (from May to mid-September), and in three periods of around three weeks each between 2018 and 2019[1]. The fieldwork included semi-structured, qualitative interviews (Edwards and Holland, 2013) and three focus groups that reached 118 actors, including workers and unionists, firms' managers and other stakeholders such as NGO representatives, labour inspectors, politicians, policy advisers, experts, firm's HRM consultants and representatives of business associations.

More specifically, the interviews in Apulia reached out 12 local unionists active in the sector, 18 workers (aged between 40 and 60 mostly women; seven of them participated in a focus group interview), two local labour inspectors, 15 managers (two of whom were also chairmen of the local branches of the two most representative sectoral business organizations; three of them took part in a focus group) together with other four representatives of local business organizations (who were not garment-footwear managers themselves). Interviews also involved three HRM consultants chosen because of their expertise in the sector (as signalled by trade unionists), one consultant specialized in working for Italian firms investing in Albania, three relevant policymakers selected for their participation in anti-informality actions at the regional level, one city councillor selected for his knowledge of the sector, three consultants/executives of the regional government's department dedicated to the relationship with Albania and two experts (economists) on the local economy. Besides interviews, I also carried out two focus groups. The first (I-35/38) brought together three managers of local firms and one specialized worker. The worker was not an employee of the three companies involved in the focus group. The second focus group gathered workers of diverse local companies. Both were organized by a local unionist who served as gatekeeper.

In Albania, I interviewed sixteen workers (all female, between 30 and 50 years of age, nine of them participated in two different focus group interviews), two representatives of the sectoral union federations, representatives of five labour-centred NGOs and of one social movement union, fourteen managers, two firms' consultants, three labour inspectors (one of whom had recently moved to the NGO sector and works on occupational safety and health (OSH)-related issues, one occupational doctor working with garment-footwear firms, the head of the most representative business organization, the head of the Albanian Investment Council, six experts (one sociologist, one lawyer, two economists and two

1 Fieldwork activities precedes the tragic earthquake occurred in November 2019 which struck Northwest Albania and killed 51 persons, injured hundreds and displaced thousands of people.

investigative journalists), one executive of the Italian embassy in Tirana, and a former economy minister. Also, in Albania, I carried out two focus groups with workers. The first gathered workers from the shoe workers from Tirana (I-64–67), and the second grouped garment workers from Elbasan (I-107/111) (see Appendix 1 for a list of the interviews and focus groups). Both focus groups were organized with the support of a local NGO.

Qualitative researchers usually reach research participants through personal contacts, gatekeepers, or directly via cold calls (Peticca-Harris et al., 2016, p. 387). I used all these three options in my research: I mobilized old contacts who lived in the industrial districts of interest and could direct me towards workers or potential gatekeepers. I cold-called potential discussants when their contacts were public, and I relied on gatekeepers.

The selection of research participants followed a logic of 'chain referral sampling' (Ram et al., 2007). To mitigate biases in selecting respondents through gatekeepers, I relied on representatives of different trade union confederations and personal networks in Apulia, on diverse NGOs, former inspectors, and social movement unionists in Albania.

Building trust with gatekeepers was also a crucial part of the fieldwork (see following sections). In Apulia, this led me to spend time in their offices whenever I could, hanging around to establish a sympathetic relationship. At some point, my presence in the unions' offices allowed me to approach workers that were consulting the unions directly and inquire whether they would agree to meet me again for an interview. In Albania, however, trade unions were not open to support me in the attempt to get in touch with workers directly. Instead, local NGOs, one OSH doctor and a former labour inspector helped me organizing focus group sessions and interviews.

Managers, on the contrary, were reached directly through cold calls from the list provided by the local Chamber of Commerce in Apulia and through the lists provided by the Albanian Investment and Development Agency (AIDA) in Albania. The logic of selection for Apulian managers was random extraction from the publicly available list. In Albania, instead, *all* the firms registered in the AIDA list that had left an email address were contacted via email, and those that responded positively were interviewed.

Interviews in Italy were carried out in Italian and in Albania in English or Italian, except with Albanian workers that were interviewed in their mother tongue with the help of interpreters. Interviews lasted between 30 and 90 minutes, followed a non-rigid script of pre-determined questions (semi-structured interviews) and were recorded—whenever research participants gave me their consent.

Through the interviews with workers, I enquired about work experience and reconstructed employment relations, the dynamics of recruitment and mobility, the labour process, and the organizing and disciplining aspects of the labour regime. The reconstruction of the labour regime went hand in hand with questions aimed at understanding the level of formalization of employment. For example, I asked whether workers had a contract, the extent to which the terms were adhered to in their everyday work experience, and how they perceived the level of formalization and informalization. The interviews also aimed to reconstruct the type of firms in which workers were employed to link specific employment relations with corresponding positions in the chain. Simultaneously, interviews enquired into the specific role of the workers within the production process and their professional growth and career trajectory. Often workers had worked in different firms with different position within the chain. This was an opportunity to ask them to reflect upon differences among employers and labour regimes.

I followed the same themes in focus groups, but I let workers more freely compare their experiences. This was fruitful both when employees had contrasting experiences and when they faced similar challenges. In the former case, I enquired indirectly but in-depth as to whether the contrasting experiences were due to different employers' positions within the chain, whether these were temporary (perhaps because of a period of restructuring) or continuous—namely, whether they described a consolidated labour regime or just a period of change.

I also enquired into the level of commitment that workers displayed toward their jobs, how much flexibility they were required to maintain, what they appreciated and what they were critical about in their work experience. In addition, I asked how productive and reproductive activities were intermingled and the factors that had led them to 'choose' and stay in the sector. Finally, I also asked workers to reflect upon their gender and how this affected their work choices and burdens, career opportunities, and employment relations. I enquired about workers' experience of employment informalization, focusing on reconstructing the level of such informalization, why they accepted it or whether and how they tried to resist it. Finally, I enquired into their relationship with employers, colleagues, and trade unions, reconstructing the channels available to express grievances, resolve conflict, or raise concerns.

With managers, I focused on the firms' structure, specialization, and position within the chain. I reconstructed the main challenges and the recent changes experienced by the company to understand how managers' strategies responded to structural changes within the sector. I also focused on the specific core activities and relations with other firms, suppliers, and clients. I investigated firms' relations with workers—namely, how they recruit, what they seek, how they set their employment relations, and what they do to cope with fluctuations and competitive pressures. I asked managers to elaborate on the relations of the company with trade unions or if the manager had any position regarding the possibility that his or her employees might unionize. Finally, I enquired into managers' position vis-à-vis the informalization of employment in the sector. I avoided asking directly whether they had ever engaged in informalized practices, instead directing my questions more broadly to the role of informalization practices at the sector level, including the kinds of practices that are more common, why other firms in the sector would rely on informalization, and whether this affected the company.

I transcribed and manually coded the interviews following first general themes, separating managers' and workers' accounts and comparing findings from different sources for triangulation. For managers the coding firstly ordered information around broad themes such as opportunities and constraints within the GPNs, investment strategies, competitive pressures, recruitment of workers, core labour activities, employment relationship and relations with employees and other firms. For workers, the first codes referred to reasons for choosing the garment-footwear sectors, core activities and skills, employment relations, experiences of informalization, forms of resistance, *reworking* or exit, levels of unionization and relationship with other workers, foremen, and managers. With time, coding became more and more specific and outlined the prevalent forms of agency and the main elements of the workplace regimes experienced by workers and managers.

Besides convenience and access, the selection of interviewees followed a principle of variation based on the attempt to collect information on the *heterogeneity of conditions* rather than the (impossible) statistical representativeness of the sample (see: Ram et al., 2007). In other words, the search for participants continued until firms with different tasks and positions within the production chains and unionized and non-unionized workers deployed in different kinds of firms were reached. A principle of *saturation* (Kvale, 2007; Small, 2009) of the most crucial aspects of inquiry determined the minimum threshold of needed interviews. I stopped the fieldwork only after research participants started providing very similar information on the labour process, their perception of structural constraints, and their pattern of agency vis-à-vis informalization.

Before getting to the findings, I will briefly reflect on how I interacted with my interlocutors while researching a sensitive and yet crucial aspect of people's lives—their work.

3.5. *Being a stranger in the field: Building rapport and negotiating access*

An interview is hardly a conversation between peers because it entails significant power imbalances that can crucially shape the data provided (Cunliffe and Alcadipani, 2016; Kvale, 2006). The researcher has the power to lead the interaction with questions and maintains a monopoly on interpretation (Kvale, 2006). Such an asymmetry, in-built in most qualitative research, is even more pronounced when dealing with vulnerable research participants or when gendered hierarchies are rooted and reinforced in the workplace, as is the case in both regions analysed (see Chapter 7). Thus, while managers had little to fear due to my interviews, workers might have perceived telling a stranger the details of their employment as quite risky.

Being a male and foreign (at least in the case of my fieldwork in Albania) researcher, investigating employment relations in a highly feminized sector—where gendered hierarchies are constantly reproduced at work and beyond—made power imbalances even more prominent. To mitigate the effects of such an asymmetry, I put in place some specific precautions to protect workers, gain their trust and rebalance the power relations of the interview.

Firstly, borrowing trust from gatekeepers was the first tool to reassure workers. Secondly, I asked all my research participants to decide the place and time of the interview. This contributed to making the interview feel like a safe space and meant the interviewees could feel slightly more in control of the interaction. Many of the interviews with workers took place in peripherals bars, trade union offices, or in their homes, usually after work or at the weekends. During the interviews, I maintained a sensitive approach and avoided pressing those issues that the interviewees seemed particularly uneasy talking about. Especially with vulnerable research participants, I did not insist asking to talk more about topics that seemed to make them uncomfortable.

To mitigate the asymmetries built into the interview setting, I made sure that interviewees had some forms of control over the interview contents as well. I clearly stated participants' guarantees of anonymity, their right to withdraw at any moment or just to refuse to respond to questions. I also made clear that they had the right to retract part of or all the entire interview and could do so at any time after our encounter. In that case, I was obliged to delete any trace of their interview and erase it from my research. This is not just a way to return some control to interviewees, but also to achieve substantive, rather than merely formal, consent to use the interview data (Sin, 2005).

Moreover, I was fully transparent about my research objectives and my inability to reward participants with immediate tangible results. Being completely honest about the fact that my research would not benefit them but just contributing to enhancing general knowledge of their situation was a way to clear any ambiguity from the interaction. This made the interview relations less instrumental and extractive because only those research participants who knew there was little to gain from the interview itself and were still ready to participate took part.

Finally, with a few key gatekeepers, I sought a frank and reciprocal exchange throughout the fieldwork. I met a few unionists and NGO activists several times, exchanging with them the partial results of my inquiry while still maintaining the confidentiality of every participant. Such exchanges were part of my iterative approach of continually reworking empirical findings and theoretical discussions. Discussing my discoveries and reflections with some gatekeepers was also a way to rebalance the power relations between them and me and to remain open to alternative interpretations by elaborating my findings with them (Harrison et al. 2001). At the same time, this practice allowed the object of the research *to speak in its own terms* about the research process, with the possibility to object and challenge the interpretation of the researcher (see: Kvale, 2006; Portelli, 1990, chap. 3).

Reducing asymmetries in the interview practice contributes to *building rapport* with the research participants. And this rapport is a crucial precondition to access richer data and stimulate the interviewee to articulate in more detail her answers. In general, this requires showing a certain level of empathy with the interviewees (or at least avoiding being confrontational), being attentive to clues and behavioural data, and being ready to reassert the researcher's trustworthiness and legitimacy and her utter protection of data confidentiality. This means showcasing (when necessary and appropriate) proof of warmth, knowledge of the argument, protection of the research participants' privacy, and a certain level of sympathy for the issues she is discussing (Dundon and Ryan, 2010; Harrison et al., 2001).

I consistently approached and interviewed management and workers separately, relying on different gatekeepers and contacting them in different ways.[2] It was crucial for me to avoid being identified with the management when I interviewed workers and with unions when I interviewed managers because this might have jeopardized the rapport-building and biased the interviewee's answers on specific topics (Dundon and Ryan, 2010).

In many cases, the interview interaction requires a continuous effort to gain legitimacy to draw out candid and sincere information. This is an issue, especially when the researcher needs to carry out the interview in a language and context with the help of an interpreter. As Meardi (2000, p. 90; see also: Almond and Connolly, 2020) puts it, interviewees dealing with a foreigner may assume he or she lacks familiarity with the field and feel entitled to be less accurate in their answers so that *everything can be told* and the researcher risks being treated as a sort of *naïve tourist*. To reduce these risks, when I interviewed Albanian workers in their mother tongue, I relied on an NGO worker and a social movement activist that the research participants knew and were already generally seen as knowledgeable in terms of workers' employment and living conditions. This provided access, legitimacy, and a certain level of trust. For Albanian managers and experts who talked with me in English or Italian, instead, I started my interviews with a short preamble right after explaining the purposes of the research and asking for their informed consent. In the preamble, I indicated my knowledge of the topic and (while maintaining confidentiality) mentioned the interviews carried out earlier with other managers, local experts, and institutional representatives. This was a way to convey professionalism and competence and avoid the risk that the participant would feel free to say 'anything'. I also took the time to prepare myself for the interviews, studying the field before getting there and interviewing experts to increase my knowledge beforehand as much as possible.

From an ethical point of view, during the preparation and carrying out the fieldwork I consistently relied on the principle of not putting in danger or causing harm to research participants. I followed a standardized procedure to ensure substantial informed consent, and I followed basic rules to secure the safe storage of collected date and guarantee the protection of

---

2 Only in one case did I interview managers and one worker together. This was in the focus group organized with the support of a local trade unionist. The worker was supposed to come in earlier on. My plan was to close the interview with him and then have a focus group with managers only. Yet the interview with the worker started late and he decided to stay also during the focus group (I-35/38). This, however, was less problematic than I expected because the worker was not employed by any of the managers of the focus group and seemed eager to express fully his own opinion also in their presence.

participants' confidentiality. I approached every potential participant by introducing myself and clearly describing my university affiliation, the goals of the research, and the themes of the interview. Then I stated the way in which I would have protected participants' confidentiality, stored and used interviews' data while sheltering their privacy. I asked for an explicit verbal permission to record or take written notes. I also clearly explained that each participant was always free to not respond, interrupt the interview, or even withdrew consent to the interview at any moments even afterwards by contacting me or a reference person in my university.

Good planning, however, cannot spare field researchers from 'ethical important moments' (Guillemin and Gillam, 2004). Unforeseen ethical dilemma can emerge in direct interactions with research participants even though pre-emptive ethical good practices have been taken. In these cases, therefore, reflexivity and ethical research practice overlap, and the researcher shall remain alert to moral tensions that can arise (Guillemin and Gillam, 2004, p. 278). Ethical important moments have emerged, unsurprisingly, during my fieldwork too. I enquired into informalization dynamics and interviews exposed me to the direct accounts of employment practices that are in breach of collective contracts and the law. I collected data about violations, however, with the intention of using it for the research in anonymized and confidential form. My commitment to knowledge production and to the confidentiality deal I had with research participants prevailed over the duty to report to authority the specific cases of violations of labour laws I was exposed to (see: Morrison and Sacchetto, 2018). At the same time, in some case I felt compelled to provide workers with the support I could, passing them the contacts of trade unionists or NGOs that could provide support in accessing justice. In my interviews with managers, instead, I avoided to ask questions about their direct involvement in informal or illegal practices. On the one hand, such direct questions would not have led to better data, as the respondents would most likely just lie or refuse to respond or even worse withdraw from the interview. At the same time, this sheltered me from the ethical predicament between the loyalty to an informant that gained from irregular actions and the duty to report him/her to public authorities.

The role of gatekeepers

If building rapport is crucial in any interview, gaining gatekeepers' sympathy and trust is even more crucial to reach participants and carry on with the research. This requires a continuous engagement and a great deal of self-reflection in the conduct of the fieldwork (Crowhurst, 2013; Peticca-Harris et al., 2016). In this case as well, the researcher has to balance the need to access data—and in the case of gatekeepers, the need to access other potential research participants—with the importance of building a respectful, trust-based relationship that avoids pure instrumentalism. I consistently rejected a mechanistic understanding of gatekeeping (Crowhurst, 2013) and instead invested my time to build stronger relationships with those actors that I considered crucial to accessing other research participants. This required a certain sensitivity in reading actors' priorities and their organizational constraints.

For example, as mentioned, to access workers in the field, I firstly approached trade unions. In Apulia, I started with provincial sectoral secretaries—to little avail. It was clear that they were either unwilling or unable to lead me to workers, and insisting with them might have impaired future access to other members of their organizations. The general feeling with provincial peak-level representatives was a sense of scepticism toward my work and the usefulness of the research. This was coupled with a sense of suspicion that constrained them to release much information. This was the case for two out of three existing unions in the sector (the third union never replied to my requests for interviews). This made me shift attention to local branch officers. It was immediately apparent that local unionists had direct contact with workers and a clearer idea of the local labour market at the level of the city or town in which they were deployed. Thus, I reached out to them *and carried out extended interviews*. These long interviews were crucial because of the interviewees' situated knowledge and to start building rapport and mutual trust (Crawford et al., 2020). In such interactions, I found more responsive unionists who showed interest in the research. I started spending more time even after the interview with these officers, often inviting them for a coffee break and a chat about the progress of my work just with the excuse that I was in town for another meeting. These repeated exchanges were crucial to convince unionists to release the information and contacts I needed and to exchange opinions on the progress of the research.

In addition, I also joined unions' local public activities, such as congresses and roundtables. In February 2019, I even took part in a national demonstration organized by the main trade union confederations against the government's economic policies (La Repubblica, 2019). For this occasion, local branches had set up buses to go to Rome, where the demonstration took place. I was able to secure a seat on one of these buses and spend one full day with unionists whom I had at first struggled to reach. Participating in their demonstration was a useful tool to gain sympathy within the organizations and did not require any form of deception since I genuinely agreed with the content of the unions' platform and the reasons for their demonstration on that occasion.

To sum up, local officers—and not provincial or regional heads—led me to workers that could speak about their experience of informal employment. These first interviews with workers were carried out in the unions' offices, without the presence of unionists in the room. Such first contacts were then the beginning of a chain referral sampling approach and represented my first step into the field in direct connection with workers. With time I could even openly tell local officers about the suspicion I perceived from their peak-level representatives. This ensued comprehension and solidarity and made mid-level unionists point out that, if I wanted to know about workers' lives, I had to talk with them rather than with the *big wigs* closed in their offices.

In Albania, in contrast, my first contact with trade unions revealed in no uncertain terms that, if I wanted to get to workers, I had to find other entry points. I, therefore, contacted NGOs and one social movement union that were more or less openly critical of the traditional unions' approach. With them I could build a similar trust-based relationship as I had in Apulia with local union officers. In addition, I participated in an event organized by a local NGO that consisted of a training course with unionists (of other sectors). I also repeatedly met the activists of the social movement union based in Tirana. NGOs and the social movement union were useful gatekeepers and even became my interpreter in two focus groups with workers.

The importance of note-taking: accounting for meta-data and dealing with focus groups

This is not an ethnographic study, and yet, gaining access and carrying out interviews required extensive fieldwork. For this reason, I tried to maximize the observational data I was exposed to during the research. Meta and behavioural data are not only aspects to consider in order to maintain a level of trust and legitimacy with research participants, but they are also important data per se (Kvale, 2007). Therefore, I kept fieldwork notebooks, using fieldnotes as a crucial addition to the content of the interviews. I took notes consistently in flexible ways according to the situation. During interviews, I jotted in my notebooks, while in other contexts I recorded audio and written notes on my mobile whenever I could not stop moving or did not want to attract the attention of strangers.

As I report in Chapter 7, for example, some of these notes describing the setting of my encounter with the interviewees and their background stories proved crucial in framing better some of the challenges faced by the interviewees which I preferred not to investigate directly in the interview in order to minimize their emotional burden. Reporting and analysing interview contents together with interactional data was even more crucial in focus groups (Morgan, 2012). In such settings, the interactions among participants can be a useful tool to interpret their answers. In such cases, I jotted short descriptions of participants' interactions and of their reactions to each other's responses, especially in those moments that seemed specifically salient to me. Interactional data provide important insights into how participants *perceive* and *compare* their experiences and themselves (Macnaghten and Myers, 2004). This is crucial to obtaining information that would probably be out of reach in traditional interview settings.

To list a few examples, in the managers' focus group I carried out in Apulia, one of the managers was the head of a thriving local lead firm while the other two managed smaller suppliers in a weaker financial and productive position. Their position within the production networks emerged from the descriptions of their activities as well as from their interactions. It seemed that managers of smaller suppliers were less keen to talk about the problems of their companies in front of a successful competitor. Instead, the manager of the lead firm was more open to talk about challenges and only after his first replies did the suppliers' managers felt free to open up a bit more about their struggles. The focus group with workers was also rich in interactional data that would hardly emerge in traditional interview settings. The participants had different careers and were working in different companies and certain commonalities and differences emerged in their behaviours even more clearly than in their responses. For instance, all the workers—regardless of their specialization and economic status—were surprised that a researcher from a prestigious university was interested in their lives. 'Why do you want to interview us?' was a question that almost all of them raised at the beginning of the session. I interpreted this as a form of *invisibilization* of their work, reflecting how local actors had internalized the marginalization of labour in public and political debates. While the skills of the garment workers were once a matter of pride for the local communities, this was now a job, precarious and informalized, as any other. Other telling vignettes refer to participants' reaction to the description of the working conditions of colleagues employed in other firms. One worker employed in a local third-tier supplier, for example, described in detail the informalization practices she had to endure at work. She mentioned bogus part-time contracts, despotic supervisors, endless unpaid overtime, and lots of unpaid idle periods. Older workers employed in local lead firms reacted with surprise and bewilderment to this account. 'These things are still happening!?', one of them queried. Their colleague's tale was familiar in the memory of these workers, and yet it seemed to me they were under the assumption that such practices had somehow completely disappeared. This vignette underscored to me the importance of being aware of the variegation of informalization dynamics and labour regimes.

3.6. *Caveats and limits*

A few specifications on the aims and limitations of this research are needed. First, this case study's research findings do not seek a broader generalization to a pre-determined population of interest but rather unveil the mechanisms of the persistence of informal employment. Second, the research findings have external validity because they can be generalized 'to the level of theory rather than [being related to] any statistical notion of representativeness' (Ram et al., 2007, p. 326; Burawoy, 1998). This research expands our understanding of informalization mechanisms and the drivers of its persistence. It also legitimates a theoretical reformulation of informalization within employment relations. Moreover, if taken to an adequate level of abstraction, the theoretical framework I propose can be transferred to analyse other industries and produce comparative analysis of different sectors.

In line with the extended case method, the research reinforces and consolidates a structuralist theory of informalization by equipping it with the analytical purchase to analyse the role of agency within local contexts. Moreover, its value lies not only in explaining what kind of agency-based mechanisms explain the tenacity of informality but also in its ability to generate a novel analytical toolkit to investigate such mechanisms. Finally, my approach contributes to the general debate—which develops beyond the specific theme of informality—on GPNs, employment relations, and labour agency by providing a framework to analyse how labour regimes within production chains can be considered interlinked and mutually constitutive. In the following chapters, I present the results of this endeavour.

4.
THE POLITICS OF INFORMALIZATION
State, Policies and the Persistence of Informal Employment in Italy and Albania

4.1. *Rethinking the institutions-informality nexus*

The new institutionalist perspective generally frames the persistence of informal employment as a result of failure to align formal and informal norms. This perspective overlooks the multiple cases in which formal institutions and policies are *deliberately* designed and implemented to favour informality, as for instance, in the multiple cases of *social policies by other means* (Seelkopf and Starke, 2019), or when informalization *is* a political strategy to increase the competitiveness of economic actors (Dewey and Di Carlo 2021; Dewey 2014; Mezzadri 2010; Hadjimichalis and Vaiou, 1990). Further, it neglects how selective tolerance of certain informal economic activities can be an electoral tool for redistribution when formal welfare reforms are out of reach (Feierherd 2020; López-Cariboni, 2019; Holland 2017). To make sense of these processes, we need to understand the relationship between informality and institutions politically. Whose interests does the persistence of informal employment serve? Which social and political groups favour, and which resist, informalization? And how do these groups access the arena of institutions and policy-making?

We cannot assume that the political actors shaping the *formal rules of the game* would generally strive to eradicate informality and therefore we cannot automatically associate the persistence of informal employment with institutional failure. Instead, we need to understand the conditions in which political actors in power pursue an eradication (or formalization) agenda and when they settle for one of the many possible intermediate positions between complete formality and complete informality. In other words, we need to account for the *politics of informalization* (Hadjimichalis and Vaiou, 1990). In this chapter, I show that an extended structuralist perspective is better suited to investigate the drivers of persisting informal employment in Italy and Albania than rival explanations. Then, I examine the recent relevant policies against informal employment in the two countries in light of the political and economic costs faced by the political actors carrying these policies out. Finally, I show that while informal employment calls for political intervention, the costs of eradication steer political actors to address the issue only partially. As a consequence, instead of complete eradication of informal employment, we witness what I call a low-compliance equilibrium in which informality persists under new forms which partially restore revenues and state legitimacy and defuse temporarily the political urgency to uproot it. At the same time, such policies leave firms' competitive strategies to increase flexibility and compress labour costs through informalization largely untouched.

4.2. *Persistence and change of informal employment in Italy and Albania*

Italy

According to ISTAT (the Italian National Institute of Statistics) in Italy in 2017, the informal economy accounted for roughly 11% while the illegal economy for 1% of the GDP (ISTAT, 2019). Both only mildly decreased in the previous three years. The situation of informal employment is, instead, more differentiated. ISTAT estimates of regular and irregular labour units—which are a proxy for the *quantity* of labour performed informally[1]—provide a picture of the informal labour performed in different sectors and regions. Despite fluctuations, the absolute number of irregular labour units remains generally stable. In 1995, there were around 3.7 million irregular labour units in Italy. By 2017, this number had fallen by only 40,000—mainly due to the massive amnesty of irregular migrant workers in 2001–02 (Megale and Tartaglione, 2006; Santoro, 2012).

The distribution of informality by sectors and regions reveals a more complex story. In 2017, the sectors with the highest number of irregular labour units were *households as employers*, the accommodation and food service sector, wholesale trade and retail, and then manufacturing,

---

1 A labour unit is the equivalent of a full-time, year-long job and it is calculated by contrasting different available measures of labour inputs. The irregular labour unit, therefore, is a proxy for the quantity of labour performed informally that might not strictly coincide with the number of workers that are engaged in informal activities. One irregular labour unit, for example, can account for one totally unregistered worker working full time, or for two unregistered part-time workers, or even for two formally registered part-time workers that perform half of their activity off the books. The labour unit is comparable to the 'Full-Time Equivalent' unit adopted by Eurostat (see: ISTAT, 2021).

construction, and agriculture. Looking at the growth of irregular labour units between 1995 and 2017, the industries with the most striking increases are human health and social work activities (+86,600), transportation and storage (+45,600), accommodation and food services (+43,500). In two decades, the manufacturing sector lost more than 865,000 labour units, of which more than 85,000 were irregular. As for the garment-footwear sector, in 1995, it accounted for 20% of total manufacturing jobs; in 2017, the share was 13%. Yet, the sector alone accounted for 22% of the irregular units in 1995 and 17% in 2017. This signals that while the overall employment in the sector and its share in manufacturing jobs has declined, the share of irregular labour has declined much slower, and the sector is more informalized now than in 1995.

Data show that informal employment can be associated with both declining and rising sectors. In the sectors with high employment growth in the 1995–2017 period, such growth in some cases (like, for example, in health and social work or transportation and storage) was driven by informal employment increases, while in other industries (such as accommodation and food services and even more in household services) regular employment led the overall employment expansion. At the same time, even in declining sectors, in some cases, irregular employment grew (as in education services) or fell (as in agriculture, mining and quarrying, and garment-footwear) at a faster rate than regular employment. In manufacturing, however, the general decline of the sector is driven by informal labour units that have decreased at a slightly faster pace than formal ones with the exception of the garment-footwear.

Since informalization is not strictly associated with growth or decline, it is useful to look at the dynamics of irregularity rates as represented in Figure 4.1. Agriculture, garment-footwear, and transportation and storage, among others, became more informalized. In all these sectors, with the addition of construction, informalization rose during the 2008 crisis, with more dramatic spikes in garment-footwear and construction and a delayed increase in agriculture. One common feature of all the sectors was the significant drop in the irregularity rate in 2003, which is also discernible for the total economy in absolute terms and coincided with a nation-wide amnesty to formalize irregular migrant workers (see: Colucci, 2018).

Figure 4.1. Change in the national irregularity rates in Italy, 1995–2017

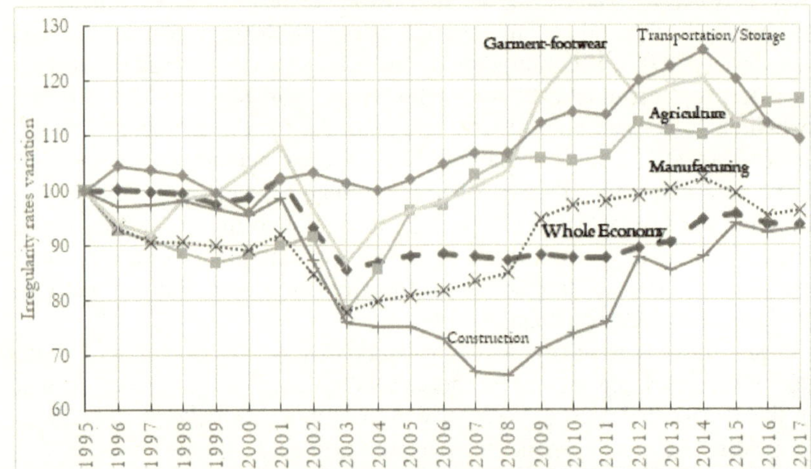

Source: Authors' elaboration on ISTAT. Base index, 1995=100. Irregularity rate: Number of irregular labour units on total labour units. Sector classification: NACE Rev 2. Manufacturing (section C); Agriculture: Agriculture, Forestry and Fishing (section A); Garment-footwear (section C, divisions 13, 14, 15); Transportation and Storage (section H); Construction (section F).

Italian macro-regions, grouping together Northern, Central and Southern regions, also show significant variation. The Mezzogiorno, i.e. the group that includes Southern regions and the two main islands Sardinia and Sicily, is consistently more informalized than other regions in all the macro-economic sectors and the economy as a whole. In 2016, the rate of economy-wide labour informalization was 10.2% in the North and 18.5% in the Mezzogiorno. The rates were 11.6% and 17.9% in services, 15% and 30.4% in agriculture, 15.8% and 23.7% in construction, and 4.8% and 11.8% in industry as a whole.

Overall, Italy's informal employment rate fluctuates, but in 2017 it was at roughly the same level as in 1995. In relative terms, the informality rate in the whole economy amounted to 16.5% in 1995 and was only one percentage point lower in 2017.

Albania

Indirect measurement techniques estimate that the shadow economy in Albania amounted to around 40% of GDP in 1991 and almost 26% in 2015 (Schneider and Medina, 2018). Alternative measurement methods estimate that the size of the informal economy was 36% of GDP in 1996, soaring to roughly 60% in the early 2000s and declining to 32.7% in 2013 (Boka and Torluccio, 2013). According to Trebicka's estimates based on the 'currency demand approach', the underground economy as a percentage of GDP between 1993 and 2013 averaged 38.4%, with a low of 29.8% in 2000 and a peak of 44.4% in 2011 (Trebicka, 2014). Even more dramatically, in 2015, the Albanian government disclosed that the informal economy amounted to 50% of GDP (Kosta and Williams, 2018, p. 9). A 2015 World Bank study (Dávalos and Cancho, 2015) confirmed the government's evaluation, estimating that in 2011, half of the total non-agricultural employment in Albania was informal. An earlier survey carried out by the ILO (2009) pointed out that around 70% of the interviewees reported engaging directly in undeclared employment activities. Survey data from the Southeast European Legal Development Initiative (SELDI, 2016) enquired into the relevance of informal employment by developing a Hidden Employment Index, based on 'the share of respondents who are engaged in a main paid activity and who hide something through a list of different informal practices' (SELDI, 2016, p. 22). In SELDI's representative sample, hidden employment in Albania reached 39%.

On the firms' side, the industrial-sector companies surveyed by the National Business Forum (NBF, 2016) declared that an average of 27% of the salaries they paid was not paid through bank transfer. This likely signals the widespread practice of envelope wages, a lack of compliance with (or the non-existence of) formal contracts and reduced social contribution payments. When asked about sector-wide perceptions, more than half of the managers interviewed declared that hiring a worker without a contract and paying employees cash are all widespread practices. They estimated that 29% of the total workforce and 43% of wages are not reported to the authorities in the sector (NBF, 2016).[2] In a similar survey, the Foreign Investors Association of Albania (FIAA) found that

2 This survey was carried out in September 2015 when the government's anti-informality campaign started, and inspections were at their peak. Therefore, the survey respondents would have likely been particularly cautious about openly stating any regulatory or legal violations.

the majority of managers operating in Albania perceives informality as a significant obstacle to doing business (FIAA, 2015). This is confirmed in a more recent FIAA survey (FIAA, 2019), in which surveyed companies list informality and corruption as their two major concerns. Moreover, in the latest World Bank Enterprise Survey (2019), 45% of firms report having experienced unfair competition from informal firms, and 93% say they began operations unregistered.

4.3. *Applying alternative approaches: Dualist, neoliberal, and new institutionalist*

Competing approaches explain informality by pointing to a lack of economic development, burdensome state regulations, or institutional mismatch. How would these analytical perspectives address the persistence of informal employment in Italy and Albania?

Italy

While informal employment in Italy is relatively stable, the factors that dualist and neoliberal approaches identify as the main drivers of informalization have shifted significantly since the late 1970s. The dualist perspective, for example, seems to hold only at a first examination when it comes to factor in the Italian territorial differences.

While Southern regions' relatively low economic development correlates with their relatively high levels of informal employment, this tells only part of the story. Indeed, employment informalty is at least partially linked to the Mezzogiorno's economic specialization. After a period of economic convergence due to active industrial policies and massive state intervention that ended already in the mid-1970s (Felice and Lepore, 2016; Berardino et al., 2016; Lüttge, 2014; Felice, 2010; Dunford, 2002; Cafiero, 1996; Graziani, 1978), the Mezzogiorno's employment structure rapidly worsened. Especially after the 2007–08 financial crisis, southern regions experienced a downgrading in the quality of jobs created which is even more dramatic than in northern regions (Gigio et al., 2021) while jobs in manufacturing as well as industrial output and value added (Banca d'Italia, 2013) declined more rapidly than in the rest of the country.

In addition, a higher percentage of southern firms produce for domestic markets (which were hit more dramatically by the 2008 crisis) and firms located in the South are generally integrated within national and global value chains in peripheral positions (Banca d'Italia, 2017; Bentivogli et al., 2018; Rizzuto and Tomassetti, 2019; SRM, 2015). This makes the crucial sectors of the Mezzogiorno's growth highly sensitive to labour costs and flexibility, and therefore, more prone to informalization.

If, alternatively, one engages with the insights of the neoliberal perspective and frames informal employment as the reaction of economic actors to burdensome state regulations, the stability of informal employment rates in Italy remains even more puzzling. The trajectory of Italian labour market reforms is one of progressive regulation until the mid-1970s and consistent liberalization afterwards (Fana and Fana, 2019; Betti, 2019; Baccaro and Howell, 2017, chap. 7; Rangone and Solari, 2012). The degree of employment protection in Italy decreased in line with other Eurozone countries in the second half of the 1990s, while the weight of temporary employment increased steadily in the last decade. Likewise, the proportion of part-time contracts increased, from 16% in 2005 to 20.9% in 2019. And while the Italian figures are lower than the average of the Euro area countries in the same years (20.3% and 22%, respectively), the share of *involuntary* part-time is much higher in Italy and has grown steadily since the 2008 crisis. This signals that firms maintain a good level of flexibility through multiple precarious and unstable employment arrangements.

Finally, another proxy for employers' increased bargaining power vis-à-vis workers—namely, the rate of in-work-poverty-risk[3]—grew. According to Eurostat, in Italy, this rate is among the highest in the EU. It was 9.1% in 2008 (8.1% in the Eurozone) and peaked at 12.3% in 2019 (when the Eurozone average was 9.2%). Nonetheless, while employment relations became increasingly deregulated and numerous flexible contractual arrangements are today at firms' disposal, the level of informalization in the economy as a whole has remained generally constant.

3 The rate of in-work-poverty-risk accounts for the percentage of workers living in a household with an equivalised disposable income below the risk-of-poverty threshold (i.e., below 60% of the national median equivalised disposable income).

Albania

In Albania, the persistence of high levels of informal economy and employment is no less puzzling than in Italy if one looks at it from a dualist or a neoliberal perspective. High levels of economic growth (annual growth averaging 5% between 1998 and 2018), a deregulated labour market, numerous bureaucratic simplification reforms, and a tax system tailored to attract foreign investment challenge the idea that informal employment is tightly linked to modernization or the persistence of burdensome regulations. While the level of informality has remained consistently high, Albania has transitioned to a market economy and became increasingly integrated into global fluxes of production, consumption and capital circulation by joining the World Trade Organization (WTO) in 2000, signing several successive free trade agreements, and undergoing sustained reform as part of the EU accession process (Bogdani and Loughlin, 2007; Choi and Minondo, 2019; Karini, 2019). A fine-grained analysis demonstrates that despite fast growth, high poverty levels remain in the country (Biscione and Caruso, 2020; Mastromarco et al., 2014; World Bank, 2015; see also King and Gëdeshi, 2020; Pere and Bartlett, 2019). However, Albania has one of the highest informalization rates in Europe and the Balkans, despite business-friendly taxation and a flexible labour market.

New institutionalist blind spots in Italy and Albania

Dualist and neoliberal perspectives fall short in explaining the mechanisms underpinning the persistence of informality. The new institutionalist approach, which relies on an encompassing correlation between informality and institutional mismatch, is also unable to address the relevant sectoral differences in informalization levels.

Starting with the Italian case, the quality of institutions, for which we can use World Bank's Worldwide Governance Indicators (WGI) as a proxy, has declined slightly in the last decades (see Figure 4.2) while informalization remained more or less constant.

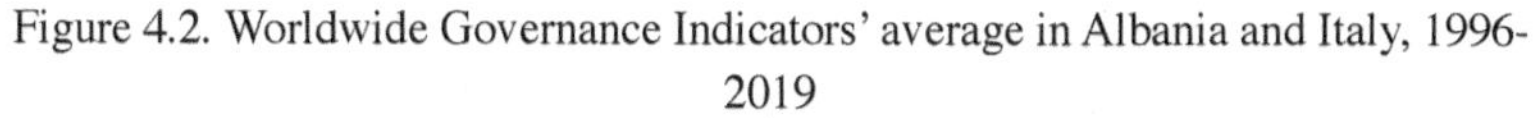

Figure 4.2. Worldwide Governance Indicators' average in Albania and Italy, 1996-2019

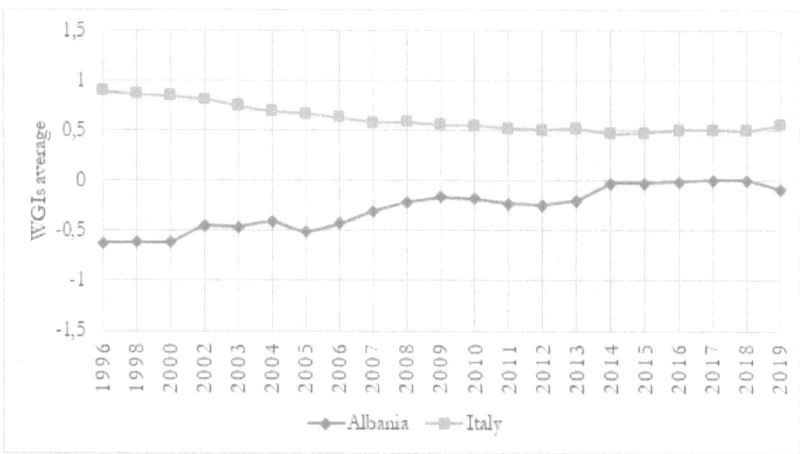

Source: Author's elaboration based on World Bank data. Note: The Worldwide Governance Indicators are estimates of the quality of governance. The indicators range is +/ – 2.50; the higher the score, the better the quality of governance. There are six distinct indicators: control of corruption, government effectiveness, political stability, regulatory quality, rule of law, and voice and accountability. The graph presents the average of the six indicators.

Another proxy of institutional quality comparable to the World Bank's indicators and disaggregated at the regional level is the European Quality of Government Index (EQI) (Charron and Lapuente, 2018). The EQI is a synthetic index of the quality of government based on survey data that measure citizens' perceptions of the quality, impartiality, and level of corruption of their local/regional institutions.[4] According to the available data on Italy for the years 2010, 2013 and 2017, the Southern regions present consistently lower levels of quality of government compared to the Northern regions, although there is a slight convergence due to the declining quality in the North. Overall, the national EQI decreased between 2010 and

4 The general IQI index contains three main indicators of government quality that captures citizens' perception on quality, impartiality and corruption. Yet, the overall index is indicated as a good proxy of all the dimensions comprising the WGI (Charron and Lapuente, 2018, p. 13).

2017, and Italy has consistently scored worse than the EU average. These indicators are largely in line with the literature that stresses how institutions in the Mezzogiorno generally work worse than in the North (Trigilia, 2011; 1992) and that Southern Italians have generally lower trust in institutions than their Northern fellow citizens (D'Attoma, 2019; 2017). Such data aligns also with cultural accounts of the North-South divide in terms of development, institutional quality, and levels of trust ((Banfield, 1958; Putnam, 1993; Bigoni et al., 2016). However, while regional differences correlate with the different levels of informalization, certain sectors are consistently more informalized than others across macro-regions, pointing again that, at best, institutional or cultural explanations can be only part of the story and overlook sectoral drivers of such informalization dynamics.

Aggregate data on Albania do not fully confirm the new institutionalist thesis either. Albania's Doing Business Indicators, which measure the ease of starting and managing an economic enterprise in the country, have consistently improved every year since 2010, with a minor deterioration in 2012. The WGIs also show mild but almost constant improvements since 1996 (see Fig. 4.10), yet the informal economy's magnitude and the role of informal employment remain daunting. As mentioned above, while Schneider and Medina (2018) estimate a considerable reduction of the informal economy between 1995 and 2015, Trebicka (2014) estimates almost a constant proportion of informal economic activities in the GDP in the period 1993–2013. Moreover, in the summer of 2015, the Albanian government disclosed that according to national estimates, the informal economy had reached almost half of national GDP (AIC, 2015; Kosta, 2018a), while in 2016, INSTAT estimated a 31.9% share of unregistered employment in the non-agricultural sector (see Kosta and Williams, 2018, p. 20). Sectoral variegation in informalization levels also persists, despite the common institutional setting. Drawing on Albanian monitoring agencies data, Karma (2019) reports that retail, hospitality and restaurant, and manufacturing, and construction are the most informalized sectors (see also EC, 2020b), while the European Commission has stressed the high concentration of female informal employment in specific sectors such as the garment-footwear industry (EC, 2020b; 2019).

The new institutionalist analytical perspective fails to explain the variegated dynamics of informalization in different sectors in Italy and Albania. While embedded in the same (clashing) institutional contexts, some sectors are consistently more informalized than others, and new institutionalist approaches provide no analytical purchase on the role of sectoral factors in informalization dynamics. A fine-grained analysis of labour informality suggests that the institutional clash thesis sits uneasily with fluctuations in informality over time and across sectors and space; it leaves crucial dynamics unexplored and does not really provide the analytical tools to investigate them further. The study of institutions alone can provide only a partial understanding of such dynamics. Besides institutions, the study of the transformation and persistence of informal employment requires an analysis of the economic structures and actors' agency behind the making of policies that influence employment informalization dynamics.

To do so, I now turn to analyse the main public policies that have explicitly addressed informal employment in Italy and Albania since the early 1990s until 2018–2019[5] to tease out the main structural and political drivers of the partial successes, failures and reversals of relevant policies. The time frame selected coincides with the transition to market-economy and democracy in Albania, and the watershed years of the Italian political system, when the consolidated parties collapsed amidst ideological crisis and corruption scandals, and a number of new political actors emerged (Ferragina et al., 2020; Ferragina and Arrigoni, 2021). For the Italian case, I also offer a brief analysis of regional government initiatives to fight informalization. Finally, in both Italy and Albania, the study of anti-informality policies foregrounds the analysis of firms' and workers' agency that follows in the following chapters.

4.4. *Italian policies against informal employment*

The persistence of informal economic activity and employment has been a constant matter of political debate in Italy since the early 1960s (Pugliese, 2015; 2009; Forges-Davanzati, 2008). Focusing on the period of the so-called Second Republic in Italy, a crucial public policy instrument to tackle informalized employment relations has been the regularization of the status of illegal migrant labourers. Measures to regularize both the residence and employment status of irregular migrants were undertaken in 1986, 1990, 1995, 2002 and 2012 (Colucci 2018; Forlani 2013). These measures had limited influence on the overall levels of informal employment except for the 2002 amnesty that formalized around 700,000 unregistered jobs, the

5 The inquiry stops before two crucial events occurred right after my fieldwork: the earthquake that hit Albania in November 2019 and the Covid-19 pandemic.

most effective policy against informality so far (Megale and Tartaglione, 2006; Santoro, 2012).

Besides amnesties, the first initiatives to target informal employment specifically were launched in the late 1980s and early 1990s in Apulia (Avola, 2007; Bianchi et al., 2003). The main trade union confederation of the garment-footwear industry (now FILCTEM-CGIL) in the Apulian province of Lecce partnered with local employers to push them to gradually comply with labour laws and national collective agreements. As one of the unionists in the regional board of the union federation at the time explained:

> Nowadays, it is quite normal to [lawfully] derogate from national contracts, but in those years, the national contract had to be fully complied with, full stop. […] Yet in the textile sector in Apulia – in the BAT and Lecce provinces – and Campania, we opened a debate after recognizing one simple truth: the practice of paying wages below the minimum was spreading. We could not think to impose a full and immediate application of national contracts on non-compliant firms. So we decided on another path: there would be agreements fixing a deadline for the complete transition to the fulfilment of the [national] contract, but the wage increases would be gradual over time. Those are the famous *step-by-step* or *realignment* contracts. (Interview with trade unionist, I-80).

The local branch of the trade union, in other words, recognized the widespread informalization of the garment-footwear and proposed a formalization procedure for those firms that intended to comply with the formal rules but were constrained by tight margins and heightened competitive pressures. With the *realignment contracts*, firms had to sign an agreement with trade unions committing to immediately comply with workers' rights standards while retaining the freedom to gradually increase wages over an extended period until full compliance with national collective contracts. In exchange, trade unions agreed to waive the immediate application of national minimum wages and monitor to ensure the transition plan was adhered to (Megale and Tartaglione, 2006).

The pilot partnership projects carried out in Apulia were reviewed favourably and so were scaled up and regulated at the national level with several consecutive laws.[6] The first laws retraced the unions' initiative and enlarged the realignment contracts instrument to the whole manufacturing sector in economically depressed areas. The firms embarking in the formalization process benefited from a 75% cut on the payment of employees' outstanding social contributions and taxes and an amnesty on

6 No. 389/1989; no. 210/1990; no. 608/1996 and no. 196/1997.

past (administrative) violations of labour and fiscal regulations with the sole condition that they had to negotiate a provincial collective realignment agreement with unions (Barbieri, 2010; Bianchi et al., 2003). Law no. 448/1998 institutionalized a Committee for the Exposure of Irregular Work (Galetto, 2007) to coordinate the local multi-stakeholder committees that drafted the contracts and supported realigning firms.

The second phase of formalization policies started after the 2001 elections when a new government came into office (Barbieri, 2010). The new ruling right-wing coalition (2001–06) introduced Law no. 383/2001 that de-facto dismantled the partnership-based infrastructure for formalization implemented by the previous social-democratic coalition (1996–2001) and replaced it with an automatic system of incentives, amnesty, and tax cuts. This measure allowed firms to bypass the negotiations with trade unions and entitled them to unilaterally apply to the relevant public agency without the agreement of workers or their representatives. It represented, therefore, a policy shift from a formalization strategy based on the partnership with labour (see: Fine and Gordon, 2010) to a formalization as an unilateral business decision. One year later, with Law no.73/2002, the government partially redrew the instruments for formalization and set up a network of Committees for Formalization of Irregular Labour (in Italian the acronym was 'CLES') in charge of drafting the provincial guidelines for the formalization plans to support those firms that decided to undertake a partnership-based path to formalization (Eurofound, 2009). While the formalization via CLES was not formally much different than the previous realignment contracts, it was less effective since the automatic procedure for formalization set up the year before remained a more appealing alternative for firms (Barbieri, 2010). At the same time, however, the right-wing government increased the administrative sanctions for firms deploying workers without registration. This 'maxi-sanction' was calculated on the number of unregistered employees and their workdays and could even reach several thousand euros per employee.

Between 2006–2008, a new, short-lived left-wing government fully embraced the proposals of the trade union confederations against undeclared work (Pinto, 2012; CGIL, CISL and UIL, 2006). The new government introduced the obligation for firms to report a new hire to the relevant agency the day before of his/her actual deployment at work[7] and abolished

---

7 This restriction eliminated a widespread practice that non-compliant firms often used to contest allegations they were using informal workers. When inspectors found employees on site without a contract, the employer would claim that it was

the automatic formalization procedure established in 2001 (Barbieri, 2010; Bianchi et al., 2003; Fasani, 2011). It also established a specific national fund to assist firms' requalification of production during the formalization process. The left-wing coalition also reformed and enlarged the application of the maxi-sanction (which was partially restricted again in 2010 by a new right-wing government) and provided labour inspectors with the power to interrupt any production activity if the inspection revealed that more than 20% of the workforce was employed informally (Fasani, 2011; Fiengo, 2012). New measures were also introduced to address the multiplication of informal employment practices within subcontracting chains. These measures established a joint liability of both the direct employers and the head of the subcontracting chain in cases of non-payment of due salaries and contributions to the employees of the subcontracting firms (Scarpelli, 2008, p. 79). Finally, a new law set a series of sectoral 'congruence indices' (*indici di congruità)* (Galetto, 2007) which were meant to provide a systematic estimate of the labour input needed for each firm according to its structure, sector, and product specialization. The indices were meant to be used for inspection purposes. Their operationalization started in 2007 amidst the opposition of the major business groups. However, they were never implemented and finally abolished by the right-wing coalition that returned to government in 2008. The formalization procedure and the laws on joint liability in subcontracting chains were also terminated (Fiengo, 2012; Pinto, 2012).

These formalization procedures, however appealing for firms, presented several shortcomings. The multiplication of different laws and the constant scrutiny of the European Commission, which criticized the realignment contracts as a form of state aid (although eventually allowing them) (Zoppoli, 2008), contributed to the ambiguity, opaqueness, and uncertainty of the formalization process (Barbieri, 2010). Moreover, under EU pressure, the existing subsidies covering social contributions for workers hired in southern regions were phased out in 1995. This abruptly increased the local unit labour costs of firms operating in Southern regions by 20% and derailed the realignment instrument (Bodo and Viesti, 1997), which was based on the premise that firms could restructure themselves before having to pay full wages and contributions (Prota and Viesti 2012, pp. 44-5).

his or her first day on the job and that the worker would be registered later that same day (see: Barbieri, 2010).

Despite these shortcomings, before the 2001 changes, the realignment contracts involved 10,000 workers in manufacturing (mainly in garment-footwear), 3,000 in services (mainly in retail) and 200,000 in agriculture. The province of Lecce alone covered 77% of all the employees engaged in a realignment process nationally. Moreover, almost all the positions formalized with this instrument concerned workers in partially informalized employment. Registered firms deploying workers under forms of partial informality participated in the realignment while fully informal firms did not (Megale and Tartaglione 2006; Bianchi et al., 2003; confirmed in an interview with trade unionist [I-80]). As for the results of the formalization procedures after 2001, against the official goal of reaching 900,000 workers, just 3,000 were formalized, 65% of whom were in Apulia alone (Santoro, 2012). Thus, the realignment and formalization policies—except for the results in Apulia—are generally considered a failure even by the trade unions that initially promoted such measures (Bellavista, 2012; Bianchi et al., 2003; Megale and Tartaglione 2006, Interview with unionist [I-80]).

After the realignment contracts policy and its subsequent modifications, no other encompassing attempt to promote formalization emerged. In 2016, however, the centre-left coalition in government passed Law no. 199, which increased sanctions and criminalized informal and exploitative gangmaster practices (*caporalato*). The law also introduced a series of active policies promoting fair employment in agriculture, such as a network of certified responsible farms and a state-backed job allocation system. Yet these measures remained underfunded and largely ineffective (Bagnardi et al., 2022; de Martino et al., 2016), and while they deter the most dramatic forms of *caporalato* and informalization, they remain unable to tackle multiple forms of partial informalization in the sector.

Monitoring and enforcement institutions

The Italian agencies in charge of monitoring compliance with labour laws have generally been understaffed, yet policy choices have influenced monitoring capacities. In 1997, the left-wing coalition enhanced the resources of the national labour inspectorate (Scarpelli, 2008), while in 2015, a major reform merged the leading monitoring agencies, the labour inspectorate, the National Institute of Social Security (INPS), and the National Institute for the Insurance against Accidents at Work (INAIL). Under the centre-left coalition, the declared aim of the reform was to make monitoring activities more effective through merging and coordination

(Simonelli, 2016). The reform led the agencies to exchange information, manage the planning of inspections collaboratively and carry out joint checks on companies (Lombardi, 2015).

Yet, the reform did not entail any increase in the number of inspectors nor their resources (Rotunno, 2018). The new governance of the inspectorate puts all the agencies under the control of the Ministry of Labour and Social Policies, which sets the guidelines for monitoring activities (Foschi and Gabanelli, 2018). The planned number of inspections is based on the political priorities set by the ministry rather than on technical evaluations. In fact, while the so-called 'business intelligence' orients inspections towards companies that are more likely to be non-compliant (MEF, 2020), such activities occur according to the goals set by the ministry (Carlà, 2019, p. 338; interviews with labour inspectors, [I-20; I-33]). For these reasons, both trade unions and inspectors themselves have opposed the reform (CGIL, CISL and UIL, 2019) and mobilized against it (Rassegna, 2019).

Moreover, the number of personnel actively involved in monitoring activities has been decreasing, and the reform did not reversed the trend. Retired inspectors have not been replaced, and in 2018 the number of active inspectors was still declining significantly (MEF, 2020, p. 203), while the harmonization of databases and work practices required the retraining of a significant portion of the staff, keeping them away from monitoring and field activities. In 2007 there were 6,463 officials involved in monitoring; in 2019, the number of active officials was 4,252—a decline of roughly 35% in 12 years.[8] The drop of active inspectors has clearly affected the monitoring capacities both in terms of the number of firms inspected and irregularities found (see Figure 4.3).

8 These numbers refer to officials in different agencies (the labour inspectorate, INAIL and INPS) and a dedicated unit of the police (the Carabinieri). After the 2015 reforms, the officials are all part of the common National Inspectorate but in the case of INPS and INAIL are still officially employed by their previous agency.

Figure 4.3. Variation index of monitoring activities, irregularities detected and revenues collected in Italy, 2006-2019

Source: Author's elaboration of National Inspectorate data. Base index, 2006=100.

The number of inspections and firms found adopting irregular practices has shrunk, as have the taxes and social contributions recovered through inspectors' activity. At the same time, the number of employees found under some irregularity has increased. These include a wide range of infringements, from OSH regulations to violations of collective contracts and the labour law (working and resting time, holidays, other contractual arrangements). Data suggest that even while resources and staff have shrunk, the likelihood of finding irregularities in inspected firms has increased. While in 2007, irregularities were detected in 62% of all inspected firms, in 2019, the percentage reached 70%. The rate of irregular employees detected for each inspected firm engaged in some form of irregularity also provide important insights. In 2007, for each firm where irregularities were detected, one irregular worker was found. In 2019, the ratio had shifted to 3.6 irregular workers per firm. Coupled with the overall data on the number of inspections and irregularities detected, this suggests that inspections have become more selective. As the labour inspectors I interviewed confirm (I-20; I-33), inspections only take place once available administrative data gathering and desk analysis suggest the probability of irregularities. The priorities set by the ministry and the shrinking staff might be increasing the pressure to raise inspection effectiveness, driving the efforts of inspectors towards those firms with more employees (see also: Iannuzzi and Sacchetto, 2020).

Furthermore, in 2007, 66% of the irregular workers were completely unregistered. The percentage shrunk to 12% in 2019. In other words, firms seem to favour partially informalized employment over full informalization. As a labour inspector pointed out:

> In cases of 'black labour' [fully unregistered workers], I get into the factory, and I find the employee working, and I see he has no contract. That situation is already sufficient proof of a violation. In the cases of grey labour [partial informality], I need the substantial cooperation of the worker, and this is not automatically granted. He has to tell me about his work conditions and status when I interview him. [...]. This cooperation cannot be taken for granted because workers often fear that problems in the workplace will follow their declarations. They fear they will be fired or face consequences. Thus, it is not easy to get the information needed to find irregularities. [...]. With grey labour, ascertaining the irregularities is more complicated because you need proof that is not always easy to find. Moreover, sanctions are usually lower [for grey labour] than for black labour. (Interview with labour inspector, I-33)

Grey labour is generally harder to identify, and if detected by the authorities, it can be lawfully rectified by the firm with a reduced sanction through an ad-hoc/ex-post regularization procedure. Further, it is not subject to the maxi-sanction. Full informalization, instead, is increasingly riskier with the maxi-sanction[9] and the *anti-caporalato* regulations. Given the overall shrinkage in inspection capacities and the difficulties in proving irregularity, the risks associated with engaging in partial informalization are decreasing. This, coupled with a lenient approach towards firms that can regularize ex-post partially informalized employment, are an incentive to *shift from black to grey* as a cover for non-compliance. Given the persistence of informalization rates in ISTAT estimates, one can conclude that firms relying on informalization strategies are incentivized to increasingly rely on partially informalized, rather than fully informal, employment.

---

9 In 2015, labour market reforms introduced a rectifying procedure in cases of detected black labour. This mandates the firm to hire the unregistered worker for at least three months and pay up unpaid social and pension contributions. With this remedial procedure the firm must only pay the lower threshold of the allotted maxi-sanction (Cascioli, 2017, p. 53).

Regions against informality

In the Italian system, regional governments have concurrent legislative powers with national institutions on taxation and job protection and safety. They also develop strategies and implement policies and laws against informal employment.[10]

In this section, I focus on the making of the regional Law no. 28/2006 passed by the Apulian regional government in 2006. I do so for three main reasons. First, the law is an unprecedented attempt to tackle informal employment comprehensively and was recognized as *policy best practice* in 2008 by the EU's Committee of the Regions (Urbact, 2008). The national government recognized the validity of the regional approach as well, drafting a similar measure (i.e., the abovementioned congruence indices) a few months later. Second, the law exemplifies the difficulties and the structural costs of eradicating informality and the weakness of the political coalitions underpinning this kind of goal at the regional level. Finally, even if the law was effectively implemented only in the agricultural sector, it formally sets the regulatory context in which the specific sectoral case study examined in the following chapters (i.e., garments and footwear) unfolds.

In a region consistently governed by conservative parties, the 2005 regional elections represented a political game-changer when a coalition of leftist forces, united under a radical social platform and led by Nichi Vendola—the leader of a minority left-wing party—won (Luca and Rombi, 2016). While widespread practices of exploitative informal employment were not new, especially in agriculture, in 2006 the conditions of informal labourers in the Apulian fields gained national attention after a series of investigative journalistic reports (Leogrande 2016; see also: Gatti, 2006). According to the head of the regional labour department (I-6), the national salience of the issue was interpreted by the newly appointed regional government as a window of opportunity to take radical action. In close cooperation with trade unions, the labour department drafted a regional law setting up a series of congruence indices to be updated periodically by a task force of experts in cooperation with local social partners (interview with the head of the labour department, I-6; interview with member of the departmental taskforce, I-74). Any firm that sought funds or

10 For more details on regional actions against informal labour see Barbieri (2010), Isfol (2011), Pinto (2012). For a discussion focused specifically on measures tackling informal *migrant* labour see Isfol (2014).

procurement initiated by the regional government had to comply with the indices. An unjustified *input-output incongruence* would be interpreted as signalling a high likelihood of the existence of informalization and would automatically exclude firms from public tenders and other public benefits such as subsidies, incentives, grants and regional or EU projects (Barbieri, 2010; Pinto, 2008). At the same time, in 2006, the regional government struck specific agreements with the financial police department and with monitoring agencies to receive up-to-date information on the conduct of those companies that had applied for regional funds or tenders (Interview with former head of the labour department, I-6). Finally, the regional labour department mobilized the realignment contracts legacy by creating programs to support firms embarking on a formalization procedure. Forms of support, however, targeted workers rather than firms and focused on workers' mobility (to and from work), language courses and integration projects for foreign workers and other activities enhancing workers' skills (Barbieri, 2010; Pinto, 2012).

The congruence indices were applied firstly to the agricultural sector because of its high rate of informalization and its structural dependency on EU and regional funds. Firms' compliance with the congruence indices was a precondition to access EU fundings and this greatly enhanced the policy's leverage. The determination of the indices, however, was a perilous task. It required the expertise of professionals (lawyers, economists, statisticians), and it needed the cooperation of local social partners. After setting the experts' task force, the regional labour department issued the indices (interview with the former head of the labour department [I-6] and a member of the task force [I-74]) but encountered resistance from employers' associations. The leading employers' organizations (Confagricoltura, Coldiretti, Cia and Copagri) refused to cooperate in the determination of the indices, and when these were finally issued, the organizations appealed against the regional law on the grounds that it impaired their freedom of enterprise (Fiengo, 2012, p. 70; see also: Pepe, 2014).

In 2009, the indices-centred policy had started to be implemented when the regional government underwent a major political crisis. A judicial inquiry on corruption in public tenders involved the manager of the Local Health Authority (appointed by the regional government) (see: Il Tempo 2009) and forced the region's president to reshuffle his cabinet to bring other parties in and consolidate the governmental majority. In the reshuffle, the head of the local labour department (member of a radical left party committed to the anti-informality reform that was not involved in the scandal) was substituted with a councillor of the moderate wing of the majority social-democratic party (La Gazzetta del Mezzogiorno, 2009). This was a move to gain the support of the moderate Centrist Democratic Union (CDU), a conservative party of which the councillor was member in the past and with which he had maintained important ties.[11]

The opposition of the business organizations, the reshuffle of the cabinet, and the removal of the head of the labour department stalemated the implementation of Law no. 28/2006. The cooperation agreements between the regional government and the monitoring agencies were not renewed, the drafting of the congruence indices did not expand to other sectors, and the indices were never fully applied to agriculture either. Weak political coalitions implementing anti-informality policies and fierce opposition led political actors in power to soften and then reverse their initial formalization agenda. As a result, the congruence indices measure was firstly not enforced and then definitely sabotaged.

4.5. *The Albanian Anti-informality Campaign*

The first attempts to curtail informal employment in post-socialist Albania occurred in 2003–2004 when, with the support of the OECD, the government carried out the first comprehensive analysis of the Albanian informal economy (OECD, 2004; AIC, 2015; Interview with former economy minister, I-48). A series of measures to improve the business climate and simplify bureaucratic procedures for business start-ups officially became part of the governmental agenda with the aim of addressing informality (AIC, 2015; GoA, 2007). The main concrete policies that followed include a reduction of taxes for Small and Medium Enterprises (SMEs), a 9% reduction on employers' payment of employees' social contributions and a 10% flat tax for firms and individuals. The payment of wages only through wire transfer was mandated, while business registrations procedures were simplified by creating an ad-hoc National Registration Centre (ILO, 2008; Mara and Narazani, 2011).

In 2008, 2010 and 2012, three amnesties addressing different kinds of tax and contribution evasion were introduced (Muceku, 2016) even though they largely failed to generate the expected revenues. In 2012, the

11 As a consequence of the reshuffle that removed from the cabinet a few representatives of the radical left party of which Vendola himself was leader, local CDU cadres abstained from voting (Il Corriere del Mezzogiorno, 2009) and the government won the approval of the CDU national leadership (La Repubblica, 2009).

government expected to formalize income worth €3–5 billion in potential tax revenues, yet the actual result brought in no more than €30 million (Muceku, 2016). These measures did not specifically aim at informal employment eradication but were rather pieces of a broader process of liberalization and reform to attract foreign direct investments (FDI).

Instead, the first comprehensive set of policies explicitly targeting informal employment was implemented between 2015 and 2017 with the assistance of the International Monetary Fund (IMF). The 2015 anti-informality campaign was announced in the summer of that year when the government disclosed that, according to national statistics, the informal economy accounted for almost half of national GDP and that fighting informality would become an ongoing priority (AIC, 2015; Kosta, 2018a). Tight cooperation with the IMF led to an action plan entailing a thorough reform of business and employment registration regulations, enforcement mechanisms, and sanctions.

The anti-informality campaign firstly focused on deterrence and enforcement (Kosta and Williams, 2018). Specifically, it restructured inspecting agencies to foster cooperation and data sharing between the General Directorate of Taxation (GDT), the General Directorate of Customs (GDC) and the labour inspectorate; it increased administrative sanctions for unregistered economic activities; and it introduced a more sophisticated, preventative approach—based on the risk assessment of companies with a high probability of engaging in irregular activities—to orient monitoring procedures (interviews with labour inspectors I-102; I-104; I-105). Monitoring activities were also intensified, and an informational campaign targeting the broader public and the business community to raise awareness of the risks and damage of informality was carried out (Kosta, 2018a; AIC, 2015). In 2016, the campaign modified the labour code requiring the parties to sign a written contract for any employment relationship and register the employment relationship one day before starting the actual work activity (Kosta and Williams, 2018).[12]

In the second phase of the anti-informality campaign, the government passed a fiscal package that zeroed or drastically reduced (according to companies' turnover) profit taxes for SMEs. Moreover, monitoring efforts started to target big companies while simplified tax-payment procedures

12 Since the 2016 amendments to the Albanian labour code, employment generally requires a written contract. In specific cases, the written contract might be signed within the first seven days following the commencement of employment. Failing to do so entails a fine amounting to 30 times the minimum wage (Deloitte, 2020; Laera et al., 2018).

for all companies and new consultation services for firms were activated within the tax authority and the labour inspectorate (Kosta, 2018a; interview with labour inspector, I-104).

While many businesses operating in Albania were unequivocal that the informal sector put them at an unfair competitive disadvantage, a few important business organizations criticized the anti-informality campaign for being repressive and detrimental to entrepreneurial activities. For example, as reported by the Albanian Investment Council (2015), the Albanian Chamber of Commerce criticized the toughening of sanctions, the German Chamber of Commerce expressed concerns about the proportionality of the sanctions, and the business association Konfindustria claimed that significant tax reform was due before the reform of deterrence and enforcement. Many entrepreneurs, moreover, consider the reform too aggressive and haphazard, lacking a clear formalizing strategy, with sanctions unevenly applied to different business (Kosta and Williams, 2018; NBF, 2016).

Nonetheless, the campaign triggered the registration of around 37,000 firms in the first year (NBF, 2016) and the formalization of 83,000 unregistered employees in the first seven months (Kosta, 2018a; see also: Hart, 2017), with 2016 revenue collection exceeding 2015 targets (EC, 2016, p. 50). At the same time, as the NBF (2016) contends, more than 100,000 small enterprises were forced to declare bankruptcy in the first year because they were unable to sustain the cost of formalization, which contributed to an initial 8.9% drop in 2015 revenues. In 2017, though, revenues were above 2016 levels (albeit below target) (EC, 2018a) and improved in the following years (EC, 2020b; 2019).

The concerns the business community expressed against an aggressive sanctioning approach were addressed in the second phase of the campaign when the government steered monitoring efforts toward larger businesses and started providing consulting services to SMEs (Karma, 2019; Kosta, 2018a; Interview with labour inspector, I-104).[13] Yet, significant shortcomings remain. The labour inspectorate, for example, is under-resourced and underfunded. In 2009, as the ILO reports (ILO, 2009), out of 140 employees in the agency, there were 95 inspectors on the ground. In 2017 the labour inspectorate relied on 155 employees, of whom 98 were in the field. As Kosta and Williams (2018, p. 43) report:

---

13 See also the Prime Minister's speech presenting the new phase of the anti-informality campaign (Rama, 2016).

> The head of SLI [i.e., the Labour Inspectorate] stressed that this institution is facing several problems which are related to limited resources (inspectors use their own cars and gasoline at their own expense because the institution cannot afford to have cars for inspectors) and very low number of inspectors. With the current number of inspectors this institution covers only 5 percent of the total registered enterprises. The Labour Inspection Law was amended in March 2017, but labour inspection is struggling with poor financial and human capacities.

The European Commission has consistently stressed this chronic lack of financial and human resources in its annual progress reports (EC, 2018a; 2020b). It also emerges from the testimonies I collected in the fieldwork (interviews with labour inspectors I-102; I-104; I-105). As one labour inspector put it:

> We have problems with resources. We are supposed to rely on our own cars, but I don't have one, so I use buses, public transport, or rely on my colleagues. The salary is low, the refund for petrol expenses is low. For the first time this year, the general head inspector introduced a per-diem bonus for the expenses related to transportation. Before, we formally had a per-diem bonus too, but we never actually received it. However, even the per-diem bonus now is very small, around €150 per year. The salary, in total, is around 4,400 Leks, approximately €350 [per month].[14] (Interview with labour inspector, I-104).

Inspections can rarely cover small villages and remote areas of the countries (Kosta and Williams, 2018; AIC, 2019). Furthermore, while the registrations of employees in formal firms have increased, the current inspection mechanisms seem unable to deter partially informalized employment practices. Registration, in fact, does not necessarily entail the eradication of informalized employment relations. Grey labour and quasi-formal employment (i.e., envelope wages and other under-reporting practices) are spread and very difficult to track for inspecting authorities (Interviews with labour inspectors [I-102; I-103; I-104]; see also: Kosta and Williams, 2018, p. 23-4). Labour inspectors' testimonies about the difficulties in detecting informalized employment seem to recall the evidence from Italy. To prove informalized employment relations, inspectors need to triangulate interviews and testimonies of the workers themselves. Yet this remains hard. As one of them revealed:

---

14 The monthly living wage for a family of four, as estimated in 2015 by the Clean Clothes Campaign (2016), was around €580.

> The workers are not open at all with labour inspectors. They are scared. We never [manage to] prove [partial informalization practices]. We just end up checking the bank accounts and transfers. (Interview with labour inspector, I-104)

In addition, while sanctions for unregistered workers are heavy (can reach 200,000 leks), informalized employment practices are punished with a fine that, at worst, equals the contributions and taxes evaded (Kosta and Williams, 2018, p. 50). Like in Italy, in other words, informal employment practices persist but shift from the total lack of registration to partially informalized employment in response to new laws, regulations, and inspection mechanisms.

4.6. *A double dependency: The structural and political role of informal employment*

Employment informalization moves the employment relationship away from laws and contracts and re-organizes it under informal rules and unfettered power relations. Thus, as I will show in detail in the following chapters, it enhances workforce flexibility vis-à-vis the employer, reduces labour costs, and increases firms' ability to navigate competitive pressures. On the one hand, it reduces tax revenues, on the other hand by boosting firms' competitiveness, it promotes employment creation (albeit informalized), exports, and economic growth. Such entangled dynamics shape the interests of the different actors that design and implement anti-informality public policies.

Informal labour remains a crucial structural feature of the Italian economy. It is engrained in a few industries that are crucial for the national productive structure. The first ten sectors (excluding public employees) in terms of occupation (measured as the average of the annual stock of persons employed in the period 1995–2018), in fact, present high or considerable informalization rates with an average that amounts to roughly 21%. Moreover, high levels of informalization also persist in those sectors in which the stock of persons employed grew in 1995–2018, signalling that informalized employment relations are still pivotal in the sectors driving job creation.

More specifically, in 2017, agriculture and the manufacturing of food products recorded rates of informality of 15.5% and 9.9%, respectively. Other sectors that are crucial for Italian exports, such as garment-footwear, had an informality rate of 10.2%. At the same time, those main non-tradable industries[15] that experienced steady employment growth, such as transportation and storage, accommodation and food services, and activities for households, have also shown persistence or even growth (in the case of transportation and storage) in the rate of informalization. This is crucial if one considers that employment creation, in Italy and even more in the Mezzogiorno, relies increasingly on non-tradable sectors. In 2000, 25% of the Mezzogiorno's employees were deployed in tradable sectors, which dropped to 21% in 2011. Northern regions followed a similar trend, and employment in tradable sectors declined from 32% to 28%. In 2011, these regions alone accounted for 60% of the national employment in the tradable sectors (17% the central regions and 23% the Mezzogiorno), and this percentage remained stable in the period 2000–2011. In 2018, the percentage of the total exports of the central and Northern regions accounted for 89% of the national manufacturing sector and 71% of the agricultural sector (against 11% and 29%, respectively, in the Mezzogiorno).

At the same time, Italian exports have increasingly originated from sectors and production activities that are price-sensitive and in competition with low labour-cost producers (Banca d'Italia, 2017; 2010). This economic specialization is even more enhanced in the Mezzogiorno, where export-oriented firms are increasingly embedded as suppliers in GPNs with their buyers in the North of Italy (Banca d'Italia, 2010; SRM, 2015; Gigio et al., 2021) and connects with the regional specialization in low-added-value tradable and non-tradable industries. Agriculture, in Mezzogiorno transport/storage and accommodation and food services are even more important than in the North, accounting for 17% of the regional employment in the Mezzogiorno against 12% in the North.

In other words, the increasing importance of low added-value specialization in export-oriented and domestic consumption sectors signals the increasing reliance of the national economy (especially in the South) on mechanisms that compress labour costs and enhance labour flexibility. Such dependency makes it difficult for political actors to comprehensively tackle informal labour since entire regions and sectors rely on employment informalization for their employment creation mechanisms and their exports (Bobbio, 2016; Dewey and Di Carlo, 2021).

15 I have classified as tradable the following sectors: mining and quarrying, manufacturing, agriculture, information and communication and non-tradable the rest.

Political decisions have shaped this restructuring and *indirectly* contributed to the persistence of informality. Declining public investment, privatization of state-holding companies, and the overhaul of industrial policies have contributed to the de-industrialization of the Mezzogiorno and increased the region's dependency on internal-consumption-oriented sectors, pushing export-oriented firms to the margins of national and global value chains. At the same time, the liberalization of employment protection has eroded unions' bargaining power in the workplace (Baccaro and Howell, 2017) and made it harder for workers to resist informalization. On the other hand, political actors have also *directly* ensured the reproduction of informal employment through their public policies vis-à-vis informalization. Since the 1990s, specific policies against informal labour have been pursued at different times, specifically by left-wing coalition governments that have been unable to maintain stable majorities for long. Constant governmental reshuffles or anticipated elections have allowed the competing right-wing coalition to reverse realignment policies, provide tax amnesties, and abolish the congruence indices. By drawing on the literature on electoral dynamics (Bulfone and Tassinari 2021; Afonso and Bulfone, 2019), one can safely assume that the right-wing coalition pivoted on the support of specific social groups that favour governmental leniency towards informality, such as the owners of SMEs, the self-employed, and the petty bourgeoisie. In line with the interests of its electoral base, the right-wing coalition has consistently undermined existing anti-informality policies, fostering a generalized tolerance toward informalization. In line with such a pattern, after the global financial crisis and Monti's technocratic government, Renzi's cabinet aimed to gain support among SMEs owners and self-employed professionals (Bulfone and Tassinari, 2021; Vesan and Ronchi 2019; Amable and Palombarini 2014) and showed a lenient approach toward informalization. It reversed the limit on cash payments and carried out the restructuring of the inspection system without addressing its structural under-staffing.

The same political dynamics have travelled across governance levels, as well. For example, the regional attempt to eradicate informality set in motion in 2006 in Apulia triggered the opposition of business organizations. The main protagonists of that reform were side-lined to consolidate a shaking political support on the regional council.

The Albanian case offers additional evidence on policymakers need to consider the economic and political consequences of informality formalization campaigns. Fighting informality was not on the agenda of the Albanian government before 2004. In that year, under pressure from the OECD, the first comprehensive study of the issue was carried out. In 2005, the first plan to tackle the informal economy was drafted; it relied mainly on deregulation and bureaucratic simplification. In the first national development strategy (GoA, 2007), the informal economy was mainly addressed as a matter of tax evasion to be addressed through information campaigns about tax obligations and an overall reduction of bureaucratic barriers for small firms. Informal employment was instead framed as a problem that concerned principally 'vulnerable groups, especially young people aged 18–25 years, women, persons with disabilities and Roma' (GoA, 2007, p. 61).

The change in government in 2013 coincided with a slightly different approach towards informality. The new Socialist Party government abolished the flat-tax-rate system, listed the fight against informality as a governmental priority, and framed informal employment as a matter of lost revenues as well as of unfair employment practices and substandard occupational health and safety (GoA, 2013). However, this anti-informality campaign was also heavily influenced by international institutions, notably the IMF (Erebara, 2015). In 2013, Albania accessed an IMF loan that entailed a fiscal consolidation program aimed at improving tax collection (curbing informality and tax evasion) and tightening public expenditures (IMF, 2017; 2016). As a result, the anti-informality campaign was primarily oriented toward improving revenues and focused on the registration of informal workers without fully prosecuting the widespread, ongoing partial informalization practices.

As in the Italian case, informalized employment remains a salient feature of certain crucial economic sectors of the Albanian economy. As reported in the 2020 EU Progress Report, informal employment in non-agricultural sectors still amounts to 30% despite the increasing number of registered employees (EC, 2020b). Considering the difficulties of identifying and sanctioning partially informalized employment, one can conclude that the Albanian anti-informality campaign has so far settled for robust action against fully unregistered employment (at least in big cities where inspectors can get to) while de-facto forbearing partially informalized employment. As noted by the European Commission, '[t]he informal economy is being tackled to some extent by fighting tax evasion and promoting tax compliance, but undeclared work is not addressed in a comprehensive manner' (EC, 2018b, p. 46). In fact, the primary goal of the anti-informality campaign—increasing revenues and insurance contribution from workers registration—has been partially achieved, while at the same time partially informalized employment remained widespread in many sectors that are crucial in terms of employment, exports and revenues, such as tourism and garment-footwear (see: Karma, 2019).

The case of garment-footwear in Albania is a clear example of such a dynamic. On the one hand, it is among the most informalized sectors in the country, to the extent that the European Commission expressed concerns 'over the proportion of women in the informal labour market, especially the textile and shoe industries, without appropriate labour and social protection' (EC 2020b, p. 93). And yet, the anti-informality campaign is unequipped to detect and deter the widespread informalization of employment relations in the sector. On the contrary, the government considers the industry a crucial driver of exports and a crucial employer for specifically vulnerable social groups (Kosta, 2018b) and was even listed as a strategic sector in the government's 2014–2020 business and investment development strategy (MEDTE, 2014). Consistently, the garment-footwear industry has also benefited from a comprehensive stimulus package of fiscal incentives and tax breaks that completely overlooked the need to raise labour standards (Kacani, 2017).

The above discussion shows that, to evaluate the effectiveness of policies against informality, one needs to take into account the specific political and structural economic factors that make the eradication of informality costly. Economically, the structural transformations of the Italian and Albanian economies make economic actors increasingly dependent on sectors that rely more and more on informal employment. Politically, the electoral coalitions in Italy relying on SMEs and the petty bourgeoisie are eager to show a certain leniency towards informalization, while alternative coalitions are inherently unstable given the crucial role of SMEs owners and self-employed professional in the electorate (for a similar argument on the pivotal role of SMEs see: Bulfone and Tassinari, 2021; Weiss, 1987; 1984). Thus, even though social-democratic coalitions have inaugurated potentially successful policies against informality, their weak electoral base has not provided sufficient continuity to their mandates. Their policies have therefore been reversed, converted or sabotaged by alternative political coalitions.

Similarly, in Albania, the right-wing Democrats have addressed the issue of informality with the tools of the neoliberal perspective. While paying more attention to the consequences of informalization for labour standards, the Socialists have been heavily constrained by the pressures for fiscal consolidation and the need to maintain the competitiveness of certain crucial sectors (such as garment-footwear) that rely on the partial informalization of employment.

To conclude, this double economic and political dependency has guaranteed the persistence of policies that favour leniency in both contexts. When informalization becomes a structural feature of important sectors of the economy, eradication might lead unambiguously to short-term loss of competitiveness, of employment, exports and even (residual) revenues. This has a clear economic and political price. Informality persistence, instead, rewards the short-term but clear interest of a crucial part of society. In Italy, while the preference of left-wing governments and their constituency was full-fledged policies against informal employment, these coalitions were unable to guarantee policy continuity. Right-wing coalitions, on the contrary, lacked altogether the intention to deprive their core constituencies of their well-engrained practices of non-compliance and consistently sabotaged or reversed eradication campaigns. In Albania, the fight against informality was mainly shaped by the pressure to improve tax collection and consolidate fiscal revenues rather than by a genuine concern to improve labour standards. Informalization's role in boosting firms' competitiveness and the crucial dependency on highly informalized sectors for exports and employment constrained the 2015 anti-informality campaign. In both cases, therefore, a *low-compliance equilibrium* has emerged, in which the state is able to recover part of lost revenues and legitimacy, firms maintain a crucial tool of labour control and competitiveness, and labour lacks enough political leverage to reshape regulations and guarantee their effective enforcement.

Against this background, consistent and significant sectoral differences in informalization and the presence of different forms of formality and informality within the same sectors persist. To address these issues, the book turns to focus on one specific sector in both countries, the garment-footwear, to tease out the sectoral constraints and the patterns of agency that guarantee the persistence of informality and transformations in it over time.

5.
SEEING LIKE A CHAIN
Global Transformations and Local Developments in the Garment-footwear Industry in Southern Italy and Albania

5.1. *The garment-footwear industry and global restructuring: A global production networks perspective*

The globalized character of the garment-footwear industry stands as a great example of a highly fragmented, highly mobile, and transnationally integrated production. This industry is considered paradigmatic of the changes many other sectors have undergone due to globalization, with a high degree of production fragmentation and international functional integration (Dicken, 2015; Gereffi and Frederick, 2010). Moreover, it represents a typical *starter industry* for national economies that are being integrated into broader production systems (Gereffi, 1999, p. 6).[1]

Fragmentation and functional integration: The basis of global production

Modern production processes in garment-footwear is segmented into distinct tasks that can be carried out separately, in different places, by autonomous actors (Lane and Probert, 2009, p. 35). Each phase of production requires different skills and specializations, coincides with different positions within production networks, and entails differentiated gains.

The planning of collections requires creativity and skills in market surveying and analysis. It also needs expert knowledge of consumption trends, raw materials supply, production time and distribution channels.

After this first phase, professional stylists and designers create the first prototype of the item (garment or footwear). This becomes the model for

1 While most of the contributions quoted in this section deal explicitly with garment manufacturing, the organization of production and its development and dynamics in the garment sector follow the same path of those in the leather-footwear industry. On Italy, for example see Dunford (2006).

a small sample run of the same item in different colours, variants, and sizes. Subsequently, 'sample-making' requires tailors that can transform the model conceived of by the designers into an initial sample series. Such samples have to adapt the original design to mass production, keeping in mind production costs and time and the availability of fabrics and accessories (buttons, patches and zips, for example). Design is usually carried out by a *buyer* or a *full-package supplier*.

The phases of cutting, assembly, ironing and packaging are the most labour-intensive phases of production (i.e., the final assembly of the item). This entails the cutting of fabrics or leather, sewing all the parts of the item together with its labels and accessories, final quality control (to eliminate excessive threads and other imperfections), the ironing of the item, and its packaging. These phases of production can all be carried out in the same production facility or distributed to contractors specialized in one or more of them.

Finally, the marketing and distribution phases entails managing the linkages between production, distribution, and advertisement. In addition, distribution requires increasingly sophisticated systems of logistics to ensure on-demand replenishment of stocks in stores.

Governance in garment-footwear: A buyer-driven production chain

As Gereffi and Frederick (2010, p. 172) argue, '[t]he apparel industry is the quintessential example of a buyer-driven production chain, marked by power asymmetries between the producers and global buyers of final apparel products'. A production chain or network is buyer-driven when 'large retailers, brand-named merchandisers, and trading companies play the pivotal role in setting up decentralized production networks in a variety of exporting countries' (Gereffi, 1994, p. 97).

Lead firms are defined as the actors that 'control access to major resources [...] that generate[s] the most profitable returns' (Gereffi and Memedovic, 2003, p. 4). They offshore all the phases of production that are easily accessible to competitors and retain the ones which maintain higher entry barriers (Gereffi and Memedovic, 2003, p. 5). The great bulk of the value-added and profits in the chain, in fact, comes from the phases that are not related to production and manufacturing. The closer a firm is to the final market, the higher the share of the surplus it gains from the whole production process. Intangible aspects of production—marketing, branding, design—are what shapes the distribution of gains and power within the chain (Gereffi and Frederick, 2010). Lead firms in the garment-footwear industry are brand owners, marketers, or retailers—namely, big buyers of items produced by someone else. Firms at the bottom of the chain, that cut and stitch items, are numerous and potentially located all over the world. Low-to-no entry barriers do not protect them from new competitors entering the supply chains and performing their tasks. Lead firms, on the contrary can actively shelter themselves from new competitors given their knowledge of consumers' habits and trends, the ownership of successful brands, or direct access to the final markets through retail chains and marketing campaigns (Gereffi and Frederick, 2010).

Figure 5.1. A stylized garment-footwear production chain

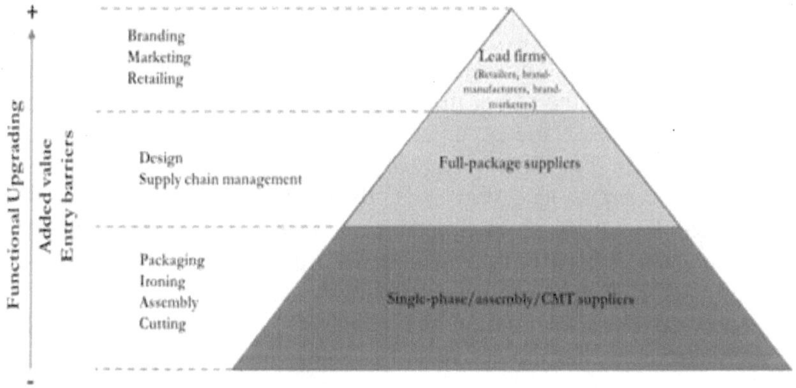

Source: Author's own elaboration

The position of firms within the production chain, the barriers protecting them from competitors and the gains they can reap from production change according to the production task they undertake (see Figure 5.1). Following Gereffi and Memedovic (2003), we can distinguish mainly three ideal types of firms according to the phases of production they carry out and to their positioning within the production chain:

Assembly or cut, make and trim (CMT) suppliers. All the materials necessary to production (fabrics, threads, accessories) are purchased by the buyer and delivered directly to these suppliers which assemble the items under the strict guidance (direct control and coded criteria) of the buyer. Such firms can carry out both the cutting and sewing of the item or just one of these phases, and they usually do not have a direct relation with the final distributor of the good but rather with an intermediary that manages the supply chain on its behalf.

Full-package suppliers. These firms receive the design and specifications about quantity, quality, and delivery time of the final product. Usually, these suppliers purchase the inputs autonomously and carry out the whole manufacturing process, including cutting, sewing, quality control, ironing, and packaging. For example, one full-package supplier might undertake all the phases of production, or parts might be outsourced to assembly and single-phase subcontractors. The products are then delivered to the lead firm or to the wholesalers/stores to be sold under the buyers' brand or within the buyers' retail chains. Recently, more and more full-package suppliers have been taking over the design and sample-making phases of production, as will be shown. Yet, they do not engage in branding and advertising activities and do not build autonomous networks of distributors.

Original brand manufacturers/brand marketers/retailers. These are the lead firms of the chain. They carry out the design and planning of their lines and then outsource the actual manufacturing phases of production. They concentrate resources and expertise in developing a brand and marketing it. In some cases, they directly control the distribution.

Different types of lead firm exist. *Brand manufacturers* own a well-established brand (or more brands) and have a strong manufacturing tradition. These firms used to produce entirely in-house or through domestic outsourcing. With increasing access to low-wage suppliers, however, they can focus on the consolidation and marketing of their brands, retaining strict control over the supply chain. *Retailers,* instead, usually own retail chains that sell different kinds of clothing and footwear, some of which might be under a brand of their property. While they own—or control through franchising agreements—the stores and malls where the goods are sold, they completely outsource the manufacturing process, design, and development of their own new lines. These lead firms rely on full-package suppliers that are able to design, develop and manufacture a ready-to-wear product under minimal guidance. Their advantage lies in the direct control of shops and stores where the goods are distributed. Finally, *brand marketers* are 'manufacturers without factories'. They own mainly their brand and focus on developing marketing campaigns and reaching different markets extensively through networks of specialized or general stores. The whole manufacturing process, like for retailers, is outsourced to full-package suppliers (Schrank, 2004).

As far as the suppliers are concerned, the main difference between full-package and CMT suppliers is that the former purchase the fabrics and accessories needed to produce the item, while the latter just assemble the inputs purchased and provided by the buyer. Usually, the first functional upgrading in the chain a firm undertakes is when it shifts from assembly to full-package supply activities. This implies an enlargement of the phases of production carried out and of the added value appropriated.

Lead firms rely on CMT or full-package suppliers according to their legacies and strategies. Contracting out to CMT suppliers entails 'pre-manufacturing investments' (Lane and Probert, 2009, p. 157): the item needs to be designed, and raw material must be purchased and delivered to the suppliers. When working with full-package suppliers instead, buyers have to pay only when the final product is manufactured and delivered because the supplier takes charge of purchasing production inputs. Moreover, with full-package suppliers, the lead time can be shortened if these are well integrated and geographically proximate to the production regions of raw materials, as in the cases of Turkey, China and Egypt (ibidem). Yet, buyers that prefer maintaining tighter control over the choice of raw materials usually rely on CMT suppliers. Buyers with a manufacturing legacy are usually more inclined to use CMT suppliers, while retailers or brand marketers prefer a full-package supplier (Gereffi, 1999; Gereffi and Memedovic, 2003; Lane and Probert, 2009, p. 157).

Trade, consumption, governance and restructuring

The transformation of the garment-footwear sector into a buyer-driven industry is related to the technical possibility to segment the production process, the importance of labour-intensive production phases and labour costs, and the low barriers to enter the supply chain. At the same time, trade policies, the active agency of retailers and brand marketers, and changing consumption habits have played a crucial role in the restructuring process.

With regards to trade policies, the phasing out of the Multifibre Arrangement (MFA) system in 1994 and the transitional Agreement on Textile and Clothing (ATC)—which lasted from 1995 until 2005—coincided with selective bilateral and regional trade arrangements and the proliferation of production in third countries to circumvent quotas (Hale and Burns, 2005, p. 210-17). In addition, specific regional trade agreements eliminated quotas and tariffs on imports of semi-finished garments that used inputs of the importer country. These trade schemes are referred to as *outward processing trade* (OPT), linking EU and Eastern European and Northern African countries (Pickles and Smith, 2016; 2011), and *production sharing*, linking the US and Central American and Caribbean supplier countries (Gereffi and Memedovic, 2003). Within these arrangements, lead firms could outsource labour-intensive phases of production and focus on marketing and branding, while foreign suppliers could carry out assembly activities but could not directly export finished goods (Hale and Burns 2005, pp. 210-17; Hurley and Miller, 2005).

This restructuring coincided with a far-reaching change in consumption habits. Retailers had massively entered the apparel and footwear market since the 1980s, driving the first significant shift of consumption and production models. Banking on experienced and easily accessible suppliers in low-wage countries, retailers could leverage their access to customers cutting inventory and production costs. The shift to 'lean retailing' and 'quick response' supply (Abernathy et al., 2006; 1999) started in the mid-1980s and entailed the application of 'just-in-time' production principles. Accordingly, the average size of production batches ordered shrinks, and sales are continuously monitored at each store. When replenishment is needed for certain lines or items, manufacturers are mobilized and must quickly produce and ship the items ordered by the retailer (Tokatli, 2008). Lean retailing increases the importance of full-package suppliers with the ability to deliver smaller batches of production with high time-responsiveness and flexibility in terms of the quality, fabrics, design and kind of items.

Such a sectoral overhaul did not occur with the same intensity and at the same time everywhere. In Europe, the restructuring was slower, and in Italy, at the beginning of the 1990s, small independent retailers still covered a relevant portion of domestic garment and footwear demand. National institutions—namely, the national mechanisms of incentives and constraints that favour small retailers over big retail chains (mainly the difficulty of getting permission to build hypermarkets in Italy)—and the specific attitudes of Italian consumers mattered in delaying the shift (Dicken, 2015; Dunford, 2006). Furthermore, different national institutions, entrepreneurial attitudes and trade policies shaped the different delocalization strategies of US and European companies (see: Lane and Probert, 2009).

Nonetheless, eventually, a common buyer-driven trajectory consolidated in Europe as well and accelerated in the early 2000s with the rise of the *fast-fashion model*. Driven by global retailers such as Zara, H&M, Mango, Benetton, and many others, the fast-fashion model relies on the power of retailers to control an increasing number of stores worldwide and their ability to set up a supply chain based on 'short development cycles, rapid prototyping, small batches and variety so that customers are offered the latest designs in limited quantities that ensure a sort of exclusivity' (Tokatli, 2008, p. 23).

Fast fashion both follows and reshapes consumption habits much more markedly than lean retailing. It values 'product *distinguishability'* instead of simple 'product *replenishability'* in that retailers 'purposefully create a climate of scarcity, the message to the customer being that "if you do not buy it now, you will lose your opportunity"' (Tokatli and Kızılgün, 2009, p. 148). Rather than producing more clothes of the same line on demand, fast-fashion chains continuously create new and diverse lines of products (Tokatli, 2008). Consumers are offered a wide repertoire of always new items to express themselves and their tastes in an affordable *and* still potentially sophisticated way. As Tokatli (2008, p. 28) explains, fast fashion is inexpensive, but *it does not feel cheap.*

Such a production model challenges mass retail chains of low-quality standardized goods, high-fashion houses, and ready-to-wear brands alike and increases the pressures along the whole supply chain, as well. Furthermore, fast fashion reduces the size of production batches and lead times and increase the pressure to be flexible and customize products together with the uncertainty of future orders (Schrank, 2004; Tokatli, 2013). The 2008 crisis has further exacerbated these dynamics, and the subsequent fall in demand in core end markets has definitely tilted the power relations within GPNs in favour of buyers (Gereffi and Frederick, 2010).

Bringing production back home? The reshoring wave

Against this background, cases of reshoring or backshoring (i.e., when production localization moves from low-wage countries back to the country where the lead firm is located) are emerging. Reshoring has been defined as 'the relocation of value creation tasks from offshore to geographically closer locations [...] irrespective of the ownership mode' (Di Mauro et al., 2018, p. 108; see also: Foerstl et al., 2016). Backshoring instead, refers to the relocation of the value-creations task to the actual home country of the firm (ibidem).

The literature generally sees backshoring either as the reversal of a mistaken offshoring decision or as part of purposive and strategic relocation (Barbieri and Fratocchi, 2017; Di Mauro et al., 2018; Martínez-Mora and Merino, 2014; Robinson and Hsieh, 2016). Often, backshoring concerns middle- to high-quality products and responds to the need to shorten the supply chain to increase its flexibility and responsiveness to demand (Di Mauro et al., 2018). In other words, backshoring ensures quality, quick lead times and thus the reduction of inventory costs (Di Mauro et al., 2018; Martínez-Mora and Merino, 2014). Finally, the 'Made in' effect is important as well, and reshoring might work as a brand-enhancing strategy (Di Mauro et al., 2018).

While the United States leads the wave of backshoring from distant supply countries—especially from China (Andersson et al., 2018; Baldassarre et al., 2014)—Italy is the backshoring frontrunner in the EU, and apparel is the most affected sector. Baldassare et al. (2014) have found that Apulia's entrepreneurs' motivations to consider backshoring—in line with those identified in the literature—are narrowing the production cost gap[2] and the unsatisfactory level of quality control over (and rigidity of) the supply chain. However, from Baldassare and colleagues (2014)'s interview-based research, it is not clear how many cases of actual ongoing backshoring concerned Apulia's apparel sector. In my fieldwork, I did not find evidence of ongoing relocation processes, and according to the Eurofound's European Reshoring Monitoring Database, between 2014 and 2019, among the 15 cases of reshoring in the ferment-footwear sector reported in Italy, only one related to firms located in Apulia.[3] Nonetheless, the supply chain disruption experienced during the peak of Covid-19 pandemic might have accelerated this trend.

5.2. *Industrial districts and global value chains: The development of the garment- footwear industry in Apulia and Albania*

The garment-footwear industry is a crucial component of manufacturing production and exports in Italy and Albania. Italy is one of the world's leading exporters in the sector, and it is by far the leading producer in the EU.

Industrial clusters specialized in garment-footwear are located throughout Italy. However, the most important production centres are in Italy's northern and central regions, specifically in Piedmont,

2 In Italy, labour costs have been shrinking (due to stagnating salaries, reductions of taxes on wages and social protection contributions) but have been increasing in supplier countries (Baldassarre et al., 2014).

3 The retailer OVS announced its intention to backshore parts of its production to Apulia (see: Eurofound, 2018).

Veneto, Tuscany and Marche. Among southern regions, Campania and Apulia account for the great bulk of production and employment. While Campania has specialized prominently in leather goods, Apulia developed a solid footwear district and a variegated textile-clothing landscape in the provinces of Barletta-Andria-Trani (BAT), Bari and Lecce.

Production profiles in the North and the South differ. The export centres of the national industry are mainly located in the North, while the distribution of garment-footwear employment is less eschewed (see Table 5.1).

Table 5.1. Share of export and employment in the garment-footwear industry in Italy, 2017

	North	Centre	South	Apulia
Export	67%	28%	4%	1%
Employment	50%	33%	17%	4%

Source: ISTAT (export) and INPS (employment measured as workers employed within the year).

While northern regions account for 67% of all Italian garment-footwear export, they account for half of national employment in the sector. The mismatch between export and employment levels signals different dynamics. On the one hand, it highlights lower productivity in southern productions and a specialization in covering domestic demand rather than foreign markets. On the other hand, as the literature (Brusco and Paba, 1997; Messori, 1989) and empirical analyses of the infra-regional trade before the 2008 crisis confirm (Giunta et al., 2012; SRM, 2015, chap. 2; ARTI, 2021), southern producers are embedded in broader production networks as suppliers of lead firms located in the North. In other words, southern producers often work as subcontractors for lead firms located in the North that export the finished product and capture higher shares of added value.

Such a distribution of roles affects the quality of employment, the levels of informalization, and the distribution of the gains in the different regions. Garment-footwear firms in the South are on average smaller, report fewer working hours per employee, and have a higher percentage of fixed-term contracts than in the North. Salaries are on average 40% lower, and the added value of Southern firms is generally half of the Northern garment-footwear companies, while even the number of company-level collective agreements is consistently lower in the South (Rizzuto and Tomassetti, 2019; see also: ARTI, 2021).

The garment industry in Apulia

While tailors and a few textile artisanal production facilities existed before, properly *industrial* textile-clothing firms emerged in Bari and BAT in the early 1950s, particularly in the Southern area of the Bari province (Viesti, 2000a). The first production facilities in the 1950s followed Tayloristic work organization principles and were highly vertically integrated. Production was carried out entirely in-house—*from the yarn to the final cloth*—and pursued scale economies. In that same period, the number of artisanal workshops shrunk due to more integrated national markets, forcing the least productive actors out of the market (Brusco and Paba, 1997; Comei, 2012; Viesti, 2000a; 2000b). Industrial companies, instead, grew in employment and production output until the end of the 1960s. They specialized in producing middle-to-low-quality garments for local and regional markets (in the southern regions of Apulia, Basilicata and Calabria). The main competitive advantages of producers in Bari and BAT were the low wages of the local workforce, estimated to be one-third of the minimum wage of workers in the same sector in northern regions (Viesti, 2000a).

At the beginning of the 1970s, however, the district experienced profound changes. The average wage increased because of growing unionization rates and workers' assertiveness in the sector and the whole region (Frey, 1975; SPI-CGIL, 2018). Moreover, in 1968 the so-called '*gabbie salariali*' (literally 'wage cages')—a salary cap established by national collective agreements that kept wages lower in the South than in the North—was abolished. At the same time, changing market and consumption habits put the highly verticalized, rigid production organization of local firms under strain (Viesti, 2000a; 2000b). At this juncture, while local producers were pushed out of the markets or heavily downsized and outsourced their orders to more agile local workshops, northern brand manufacturers started subcontracting phases of their production processes to cheaper but reliable locations abroad. Firms in the South maintained a competitive edge because of the low salaries and became accessible suppliers of labour-intensive production tasks.

In the Bari and BAT provinces, skilled workers dismissed by the big local firms in crisis met the demand for cheap subcontractors that came from buyers outside the region; small supplier workshops—often led by entrepreneurial workers that were previously laid off—mushroomed. In these years, the average size of firms decreased drastically together with unionization levels, and local producers specialized in becoming suppliers. Limited entry barriers and the widespread availability of a cheap but skilled workforce facilitated imitative processes. Subcontractors in the CMT phases of production spread widely. The local district slowly lost the phases of branding and distribution that were once carried out by the local Fordist champions, but employment increased together with informality in sweatshops and home-based work (Frey, 1975; Viesti, 2000a).

In this same period, a new productive specialization emerged when local entrepreneurs in the BAT province started small businesses manufacturing underwear. These firms were usually managed by local clothing and undergarment merchandise vendors with no manufacturing experience but direct knowledge of local distribution channels in street markets and small shops. They could bank on the supply of skilled and cheap workers and could use their networks to directly purchase fabrics from other Italian regions and abroad. Most of such workshops remained small, highly informalized and based on the low cost of the production process. They alternated production for direct distribution on local markets[4] with subcontracting activities for lead firms. Many of them usually had short life cycles, but a few grew into proper industrial firms specialized in supply and production for Northern Italian buyers (Viesti, 2000a).

By the end of the 1980s, local producers had almost entirely turned into cost-competitive suppliers, specialized in medium quality products, with the capacity to deliver small and differentiated batches of production (Viesti, 2000a). In the Northern part of Bari and the BAT province, producers of knitwear garments, sweatshirts, jackets, and a few manufacturers of 'total look' clothing[5] endured as subcontractors. In the Southern part of the Bari province, the early specialization in high-quality products—mainly suits,

4 Having direct control or knowledge of distribution channels, especially when distributors can easily keep part of their accounting in the shadows (as it is often for street marketers and small shops), represents an opportunity to informalize the production process as well. If you can sell your production to distributors under the table (because the distributors can also do the same to the clients), then you can also informalize the production process without risking a mismatch in the declared input and output of production.

5 Local entrepreneurs used the label 'total look' to refer to productions that included items for both the lower and the upper apparels. A 'total look' line, would include for example the production of trousers/jeans, shirts/blouses and coats/jackets.

dresses, shrugs, coats, jackets, and children's 'total look' garments—remained. A few lead firms consolidated, specializing in design, branding and marketing while outsourcing some parts of production to local workshops. Thus, on the one hand, the employment in big local firms kept shrinking; on the other, the aggregate level of employment in the district increased because of the multiplication of small workshop-like subcontractors (Viesti, 2000a). At this point, local subcontractors in Bari and BAT were able to deal with CMT and assembly activities as well as to design lines and realize innovative models and prototypes on behalf of other brands (Viesti, 2000a). Moreover, suppliers of ancillary phases of production such as ironing, packaging, labelling workshops, as well as firms specializing in embroidery for third parties, thrived. This offered the district an agglomeration advantage and attracted more external buyers that could keep their whole supply chain local (Viesti, 2000a).

In the 1990s, things changed abruptly again. Liberalization of trade and the rise of suppliers located in emerging economies with lower production costs pressured Southern Italian subcontractors (Dunford et al., 2016). On top of that, as some interviewees point out (knitwear-factory manager I-12; footwear supplier-firm manager I-31; president of the local footwear business organization, I-29), some of the consolidated markets for local producers—namely, those established in the prior decade in the Middle East and Northern Africa—became unreachable in the 1990s because of wars and socio-political transformations. Delocalization aimed at cutting production costs became a top priority for firms in Bari and BAT (Amighini and Rabellotti, 2006; Corò and Grandinetti, 1999, p. 898; Prota and Viesti, 2010).

As Prota and Viesti (2010) highlight, many features of the Italian production structure delayed delocalization. Firstly, the average small size of Italian firms meant they had little financial scope for greenfield investment abroad. At the same time, Italian industrial districts could already offer locally many of the advantages of lean production—namely, ready diffusion of innovation within production networks and a significant number of agile firms specialized in providing only one phase of the production process. Moreover, local suppliers allowed lead firms to retain tight control over the production process without the rigidities of in-house production.

However, in the 1990s, delocalization became such a crucial practice for local firms that Prota and Viesti (2010) refer to the so-called 'Adriatic Connection'. The Italian regions on the Adriatic shores, where most of the garment-footwear production concentrates (Veneto, Marche and Apulia), become the first in Italy to offshore relevant parts of production to suppliers in Eastern Europe. This process included limited FDI, and most of all, the intensification of OPT.

Local lead firms in Bari and BAT maintained some of the advantages of local outsourcing within the district even when offshoring production overseas. Geographical proximity and the rapid intensification of relations of Apulia's entrepreneurs with Albanian counterparts in the footwear sector that had already paved the way in offshoring helped delocalization take off. Moreover, strong social and cultural ties between the countries facilitated the building of transnational production networks. Albania's most widely spoken foreign language was (and still is) Italian, and Italy was the first emigration destination of Albanians in the aftermath of the socialist regime's collapse. As a result, entrepreneurs from Bari and BAT could establish production relations and maintain a high level of control over their Albanian suppliers and a very short lead time.

The creation of an inter-Adriatic production cluster emerges clearly also by looking at trade data.

Figure 5.2. Garment-footwear trade between the Bari/BAT provinces and Albania, 1991-2017

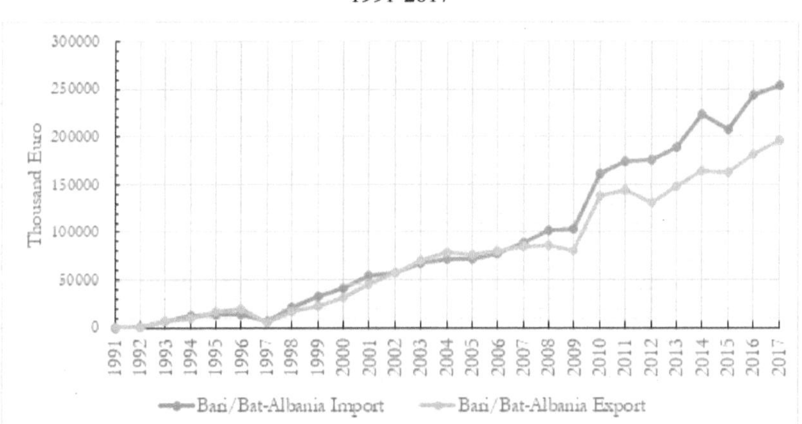

Source: Author's elaboration on ISTAT Coeweb. Note: Ateco 2007/NACE Rev.2; sectors considered: Textile-Clothing-Footwear (sections C, Divisions 13, 14, 15).

As Figure 5.2 shows, both exports to and imports from Albania in the garment-footwear sector increased steadily after 1997. The patterns of imports and exports are very similar and generally grew and decreased in parallel. This signals the presence of trade in intermediary goods and highlights the increasing importance of outward processing trade relations (see ARTI, 2020).[6]

The textile-clothing district of Bari and BAT is today fully integrated into national and transnational production networks. A few local actors reach foreign markets with their own brands (interview and focus group with workers [I-14; I-87/93]; and managers [I-95; I-97]), while the rest of the firms are integrated as subcontractors in networks led by brand marketers, retailers or brand manufacturers with a global reach. Specifically, a limited number of brand manufacturers reach national and foreign markets, and according to the quality of their product lines, either retain a significant part of their production in-house or outsource locally and to Albania (focus group with managers [I-35/38]; interviews with managers [I-22; I-76; I-97]; worker [I-14]). Other firms work as full-package suppliers for brands and retailers, carrying out design and sample-making phases while outsourcing production to different CMT suppliers in the district and in Albania (interviews with manager [I-84]; workers [I-17/18]; focus group with workers, [I-87/93]). Finally, another group of firms (the most numerous) works for local or external buyers providing a single production phase such as embroidery, embellishment, cutting, ironing, labelling, or packaging. These are greatly dependent on a few clients (usually first-tier suppliers), and so they rarely have a direct connection with the lead firm of the chain.

The footwear sector in Bari and BAT

The footwear industry in Apulia developed in the province of Lecce (that is not included in this research) and BAT, specifically in the city of Barletta and in the nearby towns. The local footwear industry did not emerge from consolidated traditional artisanal production but instead relied on imported technology, *leapfrogging,* and connections with buyers outside the region (D'Ercole, 2000).

In the early 1950s, local migrants returning from Northern Italy mobilized their networks with northern producers to import second-hand machinery and raw materials for the industrial production of standardized

6 The great bulk of Albania's total clothing and footwear exports to the EU are actually re-exports of semi-finished products (World Bank, 2009).

shoes with rubber soles (D'Ercole, 2000). The lack of an artisanal tradition in the sector favoured local entrepreneurial spirits: technology and knowledge of the production process could directly be imported and did not have to be built on long years of artisanship. Imitative processes led to the growth of local producers manufacturing rubber-soled shoes and slippers. These products were low-quality, highly standardized, and cheap. High production volumes rather than branding or designing represented the primary source of profit and growth for local firms. Local producers focused on industrializing their production process, relying on wholesalers to reach local markets in Southern Italy, retailers in Northern Europe and, through Neapolitan traders, even Northern African distributors (D'Ercole, 2000, p. 44-45). At the same time, local workshops specialized in refining raw rubber for footwear production and suppliers of moulds for the shoes' sole mushroomed.

In the 1960s and 1970s, the footwear district took off. New industrial machinery[7] increased local production capacities, allowing the introduction of plastic materials (PVC) and the creation of new products. From casual rubber-soled shoes, the main specialization of the district became producing low-to-middle-quality plastic-soled sports shoes for large-scale retailers. Firms in the district did not develop the design, marketing or branding capacities but instead focused on producing a high volume of standardized products at a competitive cost.

New ancillary suppliers emerged, such as firms specialized in the cutting and assembly of shoes' uppers and in the production of dies and metal stamps for cutting the uppers' pieces. These firms were autonomous but highly interdependent. Specialization in making low added-value standardized products required the entire district to focus on the same product in order to reach an overall output that could meet external buyers' volume demands (interviews with manager [I 31]; expert [I-2]; and business groups [I-16; I-29]). This process led to a rapid and steady increase in output, exports, new firms and employment. However, it also inhibited local employers from differentiating their production, investing in higher-quality products

7 These machines called *giostre* (literally carousels) in the local slang use moulds where liquid plastic or PVC is injected. The sole is ready after the PVC solidifies. Each of these giostre spin around continuously following the command of the operator so he or she can activate multiple moulds at the same time and produce a higher number of soles. Such machines evolved and newer versions —used widely in the BAT district's most sophisticated production of safety shoes—today creates the sole by attaching it directly to the upper part of the shoe. In this way the final assembly phase is incorporated in the production of the sole.

and gaining skills and knowledge in designing, marketing and branding (D'Ercole, 2000; Viesti, 2007, chap. 4). Cost competitiveness was ensured through economies of scale, diffused outsourcing, and agglomeration advantages, but also thanks to the high levels of employment informalization that kept labour cost low (Viesti, 2007, chap. 4; 2000b, pp. 261–3; 1998).

In the 1980s, the district kept growing as a collective supplier of a standardized, low-added-value product. Only marginal innovations were introduced in the embellishment of the uppers and in creating coloured soles to reach more sophisticated buyers and large-scale retailers (D'Ercole, 2000). In the 1990s, however, new suppliers in low-wage economies and Europe (D'Ercole, 2000) emerged while the European monetary integration process halted the currency devaluations that had guaranteed competitive leverage to Italian exporters in European and American markets. BAT's footwear entrepreneurs reacted by lobbying for protectionist measures. The European Commission imposed quotas (between 2% and 20%) on imports from China in 1994 and customs duties on imports from China, Indonesia and Thailand (Amighini and Rabellotti, 2006, p. 499; D'Ercole 2000, p. 51). However, Asian competitors were able to offer cheaper low-quality products even despite trade duties, other European competitors (i.e., Spain) were emerging, and Eastern European economies were increasingly becoming integrated into production networks led by Western European enterprises. The specialization in low-quality and standardized plastic shoes turned unsustainable for BAT's producers (Amighini and Rabellotti, 2006; D'Ercole, 2000).

The two main responses to this were delocalization and diversification of production. Firstly, a growing number of firms outsourced the most labour-intensive production phases—such as cutting and making uppers—abroad, mainly in Albania. Many of the numerous firms specialized in uppers' assembly in the district closed down or moved their machinery and activities overseas with a dramatic drop in local employment (Capestro and Guido, 2014; D'Ercole, 2000).

In line with national trends in garment-footwear, exports and delocalization grew together. In the first half of the 1990s, garment-footwear exports from Italy rose by 50% over five years, while growth in OPT in the same sector increased on average 80% every single year (Corò and Grandinetti, 1999, p. 898). At the beginning of the 2000s, the BAT footwear district was among the first in Italy to have established intermediate phases of offshoring (Amighini and Rabellotti, 2006).

For Amighini and Rabellotti (2006, p. 499), the BAT district 'replicated its own production model by displacing part of its production capacity to the Eastern side of the Adriatic Sea' without investing in higher added-value production phases. Yet, a few consolidated firms from the district did not limit their response to merely cost-saving delocalization but rather diversified and restructured their production. Some of them focused on higher-quality casual shoes—namely, trekking and training shoes for those firms working with PVC injection technologies and higher-quality fashion shoes for others. Quality shoe producers also reshaped their production process and supply chain to offer diverse products and shorter lead times, shifting to a fast-fashion kind of organization for *prêt-à-porter* (ready-to-wear) buyers (Rosato, 2015; Viesti and Luongo, 2014).

After massive investments in new technologies and machineries, other firms shifted toward producing quality safety shoes, a growing market in Europe, ensured by tightening and increasingly harmonized work safety regulations across the EU (Capestro and Guido, 2014; D'Ercole, 2000). The industrial restructuring towards the production of safety shoes was inaugurated by one of the biggest firms of the district, which had, at the beginning of the 1990s, reached high production volumes in plastic-soled, low-quality products. This firm seized the opportunity to occupy a niche but growing market. It invested in research, design and technology (to ensure products with high safety standards and a fashionable look), moved to a higher-added-value product range, outsourced non-core production activities, and built a brand and a network of distributors. Other local firms with investment capacities followed that strategy by offshoring labour-intensive phases to Albania and building alternative brands (Rosato 2015; Viesti, 2007, chap. 4).

Today, the firms operating in the district can be clustered into three groups. The first includes four/five large firms (each employing 60–400 workers locally) specialized in safety shoe production. They lead their GPNs and outsource most labour intensive production phases (usually the making of the uppers) to Albania through autonomous suppliers or branch firms. They have developed their own brands and have direct control of marketing and distribution networks. Their product is sold mainly in EU markets. The business strategies of these firms require continuous investments in technology, certifications, and design, to improve the quality, comfort, durability, and fashion appeal of the product. At the same time, cost competition remains crucial, and this drives the outsourcing of ever-more phases of production. The final assembly of the safety shoe remains crucial for the quality and certifiability of the final product and is mainly carried out in the BAT district. The rest of the locally employed workforce is employed in design, branding, research and logistics (Interview with managers, [I-29; I-82]; Rosato, 2015; Capestro and Guido, 2014). Besides the relation with few producers of special safety footwear components, those firms have minimal ties with suppliers within the district (Rosato, 2015).

A second group of firms produce fashion footwear and casual streetwear shoes. These firms work for buyers and large-scale retailers or couple the production of their own branded lines with the production as subcontractors for other buyers (Capestro and Guido, 2014). According to the product, these firms carry out in-house a significant part of the production process or just the final assembly. In addition, they mobilize short, local supply chains for 'Made-in-Italy' production or outsource abroad, usually to Albania. Finally, there are a few producers of standardized casual/sportive streetwear shoes or boots that depend greatly on buyers outside the region (Interview with manager, I-31; Interview with worker, I-86) as well as manufacturers working with their own brand and as full-package suppliers for buyers outside the district (interviews with manager, I-23; I-85).

Finally, suppliers of single operations and phases of production persist. Those are either the few remaining workshops that cut and make shoes' uppers, soles and heels or provide components for safety shoes such as protective metal toecaps (interview with manager, I-3; worker, I-94). A few workshops producing the dies for cutting the parts that compose the shoes' uppers, remain as well. However, these suppliers usually have no marketing or branding capacities and depend heavily on the volatile orders of their local clients (Capestro and Guido, 2014).

The garment-footwear industry in Albania

Albania's transition to a market economy started in the early 1990s with the collapse of the socialist regime. This was followed by a period of reform with 'exchange rate liberalization, privatizations, and the introduction of market-based institutions' (World Bank, 2015, p. 8) and generally steady growth in GDP, FDI and remittances. The period was characterized by economic and political instability, such as during the crisis of the banking pyramid schemes in 1997 (Bezemer, 2001; Bogdani and Loughlin 2007, chap. 7) and the massive influx of refugees from Kosovo during the Serbian–Kosovar war (World Bank, 2015).

During the transition, the Albanian garment-footwear industry banked on a strong manufacturing legacy built under the planned economy system and investments linked to the delocalization of Italian and Greek producers.

During socialism, this industry was a crucial source of employment with production facilities in the country's major cities (Shehi, 2023; Hylli et al., 2021; Invest in Albania, 2018). Nowadays, production facilities are still generally located where industrial centres were established during the socialist period—namely, in Tirana, Durres, Korca, Shkoder, Elbasan, Berat and Vlora (Shehi, 2017; AIDA, 2014). Old production sites were privatized and revitalized by Italian and Greek investors in the early 1990s (Anamali et al., 2015; World Bank, 2009; Shehi, 2023). FDI were crucial to maintaining industrial production, embedding industry in global production chains, renovating machinery and workforce skills, and increasing opportunities for other local firms to reach intermediaries well-integrated into GPNs (World Bank 2015; Ymeri et al., 2010).

Against this background, the consolidation of Italo–Albanian production networks was also favoured by the specific trade regime with the EU and a favourable tax system. From 1992, Albania benefited from the EU's general system of trade preferences (World Bank, 2009) while other specific OPT arrangements reduced or zeroed tariffs for re-imported goods processed in Albania (Zahariadis, 2007). Since 1999, the EU has granted autonomous trade preferences to Albania and other countries of the Western Balkans, allowing most of the goods produced in the region to enter the EU customs-free. The integration was further enhanced with the Stabilization and Association Process and different bilateral agreements with the EU. A Stabilization and Association Agreement signed in 2006 (which came into force three years later) further liberalized trade relations with the EU by constituting a comprehensive free trade area that required Albania to gradually comply with the *acquis communautaire* regulations.

In those years, Albania specialized as 'a low-cost supplier in the global production networks for mid and high level quality apparel and footwear' (World Bank, 2009, p. 15; see also: Rama and Cabiri, 2018). Since then, most Albanian garment-footwear firms (mostly assembly and a few full-package suppliers) are incorporated into GPNs through Italian intermediaries. As a result, they navigate slim profit margins and increasing competition, fully rely on the orders of buyers and intermediaries, have minimal bargaining power to shape commercial contracts, and their main competitive advantages are their proximity to the EU market and low labour costs (Ymeri et al., 2010, p. 6).

A significant number of Albanian garment-footwear firms do not own any specific brand and have no control of distribution networks (Anamali et al., 2015; Shehi, 2017). While some firms have undergone *process* and *product* upgrading, *functional* upgrading has been minimal (Anamali et al., 2015, pp. 588-89). Technological transfers from investors, for example, have been marginal because of FDI focussing on labour-intensive productions. At the same time, difficulties in accessing credits, reinforced by the dependency on buyers and the uncertainty of future orders, reduce the possibility to make further investments to upgrade production from assembly to CMT (Shehi 2023). Finally, the lack of training for workers remains a crucial inhibiting factor (World Bank, 2009, p. 24; Kacani and Shehi, 2023).

Italian buyers and intermediaries have favoured a limited functional upgrading from assembly to CMT suppliers (Pici, 2016). For Italian buyers, in fact, having more competitive Albanian suppliers means shorter lead times, a supply chain that is easier to manage, and a cheaper production process. Nonetheless, only a few firms are equipped with automated cutting machinery because investments are impaired by the uncertainty of future orders (and revenues) and the lack of a skilled local workforce (Kacani and Shehi, 2023). As the World Bank describes:

> Most of the foreign firms using Albanian CM operators are Italian manufacturers, importers or wholesalers that sell the products to retailers and thus include their own margins into the production network. This squeezes the margins of Albanian CM firms, reduces their retained earnings and, by extension, capacity to invest in upgrading. This creates further problems as labour costs increase and CM firms are not able [to] invest in new equipment that can increase factory efficiency, further undermining their competitiveness. (World Bank 2009, p. 15)

Finally, and more crucially, any further upgrading for CMT suppliers has been actively discouraged by those same buyers and intermediaries. Albanian suppliers that can autonomously create patterns and samples, manage the design phase, and directly reach retailers would make Italian intermediaries redundant. Consequently, designing and branded lines are realized only in very few firms as a marginal side of production to the predominant supply relations (Pici, 2016; Kacani and Shehi, 2023).

The 2008 economic downturn deeply affected the Albanian garment-footwear industry, even though exports continued to grow. Being integrated in European markets and (mostly Italian) GPNs in the midst of a global crisis reduced supply contracts and led to the continuous renegotiation of new contracts under less favourable terms (Ymeri et al. 2010, p. 7). At the same time, an 'increased number of contractual breaches has been noted, with buyers refusing to withdraw and/or settle orders' (Ymeri et al., 2010, p. 26). While many firms suffered economic losses and even went bankrupt, others reacted to the crisis by searching out new markets and clients, looking for new and cheaper suppliers of raw materials, renovating outdated equipment and reducing employment (Ymeri et al., 2010). Nonetheless, Albanian firms have recovered rapidly after the crisis, and the garment-footwear industry remains crucial for number of firms (see Figure 5.3), employment (see Chapter 6) and exports.

Figure 5.3. Number of registered active garment-footwear enterprises in in Albania, 2013-2017

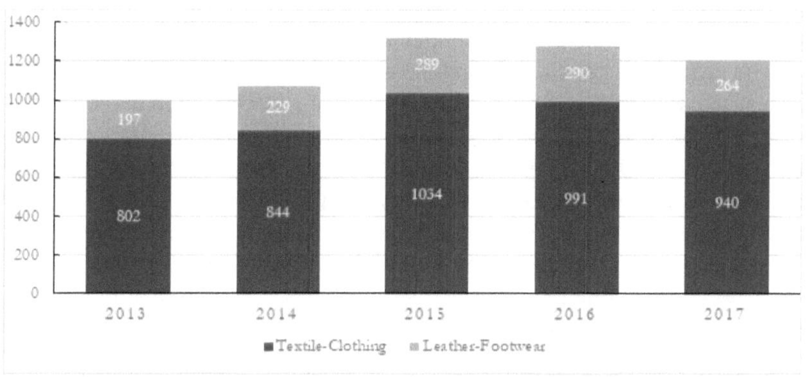

Source: INSTAT, Statistical Business Register

The garment-footwear exports kept growing before and after the crisis, and — despite a recent decline — Italy remains the main destination of Albanian garment-footwear production (taking roughly 80% of total Albanian garment-footwear exports in 2018 according to INSTAT data). In addition, garment-footwear is still the first industry in terms of exports and the only sector of the Albanian economy that maintains a positive trade balance.

Today, Albanian firms remain mainly assembly or CMT suppliers and rely on the relatively low cost of production and the ability to handle 'relatively small-scale, high-quality, and quick-turnaround production (especially for the well-established Italian market)' (World Bank, 2015, p. 25). Raw materials, designs and patterns are usually provided by the buyers or are anyway imported and the great bulk of the production involves assembling pre-cut components (MVO, 2016).

Albanian suppliers generally report growing sophistication and customization of orders together with a shrinking number of units per order and rising pressures to squeeze costs and increase quality (Anamali et al., 2015; Shehi, 2017). Tighter schedules, enhanced flexibility and customization, smaller batches of production and growing pressure to contain costs and increase quality are the main features of the industry (Gjika and Pano, 2017). The use of unauthorized subcontracting to further reduce production costs and circumvent production rigidities remain widespread and keep the supply chains opaque (MVO, 2016). A few full-package suppliers exist, and some have even developed their own branded lines distributed in local markets. As I will show in the following chapters, some of these producers have managed to reach their buyers directly, advancing in the supply-chain hierarchy and even making intermediaries and other first-tier suppliers redundant. Such cases, however, are still rare.

The trajectory of change and restructuring of the garment-footwear industry in Bari-BAT and Albania has to be understood within the processes of worldwide restructuring of the industry and within the specific historical development of the localities in which local firms are embedded. This connects macro-structures with the agency of specific firms and workers that navigate them. The next chapter analyses the challenges and structural pressures managers, embedded in specific locales, face in a changing industry and how their choices and strategies end up reproducing the very same pressures and constraints.

6.
FIRMS' STRATEGIES WITHIN CONSTRAINTS
Production Chain Restructuring and Downward Pressures through the Eyes of Capital

6.1. *The tale of winners: Upgrading for the few, pressures for the many*

In this chapter, I analyse the transformation of production chains from the perspective of the local firms. I unpack the strategies adopted by firms that hold different positions within GPNs and I outline how the structural pressures of a changing industry are navigated and passed downward by local actors in the production chain. Local lead firms (located only in Apulia), the *winners of sectoral transformations*, changed significantly to maintain or improve their positions in broader production networks. However, their upgrading strategies have had limited positive spillover effects and rather increased pressure on first- and second-tier suppliers. The success of a few firms, in other words, banks on the systemic externalization of structural pressures, uncertainty and sector-wide volatility onto local and distant suppliers.

Successful upgrading in the garment sector

Two main upgrading strategies can be identified in the garment sector. The first is to shift from production to marketing, branding, and retailing. This move is generally the preserve of retailers and 'manufacturers without factories' (Gereffi and Memedovic, 2003; see also Chapter 4). The second strategy lies in increasing the quality of production, keeping tighter control over the production process (in-house or outsourced but under strict control), and creating brands that are recognizable for their high quality in specific market segments.

In the Bari and BAT province, the clearest example of the former strategy is illustrated by Playwear,[1] a producer and retailer of children's

---

1 Names of firms, people and organizations and in some cases, places have been changed to maintain the confidentiality of the participants.

garments. Playwear started in the 1950s as a supplier for Northern Italian brands and at the time of my fieldwork worked for well-known brands under licensing contracts: the firm purchases the right to use their trademarks and autonomously manages the design, production, and distribution of the garments for the brand owners with minimal guidance from the latter. At the same time, the enterprise developed and distributed lines with its own brands through a network of wholesalers in Italy and abroad. The production process, once carried out primarily in-house,[2] has been progressively outsourced. Today the enterprise relies on full-package suppliers, keeping only design, marketing, and logistics in-house. Suppliers are located in Turkey and China (until recently also in Albania) and in Italy for more sophisticated productions (interview with manager, I-95; confirmed by worker I-35). Rather than a proper production site, the firm became a hub for developing new collections, managing intricated supply chains, receiving garments assembled abroad, and distributing them to national and European wholesalers. To these activities, the enterprise has recently added a new local branch that focuses exclusively on retail. It quickly became the most profitable. As the manager explained:

> [W]e can say that the enterprise is now split in two. There are two main companies. The first works under licensing agreements [under others' brands] and distributes through wholesalers, and the other focuses directly on retail. We have opened six stores in Italy under our retail trademark 'Guli', but many other [stores] work for us in franchising. In these stores, we sell all our own brands. […]. The production and distribution through wholesalers account for a minimal part of the turnover because we do almost everything through our retail chain […]. So now we focus almost only on retail. We do not even know if we will keep working with wholesalers since this is nowadays only a minimal percentage [of our total turnover].
>
> […]
>
> [Shifting from manufacturer to retailer] was a total transformation required by the market. After the [2008] crisis, our Italian clients [wholesalers and retailers] were not paying [for the products they purchased]. But now, they have become our affiliates [through franchising], and we can get our credits back easily. That's all. In this way, we can guarantee a lower price to the customer […]. If you consider that we used to sell to a client that had a mark-up, and this client had to sell to the customer retaining another mark-up, the final price used to be higher. Instead, if we sell directly, like Zara—I am just saying […] we are not at the level of Zara, of course—but it is clear that the chain gets shorter. And

2 In the period of greatest growth in the late 1980s, Playwear's workforce reached about 300 partially unionized employees (interviews with trade unionists I-24; I-79; and a worker I-35).

> if the chain gets shorter, you can guarantee a lower final price to your customer. This is a winning strategy. (Interview with manager, I-95)

As this manager points out, by shifting to retailing activities, the firm cuts the risks and costs of relying on third-party wholesalers and distributors, has direct control over distribution and marketing, and offers more competitive prices in stores. At the same time, however, the firm is progressively abandoning its role as a manufacturer. While at the time of the interview, Playwear still carried out the design and sample-making activities (albeit only for a few of the licensed brands), it seems the future will bring a complete shift to retail and marketing activities:

> Now the trend is to outsource everything. We still have everything in-house, but the future is outsourcing everything: logistics, staff, style, sample-making. You should have a minimal core workforce and buy everything from external consultants. This is the future, I am sure! Because in Italy labour costs way too much. This is the problem, and firms like ours are outdated. At the moment, with the two companies, we have 120 employees. But this kind of company is virtually extinct; in fact, we are now changing course. [...]. [We will keep in-house] not even the design. Nowadays, there are plenty of stylists working freelance. So medium and small to medium-sized enterprises like ours cannot afford [to keep them on the payroll...] I mean, we still have ten stylists in-house, but it makes no sense anymore. If I had to give a piece of advice to a start-up, I would not advise them to keep stylists as direct employees because they need constant upgrading. Of course, you could employ directly a style coordinator, but besides that, you should rely on external [designer] firms. (Interview with manager, I-95)

Playwear followed the course of the sectoral transformation. A manufacturer that once had a substantial role in the province's employment, deploying hundreds of highly skilled female workers, tackled the industry's transformation by focusing on the most profitable production phases. While this is a successful strategy for the firm itself, it has profound local implications: downsizing and moving significant parts of manufacturing overseas in search of cheaper suppliers. This also affects the few remaining local suppliers that have to navigate such global cost competition. As a retailer, Playwear can now place its production orders to the supplier that provides the best offer without any further burden or responsibility. When I asked the manager whether they retain long-term relationships with the same suppliers, the response was:

> It depends [...]. There is not a fixed response [to your question]. Many [suppliers] close down unfortunately, so... (Interview with manager, I-95)

Brand manufacturers represent a successful alternative to the retailer's path. These firms develop a recognizable brand but keep manufacturing their products in-house or under tight control. Such a strategy mixes *product upgrading*, moving to higher-quality products, and *functional upgrading*, incorporating higher added-value production phases such as creating a brand or investing to reach new markets and distributional channels. These firms, however, unlike Playwear's example do not directly own a retail chain; they rely on third-party stores and distributors and invest heavily in multiple branding strategies. As the manager of one manufacturer of high-quality wedding dresses explained:

> We own four brands. Actually, at first we had only two. I mean, historically, it has always been two. We introduced two more for the Italian market in order to, let's say, expand a bit our network of distributors. We guarantee to each distributor of one of our brands the exclusive right to sell that brand [in its region]. However, often, especially in the last few years, some of our good old retailers started to lose momentum and decreased sales while new and stronger competing retailers came up. Thus, we created two additional brands to acquire a position in these new stores while we were losing in the others. (Interview with manager, I-36)

Creating multiple branded lines and producing both men suits and men/women outerwear was the strategy another brand manufacturer (I-97) followed to increase turnover and stabilize production over seasons. The firm, at the same time, operates as a full-package supplier for luxury brands. Being a reputed, reliable supplier and having an increasingly popular brand was deemed crucial by the manager to connect with new buyers, especially through participating in international fashion fairs with his own collection.

Similarly, a local brand marketer (interview with manager, I-22) that operates the designing, style-creation, marketing, advertising, and sample-making phases in-house while locally outsourcing the rest of production affirmed that covering more market segments helps consolidating the reputation and recognizability of the brand itself. His firm owns a branded line of high-quality suits, an elegant total look line for men and one for women. On top of this, the firm acquired a multi-year licence to design, produce, and distribute garments for a third luxury fashion brand. This strategy banks on the reputational capital of an affirmed trademark that also makes other brands more recognizable to the broader public (manager and president of apparel business association, I-22). In a similar fashion, another local, high-quality manufacturer used to work for brands under a licensing regime to 'win' new markets:

> Our brand, for example, was basically unknown in the US. In order to access this market more quickly, we had to [start producing under the] license [of] a brand owned by some Australian stylists who dress well-known celebrities. This enabled us to get into the six or seven most important sale points in the US. Thanks to this strategy and this brand we licensed, we accessed the boutiques, and now clients also buy our own product. [...]. This was the 'Trojan horse' that let us in the most important boutiques. And now we continue to work in this way. (Interview with manager, I-36)

If distribution is important, style, quality production and the *Made-in-Italy effect* remain crucial for these local lead firms. Fabrics and accessories, certified Italian manufacturing, and a significant investment in design are the main features that local brand manufacturers rely on. As a manager explained:

> In our case, [the most crucial phases of the production process are] design and style. We invest everything in that because a firm producing exclusively Made-in-Italy products either makes dresses that are *really* different, or it will just be wiped out because there is always somebody that can do it for a lower price. Only with the most exclusive materials, lines and designs can you actually compete. (Interview with manager, I-36)

At the same time, producing only the finest quality garments increases the need to find new national and niche markets, requires more investment in branding and marketing and leads to restructuring. On the one hand, lead firms shift resources to new activities and cut labour costs by containing the number of direct employees in the production lines. On the other hand, they need to tightly control the production process and outsource exclusively to trusted and controlled suppliers only when necessary (i.e., during the months of peak production). As one manager explained:

> [Our production] is all in-house. For the last few years, we worked with some [supply] workshops located here in Apulia, though. You know [these are] workshops with all regular contracts. [We outsource to them] only when we have production peaks, and we can't cope with these peaks with our own workers [...]. You know, recently I had to downsize and dismiss some of my workers because I could not guarantee them enough work all year long.
>
> *Ok. Which phases of production are usually outsourced?*

The sewing. Everything else—cutting, sample-making—is done in-house. We outsource only the sewing, but only part of it and not always.

So only in the period of production peaks?

Yes, only in those 3 or 4 months per year, when we have to produce for those orders that were supposed to be delivered...yesterday [laughing]. Yes, we do have this problem.

And those subcontractors, do they work only for you or also for other clients?

Well, they are very small workshops, they have like five workers, three workers...the biggest maybe has ten workers.

And how would you assess your relationship with these subcontractors?

We have worked with them for 3 or 4 years now. In the past, we used to do everything in-house. So far, [this supply relationship] is lasting [...]. Let's say that the subcontractors who work for us work *mostly* for us because they are micro-enterprises. I mean, the firm with only two workers, of course, works only for you. Perhaps, the one with ten workers gets some orders from another client [...] two clients maximum. (Interview with manager, I-36)

Outsourcing might also serve the need of lead firms to diversify and add new items to one's own collections:

Five-six assembly suppliers in [the nearby city of] Martina work for me. This is important. Not only are we 130 [workers] here, but all around, another 200 workers depend on us. [...] So, I do the cutting, then I bring the pieces [to the suppliers], they sew them, I go and take everything and I do the ironing here so I can check them out. [...]. I also have one subcontractor that makes the coat, one that realizes the gilet, one specialized in the trousers or the jacket. (Interview with manager, I-97)

However, high-quality production requires stringent control over the supply chain. Therefore, suppliers are purposely located in the region so that lead firms can rely on their reputation and easily control them in a direct way:

What are the most important requirements you look at when you choose a subcontractor?

Well, the quality [of the product] should be like mine. I give you a sample, and I want a product that matches it. I want that. If you are up to the task, it is good; if you are not, goodbye. There is no space for [...] I mean, I even have a technician checking the subcontractors every day.

A quality inspector?

It is a permanent quality inspection (Interview with manager, I-97).

Brand manufacturers directly train and tightly control suppliers to maintain uniformity and high-quality standards. As a result, the products need to 'look like children of the same mum' as a manager asserted (I-36). Similar strategies are used by other local brand marketers that develop 'total look' branded lines of a lower quality. In these cases, however, suppliers' capacities and the need for quality control are less stringent. Therefore, the competition among suppliers increases and supply relations become more uncertain and short-lived (interviews with managers [I-76; I-22; I-14]).

Subcontractors, in fact, in these cases depend entirely on the orders of the local lead firms that have an interest to outsource only when their internal productive capacity cannot cover the demand. As a manager points out:

> [Our suppliers] are small enterprises, sometimes even family-based, but they all have workers with a regular [social and pension] insurance. Maybe they have fixed-term contracts since they work for six months only, and then they stay at home. That is their problem. I mean, they ask me: 'won't you give me more orders?' referring to the periods of low production. Thus, we try to give them some small orders just to keep connected to them. [...]. But of course, I still carry out the big bulk of production in-house because I have no interest in outsourcing it. It [the small orders] is just to keep a relationship with them. (Interview with manager, I-36)

While the brand manufacturer has an interest in keeping a long-term relationship with a reliable supplier in order not to lose its expertise, suppliers remain the first to be cut if demand drops as brand manufacturers prioritize in-house production and make sure that every employee's labour power can be fully mobilized and idle periods can be minimized. Only when demand exceeds internal capacities, for some months per year, is production outsourced to the suppliers.

Against this background, suppliers remain in a highly vulnerable position. Not only they have to cope with a structurally discontinuous production process, but they also have to remain competitive and reliable vis-à-vis other potential suppliers that might win over the lead firm's trust and its next order. On top of this, production cyclicity is a structural feature of the sector and manufacturing is patterned along under- and overproduction periods. As a producer of 'total look', middle-quality apparel explained:

> In some periods, there are always some overlaps. Now, we are producing the summer collection, but we are also creating the samples that are actually crucial to get the orders for the winter season. […]. And the sample creation is actually a priority because if you don't send out the samples, you will not get any orders, ok? So, in these periods, in order to cope with the delivery of summer batches, we outsource the surplus production. (Interview with manager, I-76)

The winning strategies of a few local firms have multiple and often adverse spillover effects on other local actors (see Table 6.1). The restructuring pursued by both retailers and brand manufacturers curbed and modified dramatically the local employment in the sector. Most of the production phases are now outsourced outside the region by retailers or are reduced and upgraded in quality in other cases. Brand manufacturers use still small local workshops to produce parts of their production to diversify their products or cope with structural cycles and peaks of production. However, despite the high quality of their work, local subcontractors are highly dependent on their local lead firms: they often have few stable clients and work only in the months of peak production of those clients.

Winning strategies in the footwear sector: insulated upgrading and de-localization

The best performers in the local footwear district in terms of export and revenues are the companies that converted their production to the niche market of safety shoes and protective wear items (see Chapter 5). Their restructuring entailed *a process upgrading*, which required investments in machinery, technologies and workforce skills, as well as a *functional upgrading* to develop their own brands to reach foreign markets. The shift in the district's specialization from a standardized, low-quality shoe for mass retailers to a sophisticated and certified footwear item was initiated by the biggest local firm of the district in the early 1990s (Rosato, 2015). The upgrading of this firm paved the way for a few other local firms to follow (Rosato, 2015). As the engineer who headed the safety shoe division of the frontrunner firm, SafeShoes,[3] explained, massive investment in technology

3 SafeShoes (fictional name) is now the biggest firm of the district with around 400 employees in Italy and more than 2,000 in Albania.

Table 6.1. Upgrading strategies and their impact on suppliers in the garment industry

Local lead firm	Upgrading strategy	Features of the supply chain
Retailer	Ownership/control over distributional channels; Full outsourcing of production; Relatively looser quality requirements.	Long supply chain; Weak lead firm/supplier linkages; No specific requirements for suppliers' localization; Short-term, cost-based supply relationship; Worldwide cost competition.
High-quality brand manufacturer	Focus on branding and reaching new markets; Focus on design; Focus on high-quality production (quality raw materials, tight control over production, Made-in-Italy).	Short and tightly controlled supply chain; Outsourcing *only* when in-house capacities are not sufficient (in peak seasons); Long-term, trust-based supply relations; Suppliers' dependency on one/few lead firm/s.
Middle-quality, multiple brand manufacturer	Development of differentiated brands to reach new and diverse markets; Enhanced responsiveness to demands' fluctuations (quick response and ready-to-wear production).	Differentiated supply chains according to the different brand lines; Relatively loose quality control and crucial lead-time reliability; Enhanced seasonality/fluctuation/flexibility of orders/production.

guaranteed very high productive capacity exactly when European buyers started to move their supply networks from Apulia to Eastern Europe and Asia. SafeShoes trajectory showed to other local firms the need to change their specialization:

> We started working on this new product [safety shoes] at the margins. The game-changer, however, was when we became the first to implement the European Directive for safety footwear that at that time was non-compulsory. We were actually the first to implement the novelties of the Directive and to get this certified. What was the reason? Well, at that time, it was customary to follow the German

> DIN regulations,[4] which detailed the safety standards but also the production process and the materials to be used. Basically, you had no leeway; you could just follow what was set in these norms in terms of standards, production processes and materials. On the contrary, the European Directive established only the shoe's safety and final ergonomic requirements, leaving us more freedom vis-à-vis production processes and materials to be used. […] It was very easy for us to give the safety shoes a sporty look. With the European certification, we were the first to present a fresh, youthful, cool, colourful and sporty product that would target young workers who were hardly inclined to wear safety shoes. […]. I would say that the other strategic move was for us to shift from being a supplier for private labels to develop our brand and organize our sales network. […]. This expansion was accompanied by delocalization that was necessary, at that time, for some production phases. (Interview with manager, I-82)

When orders dropped, high productive capacity facilitated the shift to a new technological product while expertise in a fashion-sensitive market (the sneaker) allowed the local firm to add new value to the production of safety shoes. SafeShoes anticipated the requirements of a new and not yet compulsory EU regulation and invested in branding and marketing activities. Other local firms followed and found their space in the safety footwear niche. The new product specialization triggered increasing investments in technology and product upgrading and banked on the presence of local suppliers and workers that could easily be converted to the new production (interview with manager and representative of business association, I-29). However, in the first years, follower firms did not develop any brand strategy:

> Our main concern was to gain specific know-how we did not have. Thus, we were chasing the need for product innovation much more than branding strategies. We had to renew our equipment; we wanted to comply with the newest product certifications, and we had to build from scratch new distribution networks with clients. All this required certain technical skills we did not have. So, the energy of [local] entrepreneurs focused on these things rather than on branding. (Interview with manager and representative of business association, I-29)

The upgrading strategy makes the direct control of certain phases of production and the qualification and training of workers crucial. Firms created in-house laboratories to test products, developed process innovations,

4 DIN is the acronym of the Deutsche Institut für Normung (the German Institute for Standardization), which is now the ISO member body for Germany. As illustrated on the DIN's webpage, a DIN standard 'is a document that specifies requirements for products, services and/or processes, laying down their required characteristics' (DIN, 2020).

obtained product certifications, and improved the final product (interviews with managers [I-29; I-82]). New professional figures were also deployed, as the engineer that led the restructuring in SafeShoes explained:

> I would say that in this new [safety shoes] division, we had the opportunity to experiment, develop and train a series of new professional profiles. For example, the supply-chain manager, customer service, the management of production and of sales outlooks; all these profiles we developed from scratch. (Interview with manager, I-82)

Later, branding activities became crucial. Local firms, in the years of my fieldwork, produced more than half of their output under their own brands (interview with manager and business association representative [I-29]). Besides upgrading, however, cost containment was the other pillar of the restructuring and relied on outsourcing the most labour-intensive production phases to Albania. As the president of the local footwear business association argued:

> All the labour-intensive phases of cutting and pre-assembling before the final assembly are carried out there [in Albania]. Then the goods are re-imported through the outward processing mechanism, and so we can keep the Made-in-Italy label, ok? […]. There were no alternatives [to delocalization]; I challenge anyone to prove me wrong because our product has a high technological content only at the top of the production process. I mean, there are shoes that can be sold at €180–200, but it is just a very small niche. The great bulk of the demand is for the construction sector, and therefore [the shoes] have to be cheap, or for the automotive sector, for example in Germany, and they need to be technic and light. This enabled us to segment our markets and realize different products at the price that markets are willing to pay. […] For us, Albania has been a lifeline. It allowed us to strengthen our supply chain. Without Albania, I believe, the existing firms would not have survived. (Interview with manager and business organization representative, I-29)

Local footwear lead firms maintained control over the most technological and strategic phases of production—which in the case of safety shoes is the final assembly—and outsourced the rest. Thus, offshoring to Albania followed a mixed strategy of greenfield investments in the capital-intensive phases and full outsourcing for the cutting and assembly of the uppers. As the former engineer of SafeShoes put it:

> The delocalization process was carried out partly through subcontracting contracts and partly through foreign direct investments because the company really had lots of capital and resources. Therefore, it had the capacity to

> invest without many problems. [...]. The most important phases were directly controlled while those more labour-intensive [were not...] because we had to curb high labour costs, and those phases were passed to subcontractors. (Interview with manager, I-82)

The broader effect of the upgrading process in terms of local employment was dramatic. On the one hand, local lead firms rely on a more qualified workforce that engages with capital-intensive production phases. On the other hand, the labour-intensive phases have been offshored to Albania, and the Apulian complex of suppliers—specialized in the cutting and assembly of shoes' uppers for the local shoe factories—has almost completely disappeared (see Chapter 5).

Besides the safety shoe production in part of the district, a few local firms pursued an alternative strategy of upgrading. They maintained their initial specialization in the manufacturing of casual streetwear shoes but shifted from standardized, low-cost suppliers to lead firms that manage the phases of design, branding, and marketing. These firms can be considered small *footwear brand manufacturers*. As in the garment industry, they retain a great deal of the production in-house, focus on design and branding, and invest resources to consolidate a network of retailers. Often the design, branding, and style development—as well as the making of samples to be presented to clients—are carried out in-house, the production of uppers and soles are fully outsourced, and the final assembly is carried out in-house so that the product can be screened in a final quality check, packed, and send to the stores. Footwear brand manufacturers also develop multiple branded lines to reach different networks of stores and multi-brand boutiques. As the manager of one local brand manufacturer (I-85) stressed, these firms start the production only after receiving the orders from the networks of stores in the quantity and amounts ordered. This cuts inventory costs and the risk of unsold merchandise but enhances seasonality and increases pressures on production times. As the manager explained:

> For our production, we really have the problem of cyclicity that is tied to the periods of purchase [by the stores]. Next Sunday, we officially start our sales campaign for the 2019–2020 fall season. We go to the MICAM[5] fair in Milan, and there we officially start our sales period. This [period] lasts until mid-April. We get all the orders [from the stores], and we order the raw materials we need

5 The interview was carried out at the beginning of February 2019, just before the MICAM fair. MICAM is one of the world's most important exhibition fairs for fashion houses and footwear producers. It is held twice per year, in February and September, and it is a reference point for brands, buyers and manufacturers.

[...]. We work only on order. Then we start the production, and we deliver the product between the end of June and early September [...]. The most difficult period is the shift between fall and summer. We produce the fall collection until September, and then in September, we start the sales campaign for the summer collection. So, we have those 2 or 3 empty months that are a significant problem [...]. We tried to present our collections [to the stores] a bit earlier in some markets, but it did not work. We make a middle-to-high quality product, and our client wants to really have a clear idea of what to buy. He needs to see more collections from more producers and assess what to buy and in which amount. Thus, there is this gap [in production] that is difficult to fill, at least if you work only with your brand.

So, is the high quality you produce what increases this seasonality problem? I mean, does producing a middle- or low-quality brand make it less sensitive to this cyclicity?

Well, yes. At least it used to be like that because the client that buys low-middle-quality goods usually buys in advance the merchandise compared to those working with higher quality.

Why is that?

Because our client is a boutique, a single store, while in the case of low-quality goods, the client is a mass retail chain. (Interview with manager, I-85)

The lead firm copes with production peaks by adopting multiple strategies. Firstly, during the periods of non-production, administrative, sales, and design departments keep working full time while workers with open-ended contracts at the assembly line stop working and are covered by the temporary layoff-fund scheme.[6] Secondly, during the peaks, new workers are hired with fixed-term contracts (even with multiple temporary contracts per year). This strategy was under pressure at the time of the interview after the so-called 'dignity decree' (Law-Decree 87/2018)[7] mandated a limit to the use of such employment arrangements. A third strategy to cope with production peaks is further outsourcing.

6 This refers to the *Cassa Integrazione Guadagni Ordinaria*, a temporary layoff fund, financed by firms and workers. It covers up to 80% of workers' salaries in periods when workers are not working due to temporary drops in firms' production.

7 Law Decree 87/2018 (known as the 'dignity decree') establishes the obligation for an employer to hire with an open-ended contract any employee who has already been employed more than four times in a total of 24 months in the same company under temporary contracts (see Menegotto et al., 2018).

Table 6.2. Upgrading strategies and their impact on suppliers in the footwear industry

Local lead firm	Upgrading strategy	Feature of supply chain
Safety shoe producer	Research & Development; product and process innovation; Internal testing labs for certifications' requirements; Direct control (in Italy directly, in Albania through branch firms) of technological, knowledge-intensive phases of production; Outsourcing (abroad) labour-intensive phases of production (cutting and making of uppers); Branding and consolidating marketing networks in Italy and abroad.	Suppliers of uppers' cutting and assembly entirely moved overseas, in increasingly (worldwide) cost competition and short-term supply relations; Final injection-technology assembly phase retained in Italy or Albania through branch firms (stability of orders for suppliers, but total dependency on the strategies of the headquarter/lead-branch; cost competitiveness remains crucial).
Footwear brand manufacturer	Focus on branding, consolidating and widening the network of client stores; Resources and skilled workforce dedicated to design; Focus on middle-to-high-quality production (specific raw materials, tight control over outsourced production of uppers and soles, Made-in-Italy). Final assembly (and control) carried out in-house; On-demand and just-in-time production (production starts based on stores' orders).	Enhanced cyclicity (periods of over production and underproduction); Need for time-responsive, reliable suppliers of soles and uppers; Outsourcing of the final assembly only when in-house capacities are not sufficient or short-term employment is impossible; Crucial lead time reliability.

Success stories in the footwear sector, however diverse, are again stories of displacing employment and increasing uncertainties (see Table 6.2). Focusing on certain phases, products, or markets, retaining only the most pivotal workforce, and outsourcing all non-core activity, are the common features of upgrading. In addition, the pressures of fast-changing consumer markets, enhanced by the asymmetrical governance in GVCs and the possibility of moving production relatively freely, enable lead firms to pass the burden to respond quickly to uncertain, volatile, and just-in-time orders the suppliers in an increasingly competitive market.

6.2. *Between success stories and those left behind: Suppliers navigating pressures and passing them down the chain*

Suppliers in the chains carry out different tasks and hold differentiated positions. As detailed, different types of suppliers exist—full-package, CMT and single-phase—and being a supplier might be a strategic retrenchment decision or the first step in an upgrading trajectory. A supplier might be a brand manufacturer that undergoes an adaptive or a strategic downgrading[8] or a firm that is developing a branded line but has not yet abandoned its role as a supplier within the chain. Alternatively, it might even be a crucial intermediary that manages, with a certain level of autonomy, multiple supply chains on behalf of the buyers. Nonetheless, whether being a supplier represents an improvement in the trajectory of individual firms, a survival strategy, or a strategic move to increase profitability, every supplier in a buyer-driven GPN has to cope with the requests of lead firms with access to the final markets.

A multifaceted production strategy: Branding and supplying different market segments, product qualities, and clients

For suppliers, versatility is crucial to stay competitive. For example, a local quality shoe manufacturer, Rebel Footwear, mixes branded production

8 Following Blazek (2016, p. 862), I define *adaptive downgrading* the situation in which a 'firm is unable to sustain competitive pressure and is forced to focus on lower/smaller market segments or on production of components instead of final product'; and *strategic downgrading* as a 'carefully planned move by a profitable firm to a specific market segment to make maximum use of its core competence and thus to increase its profitability even further'.

and full-package supply for external buyers to reach sufficient levels of output and turnover and to attract more clients:

> The company has two brands of its own: the first is 'Ares', and it is the brand for our male footwear, and the other is 'Athena', which we use for women's footwear. Also, we work as a supplier for other brands as well. [...] Today, it is impossible to work only with your own brands. But, if your own product is appreciated, you can get to work for other brands under their own trademark, their image, and their identity with some specific customization. So, you work more. (Interview with manager, I-23)

For *pure suppliers* with no brands, covering different market segments and product qualities remains pivotal. As the manager of a full-package supplier of high-quality, made-in-Italy knitwear (wool and cashmere) garments explained:

> We produce knitwear cloth for every kind of item, from the small house-shoe to the hat, to the jacket [...] everything that is knitwear. [...] You've got to organize [yourself] to serve different clients. There are clients for women [garments] that need productions in specific months, and clients for children [garments] that need deliveries in other months, so you have to juggle them, to mix them in order to have a continuous production for your firm. (Interview with manager, I-13)

Hybrid strategies are crucial for *suppliers-without-factories*, as well. These firms deal with design, sample-making and supply chain management, work as intermediaries and offer a ready-to-wear product to buyers. Yet, they outsource almost completely the actual production phases. As an employee of this type of supplier noted:

> The enterprise where I work is specialized in making shirts for men. We also made children garments, actually. And in the very last season, we actually designed and realized the samples for a collection of children dresses that had some commonalities with our own production of shirts. [...]. We work for our own brand. I can even tell you the name: 'Peterson'. And then we work for others, as an intermediary for other brands: Luke-ho, Bormar, and many others. We are a small firm: ten, twelve persons between offices and the workshop where we carry out a minimal production, namely, the making of samples. The *real production* is entirely outsourced. (Interview with workers, I-17/18)

Suppliers-without-factories' core activity is responding to the multiple preferences of clients. As the employee managing the supply chains in this kind of company explained, they mobilize diverse supply chains on demand; they can source raw materials from Italy or China and activate multiple workshops in the region and beyond:

> We have a couple of different assembly factories: one in Andria, one in Alberobello[9] [...] and then we have two or three in Albania, in case one [buyer] wants a shirt without the Made-in-Italy label but with a lower cost. (Interview with workers I-17/18)

Some suppliers, instead, target luxury brands in search of higher returns, as the manager of a local company specialized in embroidery and embellishment explained:

> I am trying to work only for high-quality brands now. Because, well, in Italy our production costs are the highest, so either you work for the fashion-luxury brands that can afford a Made-in-Italy production or you don't get any profit. The middle-to-low-quality brand cannot pay for your expenses. (Interview with manager, I-84)

However, reaching for higher-value brands requires investments in production and self-promotion through participation in international fairs and the deployment of sales agents. It can even enhance seasonality and discontinuous production. To cope with that, the firm mobilizes different production chains for different clients: higher-quality production is carried out in-house, while lower quality, labour-intensive embroidery and embellishment are offshored to an Albanian branch that further outsources to local Albanian workshops during production peaks:

> I want to cut [production] as much as possible here in Italy and work only for luxury brands. There in Albania, I can hire as many as 200 persons. They cost me €250, and I don't even have to pay them severance when they leave. (Interview with manager, I-84)

Increasing control, risks, and uncertainty

Working for buyers requires planning and coordination but also customization and flexibility. In the words of a full-package shoe supplier's manager:

9 Both cities are located in the Bari and BAT provinces.

> When you work for brands, everything gets more complex because, first of all, you have to develop a customized collection tailored to them. [...] You have to do specific prototypes, and you might have to use some exclusive materials. And the materials you used for one brand cannot be used for another. You have to cope with the requirements they choose. For example, if they want a specific sole that we [and our usual suppliers] don't have, we have to readapt the uppers of the sandals, specifically on this new sole. So, the development of design and samples is really very complex. Moreover, you have to keep a record with photos and information sheets for each collection. Then you have to actually make the samples they want to present in the luxury brands' international fairs. [...] Working for them means a great deal of specification and requirements to respect. We really have to do what they ask. I mean, they give you instructions on everything: size, colours [...] we even develop the packaging in the box as they want; otherwise, a non-compliance situation arises. (Interview with sales manager, I-23)

Buyers often impose long-term investments on their suppliers before placing their orders and rarely commit to supply contracts that last more than one or few seasons. Lead firms can therefore maintain a wide repertoire of different supply options without having to make the pre-production investments needed for such level of diversification. For suppliers, in stark contrast, this means increased risks. These dynamics were neatly captured by a local shoe factory worker and shop steward (I-86). As she explained:

> We had a massive order from Marathon.[10] They made us set up the plant and equipment according [to their requirements]. We fixed the machines, and we purchased everything needed and more. Then at some point, Marathon decided to move production to Serbia on cost grounds. So, all the work we used to do for them—from the small children's shoe size 18 through to men's shoe size 47—was taken away. Once Marathon left, our firm's ordeal began. Just yesterday, we finalized a collective dismissal procedure for 16 workers. Just yesterday! (Interview with worker and shop steward, I-86)

Marathon asked the supplier to find a new warehouse that would comply with its high standards of workplace safety and the needed production capacities. In the words of the worker, this was necessary 'because either you work this way for Marathon, or you don't work for them at all' (interview with worker and shop steward, I-86). However, after a few seasons, Marathon reduced and then entirely withdrew its orders. As a result, the supplier was left with a big rent bill and the cost of the

10 Fictional name for a global retail sportswear chain.

investment to restructure the new warehouse, but with no orders and revenues to amortize them.

Besides this specific case, any new batch of production requires specific technological adaptations and a reworking of skills. There might be, for instance, a need to train the workforce for specific operations, for shoe production, suppliers might need to create (or purchase) the stamps to cut the different components of the uppers. New production procedures also require some time to learn and increase productivity.[11] These costs become crucial when batches of production shrink in size and grow in customization. As the shop steward put it:

> [W]e do not do that [work for big fashion brand] anymore 'cause it is not worth the hassle. We manufactured the punching stamps; we did everything. And those things, in the long run, turned out to be burdens for us. We also worked for Roberto Artini[12]—we did two or three orders of around twenty thousand pairs [of boots]. But in order to meet those orders, we had to change all the stamps because Roberto Artini needed the stamps to be tall, and we had only those for the shorter boots. We had to buy their original fabrics because the internal lining always has this pattern, you know? We had to train the girls who package the boots as well. (Interview with worker and shop steward, I-86)

Suppliers have little bargaining power vis-à-vis buyers, even when they offer high quality and quick lead times. Prices, timing, and quality specifications are a given and suppliers either cope with such requirements and get the orders or stay idle. As a manager put it: 'it is the buyer that decides everything. They work in this way and keep going […]. Their attitude, their governance, is just like that. And you are either in or out' (interview with manager, I-13).

Suppliers, in fact, report that quality, speed, reliability and low prices never seem enough to guarantee the buyer will confirm the next order. As a manufacturer of sneakers and sandals for mass retailers jokingly told me when I ask about the main demands from his buyers:

> Timing, quality and product. [It is about] a menu of services that you offer to the buyer […]; once it was all about the delivery time, and even if you sent two left-foot shoes in the same box, they would buy it. Now you have to design

11 As a high-quality Albanian assembly manufacturer of coats and jackets for global retail chains explains, workers and machines have to adapt to the different fabrics and materials sent by the lead firms. This implies lower productivity and errors in the early production runs (interview with manager, I-69).

12 Fictional name for a worldwide known Italian haute couture brand.

for them, and even if you were to put some banknotes [as a gift] in the box, they would still bargain for more. (Interview with manager, I-31)

Keeping a buyer happy remains crucial, even when this means reducing mark-ups, as the manager of a shoe manufacturer reported:

> [T]here are still brands that need to sell quality [products], but it is obvious that you need to contain costs. Thus, we also try not to increase our prices. You know, our profits have shrunk. We went down of a couple of percentage points. I mean, the enterprise still makes a profit, but less [than before]. Unfortunately, in order not to increase our prices, we accepted less profit. Yet, it is crucial to maintain your markets. Better times will come, we hope. (Interview with sales manager, I-23)

Passing pressures down to subcontractors and second-tier suppliers

First-tier suppliers are not the last tier in the chain. On the contrary, they can address fluctuating and volatile orders or even stably patterned production through further outsourcing to second and third-tier subcontractors. As reported by some respondents, the relation between the first- and second-tier suppliers is often short-term because subcontractors usually have short life cycles due to tight mark-ups and long idle periods (interview with managers, I-95; I-84). They buffer the vagaries in production for their clients and are the first to be cut out when demand shrinks. Even when the subcontractors have a long-term, trust-based relationship with a first-tier supplier, production conditions remain daunting. They are usually dependent on very few clients and work only a few months per year during the peak-production outsourcing of first-tier suppliers. A good example of such dynamics is Rebel Footwear, which, as mentioned above, is a first-tier supplier of high-quality shoes for luxury brands. When orders cannot be dealt with by its own workers, the company relies on one particular supplier to manufacture uppers. Even though this supply relation is long-term, the challenges for the subcontractor are evident since it faces highly concentrated orders coupled with total uncertainty about the prospects for future production.

> We have just one subcontractor assembling the uppers. It is a lady in Corato;[13] I can tell you that.

13 A city in the BAT province.

> *Ok. Does she work for you only or also for others?*
>
> Well [...] she works a lot for us because we order a lot of uppers in the peak production period. But it could be she also works for some other shoe factory.
>
> *And you, how do check how your subcontractors manage their workforce—if they are punctual, and if they have a good reputation? I mean, how do you control your subcontractors?*
>
> So, first of all, they have to be on the Chamber of Commerce lists and be formally registered. This is particularly important because anyone who works for us has to be registered and be in line with the requirements of INPS, INAIL and the like. Then, of course, we check if they are punctual because we also need to respect delivery deadlines, and we ask [subcontractors] to respect some specific daily threshold of production. (Interview with sales manager, I-23)

Even in those markets where seasonality is less severe, production responds directly to consumption trends and therefore remains uncertain and volatile. First-tier suppliers, therefore, strategically pass such fluctuations onto their subcontractors. This was well illustrated by an interview with an employee working for a full-package supplier of undergarments. Since undergarment sales are less sensitive to seasonality, production is expected to be less cyclical, yet it is not necessarily more stable. Changes in sales lead to fluctuating orders from wholesalers that are reflected in fluctuating batches of production for the final subcontractors. As an employee of the firm explained:

> Since we make undergarments, there are no seasons unless you work with knitwear, and you have the warmer one, the brushed one and some dedicated production for the summer and the fall. However, there is always fluctuation in orders. I don't know why; it is a strange market dynamic, but [...] if our clients are not selling, they will not buy from us, and we will not give orders [to subcontractors]. (Interview with workers, I-17/18)

Beyond the Adriatic, Albanian firms face similar dynamics which intensify competitive pressures on local suppliers.

Albanian suppliers: Hard-won gains, constrained upgrading and amplified pressures across-the-board

Like their counterparts in Italy, Albanian suppliers face shrinking mark-ups, increasingly demanding buyers, shorter lead times, and smaller production batches. The great majority of Albanian firms in the sector are assembly suppliers. They specialize in the assembly of garments and the making of uppers in footwear. A few successful firms have undergone a process of *learning by exporting* (see Benkovskis et al., 2020) and can offer finished goods on demand (interview with GIZ-Albania consultant, I-44). Yet, their upgrading trajectory remains highly constrained.

To reach high-quality production and shift from assembly to CMT supply, for example, firms need software-driven cutting machinery. However, such machinery requires investment and skilled workers. The former is discouraged because of the uncertainty of future orders and revenues; the latter requires resources to train workers or hire foreign (often Italian) technicians who can handle the equipment. As the manager of one garment assembly factory explained:

> We used to do the cutting [manually], but now my clients in Italy [intermediaries] have automated their cutting operation reducing their cost. Plus, [by doing the cutting] they can control the quality of the fabrics […]. Anyway, the automated cutting requires an investment that I can't afford right now […], you need the maintenance, the software […]. And if the machine stops working, you might have to stop the production while waiting for the technician since [he is] certainly is not based here in Albania. (Interview with manager, I-60)

Besides that—as highlighted by other CMT suppliers (Interviews with managers, I-58; I-72)—automated cutting massively increases productive capacities and that requires the prospect of future and stable orders to pay the machineries investment back:

> [Y]ou need to have orders if you want to amortize the investment. It is not just about having the money to buy it. The automated cutting enables you to produce four times more pieces than what four workers can do manually. This means you need an output to use it and to amortize your investment. (Interview with manager, I-69)

Furthermore, upgrading to full-package supply requires the capacity to deal with design, sourcing of raw materials, and the management of complex international supply chains. While this would allow Albanian firms to cut out (Italian) intermediaries and deal directly with retailers and brands, it is also seen as a very risky strategy. As an assembly manufacturer's manager explained:

> First of all, one needs the right networks to source the raw materials to become a full-package supplier because that's the lion's share of production costs. Once you have that, half the job is done. But we have no such networks because we always worked for other intermediaries that managed the supply chain for us [...]. Besides, there is also the issue of credit. To buy fabrics abroad, in China or wherever, you need to access bank credits because the suppliers [of raw materials] will not work with you if you have no bank guarantees. (Interview with manager, I-58)

Even the most successful firms, with high-quality production and years of partnership and tight contacts with global retail chains, highlighted the risks of upgrading to a full-package supply position in the chain:

> I have had a direct relationship with some retailers for many years now. They come here to check our work and meet us and see the factory. However, there is always an [Italian] intermediary because they require a full-package product. This means purchasing materials, fabrics, accessories...[which are] all very expensive things that I don't feel like doing by myself. It requires considerable investments. [Suppliers of raw materials] require [financial] guarantees, and that's why I rely on the Italian intermediary [...]. I actually have the contacts and the networks [of suppliers]. It is just a matter of economic risks that I don't feel like taking. (Interview with manager, I-69)

One footwear supplier stressed the risk of not finding trustworthy clients or sub-suppliers and the difficulties in accessing legal protection in GPNs (interview with manager, I-73). Power asymmetries within the chain do not only manifest in small mark-ups and volatile orders but can also take the form of scant legal protections for Albanian suppliers and widespread predatory commercial contracts. As Pici (2016) reports, if an Italian client faces a company crisis, changes managements, or goes bankrupt, Albanian suppliers find it very expensive to seek legal remedies to pursue payment for already delivered orders. At the same time, commercial contracts with Italian clients are strict and generally unfavourable to them. Many requirements in terms of quality, time, processes, and procedures have to be respected, and the opportunities for predatory practices to avoid paying on the grounds of some alleged violation of the contract remain (interviews with managers, I-101; I-73). In these cases, Albanian suppliers reported having very little power to defend themselves in court, and even when they do, the length and uncertainty of litigation processes make it very hard for the firm to survive in the meantime. This discourages negotiating directly with Italian (or other) suppliers of raw materials and leads Albanian firms to rely on trustworthy Italian intermediaries that will take care of that for them:

> If your supplier [of raw materials] confirms everything, but then you start the production, and then he tells you that the quality or price negotiated is no longer available, what can you do? You lose money because you cannot tell your client you won't deliver the shoes or that you need to increase the price. The supplier [of raw materials] can do that because you are not a significant buyer for them [...]. Once this happened—we delivered the shoes as we could, and we paid penalties to our client for the delay, and the variable quality, etcetera.
>
> *Can't you sue the fraudulent supplier, then?*
>
> We tried. We wasted time and money. (Interview with manager, I-73)

Thus, some Albanian suppliers manage to upgrade to higher-quality production and carry out the whole production process but relying on Italian intermediaries remains crucial to keep a better grip on the whole chain, dealing with clients and raw material suppliers at the same time (interviews with managers, I-72; I-73; I-69; I-58; I-59; I-60).

Against the background of these few hard-won gains, further upgrading to design, branding or retailing seems almost impossible to most Albanian managers and experts. Firstly, becoming a retailer requires massive investment and the ability to access consumer markets in which other retailers are already strong. Secondly, design needs specific skills, fashion houses, and the promotion of certain cultural and commercial events (fashion fairs, catwalks, and alike) that do not exist yet in Albania (see Chapter 5). Thus, upgrading is truncated for Albanian firms and generally stops at the level of full-package supply with limited design activities required. As a full-package footwear supplier that managed to bypass intermediaries and reach retailers, explained:

> We started with the cutting of uppers; then we sewed them, then we did the shoe assembly, then the sample-making and design [...]. We thought about creating our own branded line, but it is costly, and the market is saturated [...]. Therefore, we are focusing on creating alliances with existing brands. We guarantee reliable production, and they feel safe with us. This is our strategy now—to join forces with existing brands. (Interview with manager, I-68)

Amidst stories of truncated upgrading, the whole sector faces enhanced seasonality. Some address the issue by accepting reduced mark-ups just to avoid keeping production lines idle (interview with manager, I-73), while others bank on local subcontractors to address production peaks so that they are only limitedly hit during production drops:

> I [use outsourcing] as a relief valve. I rely on colleagues because employing more workers is impossible. We [have no resources and time and] cannot train them [...]. We cannot even find them since there is a lack of skilled workers in Albania now. (Interview with manager, I-60)

In some cases, outsourcing is openly described as a strategic process of offloading risks and burdens. As a CMT producer of undergarments for European brands, explains:

> [W]e decided to build a production network comprised of former employees and technicians of ours. We lend them machines and know-how, and we lead them in managing the production line. We send quality inspectors [...] we do everything. But they are private and autonomous subjects. Yet, they rely on our orders for about 70% or even 100% [of their production]. In this way, we are more flexible and have no outstanding stocks [...]. If we needed to increase production rapidly or hire more employees [...], it would be difficult to manage 400–500 workers in-house. However, it is another thing altogether to have six [supplier] companies with 60 or 100 employees each [...]. It was a complex decision. We considered all the variables. But if you have a fall in production, what do you do with 500 employees? And vice versa, if we have to double the production for one month, how do you do it? You are constrained. You have this number of workers, this warehouse, these facilities. But if you have five or six different companies [working for you], you are more flexible. (Interview with manager, I-54)

As in Apulia, the successful strategies of some firms increase the vulnerabilities of others down the chain. As the manager of a footwear supplier that avoids outsourcing in order to tightly control the production quality put it:

> I think that 99% of firms outsourcing locally have two aims. First, if you outsource, you have no burdens to pay social contributions, rent, electricity, etc. Second, you don't pay immediately, and you can say: 'I will pay you as soon as my client pays me'. (Interview with manager, I-101)

Second-tier subcontractors, thus, depend on one or few clients, face very tight mark-ups and periods of patterned over- and underproduction, and have no real opportunity to upgrade (interview with manager [undergarment assembly subcontractor], I-56).

Finally, a different form of integration in GPNs is represented by local branches of Italian brand manufacturers (as in the case of Apulian safety shoe producers) or autonomous firm that are in a de-facto exclusive partnership with one specific Italian client, usually through multi-year licensing contracts, as is the case with a few undergarment factories (interviews with managers, I-72; I-54). These firms specialize in labour-intensive production phases and are the result of a cost-saving strategy of their lead firm. Consequently, their main competitive advantage is the low cost of labour and their existence and potential upgrading totally depends on the production strategies of the lead firm.

To conclude, the effect of Albania's integration into Italian production networks has been twofold. On the one hand, moving production to Albania was pivotal in the success of Italian lead firms' upgrading. On the other hand, the availability of cheaper but increasingly reliable suppliers in a nearby region wiped out almost completely the suppliers of labour-intensive production tasks in Bari and BAT. For the few remaining assembly and CMT suppliers in Apulia, the increasing competition from overseas and the demands of buyers are daunting. Full-package suppliers and suppliers-without-factories are similarly challenged by the upgrading trajectories that a few Albanian counterparts have managed to undertake, and that might make them redundant. At the same time, Albania suppliers are stuck in a truncated upgrading trajectory or deal with the most precarious and labour-intensive phases of production.

All in all, lead firms can cope with the vagaries of competitive markets by mobilizing suppliers at need, offloading onto them the uncertainty of production and the volatility of orders. First-tier suppliers have still some leeway to pass the pressures of their clients onto subcontractors, as well. However, second-tier suppliers and all the rest of the chain have no buffer left. The entire chain, its responsiveness to volatile markets, and the strategy that lead firms adopt to upgrade (and full-package suppliers use to survive) are built upon outsourcing and the subsequent reduction of rigidities and responsibilities that would entail carrying in-house more productive activities and employing workers directly.

Amidst the structural changes in the sector, firms remain crucial. They navigate the pressures that the sector poses, and *they do have agency*. They make plans, develop strategies, make decisions and act, and their actions coincide to shape the structures other actors have to navigate. However, with their upgrading or survival strategies, firms reproduce and enhance the structural pressures of just-in-time production by displacing and unloading risks and uncertainties over other firms in the chain.

7.
PUTTING LABOUR IN ITS PLACE, INFORMALLY
The Function of Informalization in Precarious Production Networks

7.1. *The garment-footwear industry through the eyes of labour: Segmentation, vulnerability and informalization*

As the previous chapter illustrates, firms retain agency despite constraining structural changes. The upgrading of few companies, however, entails increasing downward pressures in terms of prices, flexibility, responsiveness to complex production requirements, and suppliers' dependency. Such pressures profoundly influence employment relations throughout the chains. In this chapter, I reconstruct the production networks through the eyes of labour. First, I outline the local labour markets, the profile of garment-footwear workers, the magnitude and variegation of informal employment practices. Then I stress the disciplining function of informalization by framing it as a tool of labour control rather than as a mere cost-cutting strategy. Finally, I analyse the most common forms of workers' agency vis-à-vis informalization.

The garment-footwear workforce in Bari and BAT provinces is highly femininized, especially in clothing firms (Bagnardi et al., 2022). According to ISTAT/ASIA data (2017), women in both branches of the sector account for 5% of the total female employment in the private sector against roughly 3% at the national level, while provincial levels of female unemployment are much higher than the national average and provincial employment rates are much lower (see Table 7.1).

Table 7.1. National and Provincial rates of employment and unemployment in Italy and Apulia, 2018

UNEMPLOYMENT RATE (%)			
	Male	Female	Total
Bari	11.9	14.4	13.0
BAT	12.0	18.4	14.2
Italy	9.7	11.8	10.6
EMPLOYMENT RATE (%)			
	Male	Female	Total
Bari	49.9	28.5	38.9
BAT	47.1	22.8	34.7
Italy	53.6	36.3	44.6

Source: ISTAT/ASIA; cited in: Bagnardi et al. (2022, p. 46).

The garment-footwear industry is also highly informalized. As Figure 7.1 shows, Apulia scored consistently higher than the Italian average in the rate of irregular employment both in the whole economy and in the industrial sector as a whole.

Figure 7.1. Irregular employees as a share of total employees (%) in Italy and Apulia in the whole economy and in the industry, 2011–2016

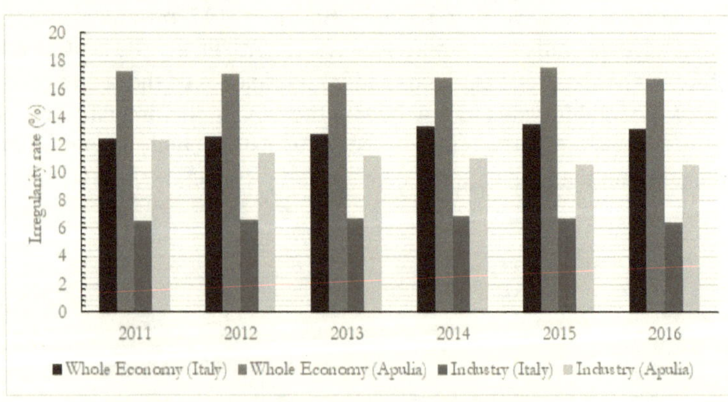

Source: Author's elaboration on ISTAT

Such data needs to be considered as a conservative proxy of the actual share of informal employment in the garment-footwear, which is probably higher. Where more detailed data are available (at the national level), the share of informal labour units in the total number of labour units (regular and irregular) is, in fact, consistently higher in the garment-footwear than in the industrial sector overall[1] (See Figure 7.2).

Figure 7.2. Irregular Labour Units per 100 Total Labour Units in Italy, 1995-2017

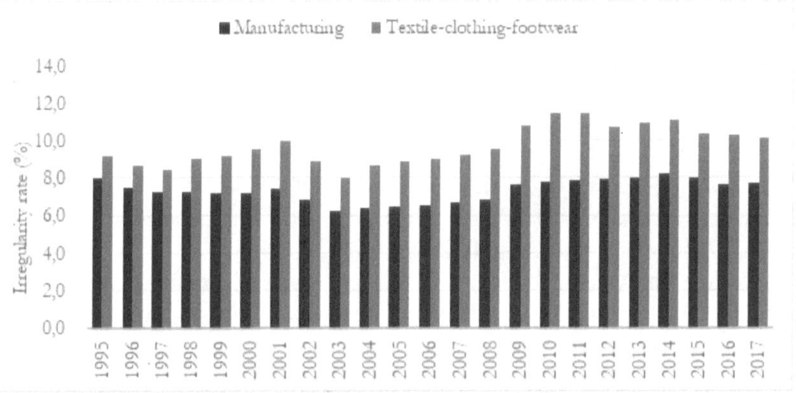

Source: ISTAT; Bagnardi et al. (2022, p. 47).

Moreover, according to data from the Bari and BAT local labour inspectorate, while the garment-footwear industry receives only a marginal share of the total number of inspections (between 14% and 9% of total inspections in the period 2012–2018), the rate of ascertained employment irregularities is higher than the average of all economic sectors. The garment-footwear sector in Italy, and even more in the Bari and BAT provinces, relies on a segmented and vulnerable workforce: it is segmented because of the feminization of the sector; it is vulnerable because of the high rates of informalization and the narrow employment alternatives that women have in the local labour market.

In Albania, according to INSTAT, the garment-footwear sector in 2016 officially employed 46,615 workers (Kosta, 2018b), even though other sources estimates the effective number of formal and informal employees as

1 According to the Ateco 2007-Istat classification, industry (B and C) includes all of manufacturing together with the extractive-mining sector.

more than twice that number (MVO, 2016). Garment-footwear production is concentrated in the industrial districts located in Tirana's peripheral neighbourhoods, and in a few other cities, such as Shkoder, Durres, Lezhe, Berat, Fier and Vlora (Arqimandriti et al., 2016). The workforce employed in the sector is predominantly female and young. According to INSTAT, women in the sector amount to 83% of the total (Kosta, 2018b), yet contrasting estimates exist. MVO Nederland and the AIDA (MVO, 2016) report that 91.7% of workers are women with a median age of 33 years in 2015, while Arqimandriti, Llubani, and Ljarja (2016, p. 20)—quoting information from the Albanian Chamber of Façon, a business organization[2]—report an even younger (31 years old on average) and highly feminized workforce (95% female). More recently, referring to the garment sector only (excluding the footwear industry), the Albanian Investment and Development Agency (AIDA, 2019) confirms that the share of women in the workforce is 90%. There is a consensus on the low level of formal education of the garment-footwear workforce among the studies surveyed (Arqimandriti et al., 2016; MVO, 2016; Papa and Kongoli, 2016; ACIT, 2010).

Women in Albania experience a high level of unemployment even though their participation rate is relatively low compared to men (see Table 7.2). Moreover, disaggregated data show that the participation rate is even lower if one considers women with primary education (45.6%) and grows with the years of education (reaching 71.9% for those with higher educational attainment). Therefore, the garment-footwear sector is crucial because it employs women with lower levels of formal education that have rather few alternative job opportunities in the Albanian labour market and relatively low rates of participation.

Table 7.2. Employment, Unemployment, and Participation rates in Albania in 2018 (%), group age 15-64

	Participation rate	Employment rate	Unemployment rate
Female	59.7	52.4	12.3
Male	76.9	66.7	13.2
Total	68.3	59.5	12.8

Source: INSTAT Labour Force Survey

2 'Façon' is the name given to the *active processing regime* and more broadly to the garment-footwear sector in Albania (Kosta, 2018b).

The garment-footwear industry alone accounts for approximately half (between 45% and 49%) of all Albanian manufacturing employment, and it is more informalized than the rest of the non-agricultural sectors (Doci, 2018; EC, 2020b; 2019; 2018a; Kosta, 2018b).

7.2. *Varieties of informalized employment*

Fieldwork analysis reveals that one of the most common forms of employment informalization mentioned by interviewees in Apulia is a well-entrenched informal system called the *pacting (or pacted) regime*. This is the literal translation of the local slang phrase 'regime del pattuito', which participants frequently used in interviews and informal conversations. It refers to an actual regime regulating employment relations based on a verbal agreement that oversees the terms of the written contract that still exist and is signed by the parties. The phrase *regime del pattuito* is so common and well-understood in both the Bari and BAT provinces that it required no further explanation when I mentioned it during interviews and informal conversations. The well-established and shared meaning this term has acquired, as well as the reference to an actual 'regime', signal the spread and stability of the practice.[3] As a local trade unionist described it:

> I am talking about the textile and clothing sector: there are firms that pay €5 [per hour] in the best case if you are perfect [in your work…]. The rest earn €3, €2.50 or €2. Do you get it? This is the thing. Then in the footwear sector [it's] the same. Everything is based on […] let's say, on *pacting* […]. The word says it all! You come, and I [the employer] tell you: 'I can't pay you according to the contract. I will pay you €5 [per hour]'. This means that you work 8 hours or 9, or 10 or 11, whatever, and I pay you €60 per day or 50 […] whatever it is. But I hire you [officially with a contract] for 2 or 3 hours [per day] just because I have to show [that I hired you formally]. Then, I give you the payroll. How much is the payroll? €300. How much is the total of your actual work at €5 [per hour]? €1,000. I will give you the difference of (Interview with unionist, I-8; see also Bagnardi et al. 2022, p. 47)

In the words of an informal worker with more than 25 years of experience as a sewing-machine operator in both the footwear and the garment sector:

---

3 As Ledeneva (2018) puts it in the *Global Encyclopaedia of Informality*, a worldwide repository of informal practices, informal practices 'are invisible to the outsider' but 'ubiquitous' and 'expertly practiced by insiders'.

> [My contract] was often full time, but the paycheck, I mean [...] basically, on your paycheck they put the minimal pay that you were entitled to, but in reality, they would never give you the sum that was written on your paycheck. (Interview with worker, I-15)

In the same fashion, a trade unionist from a different confederation explained:

> Just before coming here [for the interview], we started a labour dispute over exactly this kind of situation. First, there was a full-time [contract] at the hiring. Then, with the coming of the [economic] crisis, the employer proposed [to the worker]: 'Let's reduce the official working time, and if there is need for extra working time, of course, you'll do it [informally]'. Here, you know, if you have a family and you have no alternatives, willingly or not, you are constrained to accept a 'blackmail' like this. (Interview with unionist, I-24)

In other cases, the pacting regime does not lead to the situation in which the employer pays part of the wage off the books but the opposite transfer occurs. The employer benefits from certain fiscal incentives for hiring new employees and officially pays entitlements like the thirteenth-month-pay, paid leave, and the monthly rate of accumulated severance pay to the workers. However, if the formal salary, including all the benefits, exceeds the actual salary established through pacting, the worker is required to return part of it in cash to the employer. At the end of the employment relationship, the employee will not be entitled to any severance pay since this has been officially paid monthly.

> Look, this is another firm: the Grand Textile Company [finger-pointing at the heading of a payroll]. You see, this guy [the employer] puts in here [the payroll] paid leave, thirteenth-month-pay, extra payment for working on public holidays...She [the worker] does 173 hours [per month], which is the minimum, so the payroll says. However, she [the worker] maintains that she never received €800 or €900 [in a month]. So if the gross wage is €1,200 [as the salary recorded in the payroll], minus the 23% [for taxes and contributions], you will get €800. And if she works not too many hours and the payroll is around €1,000, she will actually get €500. So she will receive the paycheck [of €1,000] and give back some of the money.
>
> *In cash?*
>
> Eh[xactly]! (Interview with unionist, I-8)

This practice persisted, as a local labour inspector explained, notwithstanding the obligation introduced by a national law to pay all salaries through wired money transfers:

> Today the lawmakers gave us an additional instrument [for monitoring purposes] because, from July [2018], all the payment of workers' remuneration must be traceable. All the money transfer for workers' remuneration must be done with traceable means: wire transfers, bank cheques, charges on debit cards. This tool helps us but does not rule out abusive practices because it happens that they [the employers] give a cheque to the worker, he goes to the bank and cashes it and returns part of what he cashed [to the employer]. (Interview with labour inspector, I-33)

The spread of the pacting regime and the (albeit decreasing) persistence of totally unregistered workshops were confirmed in most of the interviews with trade unionists, workers, labour inspectors and even firms' labour consultants. Moreover, all the unionists interviewed confirm that multiple other forms of partially informalized employment persist. As the list of one unionist went:

> [B]ogus part-time [arrangement], unpaid overtime, envelope wages, not respected paid leave, arbitrary production bonuses, some bogus collective agreements [...]. If I look at the payroll, everything is all right, but if we start a dispute, you discover [numerous violations]. (Interview with unionist, I-26)

As another union representative (I-24) explains, the 2008 economic crisis triggered the downsizing and closure of many local companies. Yet, some of the workers that lost their jobs in the sector, especially the most experienced and skilled ones, have started their own family business in the trade. Such firms are often totally or partially informalized and hire workers with no contracts (as confirmed by accounts from interviews with workers I-4; I-15; I-81 and focus group with workers I-87/93). In the cases of fully undeclared employment, employers and workers might collude and agree to not pay social contribution obligations or to keep cashing unemployment benefits while working off the books (interviews with trade unionists, I-24; I-26).[4]

Similarly, in Albania, garment-footwear workers are often hired without contracts or they are not allowed to see and retain a copy of the contract when there is one. Moreover, workers report the widespread use of envelope wages and consistent violations in terms of pay, overtime, leave, social insurance payments (IndustriAll, 2019; Doci, 2018; Arqimandriti et al.,

4 One unionist revealed that he was exposed to situations in which the worker was compelled to quit, and then was informally employed again by the same firm so that he could monetize the unemployment benefits and keep working informally for a lower wage (interview with trade unionist, I-7).

2016; Clean Clothes Campaign, 2016; Filipi and Balla, 2011). In a survey involving more than one hundred workers in the footwear industry in the city of Vlore (Qendra Aulona, 2019), around 80% of the workers reported having a contract, around 16% reported not having signed a contract for their current employment, while 4% did not know whether they signed one or not. According to a 2014 survey on the whole garment-footwear sector (Papa and Kongoli, 2016), one in every two workers reported being employed without a formal contract, four out of ten employees reported not having received their wages fully through traceable banking systems, 68% reported experiencing problems with the payment of their wages in the previous 12 months, and 60% reported that the pay was determined unilaterally by the employers with no collective agreement or possibility for individual bargaining.

According to the same survey, 11% of workers in the garment-footwear or 'façon' industry reported not receiving any social contributions, while 4% did not know about it. Moreover, around 21% of employees reported receiving social contributions based on the minimum wage even though earning more (receiving, therefore, an envelope wage), while 14% reported earning less than the minimum wage even though their social contributions were paid on that threshold (Papa and Kongoli 2016). Finally, according to different sources, often wages are below the Albanian legal minimum if workers do not systematically work overtime (Arqimandriti et al., 2016; Clean Clothes Campaign, 2016; Qendra Aulona, 2019)[5], and the 2014 survey data reveals that 99% of the workers in the 'façon' sector experience at least some difficulties to meet their household's needs relying on their wages (36% reported experiencing *great* difficulties) (Papa and Kongoli, 2016, p. 45).

Clean Clothes Campaign (2016, p. 4) reports that 'workers do not have a copy of their labour contract and are sometimes not even allowed to read it'. As one NGO representative (I-50) I interviewed put it:

> [The workers] don't have a contract at all, or they have a contract, but they have never seen the contract. They tell us: 'a person [from the management] came and said to us: 'Sign, sign here'. But the page is blank. And the worker asks 'what is this?' and is told 'this is your contract. 'Sign! Sign! Quickly!' (Interview with NGO representative, I-50)

5 The legal minimum wage in Albania was 22,000 lek between 2013 and 2016 and was raised to 24,000 lek (around €200) in 2018 (Doci, 2018). Note that the monthly living wage for a family of four as estimated in 2015 by Clean Clothes Campaign (2016) was around €580.

Consistently, an NGO representative working with women employed in the garment-footwear industry in the South of Albania explained:

> [the workers] tell me: 'I was working, and a person came, I just signed [the contract]'. And if they ask: 'can I read it?', [the response is] 'No, you can't. Just sign here'. So, they never read it. (Interview with NGO representative, I-106)

The practice of not holding a copy nor having the opportunity to bargain or being well informed about its terms was confirmed by NGOs (I-41; I-45; I-50; I-107), unions (I-51; I-71) as well as by workers themselves (focus groups I-64/67; I-107/111; and interviews from I-112 to 118).

Full informality—that is, cases of employment without any contracts or social insurance registration—also persists even though it is hard to quantify its share on the total of informal practices. According to a Tirana-based NGO (I-41) and a former labour inspector (I-49), total informality is shrinking as a response to the anti-informality campaign started by the government in 2015, while partial informality is holding steady (see also Chapter 4). In one of the focus groups with workers, it emerged that employees continue to work without contracts, but this is more common in the first months of employment (focus group with workers, I-107/111; interview with NGOs representatives I-106). Workers are accustomed to starting work under the promise that in the future they will receive a contract even when they have previous working experience in the sector.

7.3. *Normalizing informality for a gendered workforce*

As Paola (I-4)—a former sewing-machine operator who worked for various local suppliers—explained, some form of informality has always been the norm throughout her career:

> [I]f you threaten to quit, they just tell you: 'take it or leave it' [...]. Everywhere was the same. If you said: 'I want my social insurance contribution paid, and this and that', they would reply: 'You need to look for work at the cement plant. There you can get those things, not here [in the garment sector]'. (Interview with worker, I-4; quoted in Bagnardi et al. 2022, p. 46)

This was a shared experience for many research participants. As another worker explained:

They were all the same; also in other companies [not only in the ones I worked for].

All? Did you have cases of acquaintances or friends with more positive experiences, or can you tell it was a generalized situation?

All! That's why I told you, here it is like a mentality that is wrong. And it is also wrong from our side as workers that, in the end, we let this situation dominate us, and hardly anyone has the courage to address it. Because many of us [workers] would like it to change; but in the end, they don't act, they back down in order not to lose the job [...] and all the other things. And it is legitimate, especially now that there is not much around [in terms of employment], so one thinks: 'All right, this is better than nothing'. But in this way, they [the employers] get even more greedy; they think they can do whatever they want. (Interview with worker, I-15)

This interviewee revealed she liked making shoes as she felt experienced and talented. Nonetheless, the employment terms that were offered and the complete lack of clarity about remuneration made her give up and shift to the garment sector. However, the employment conditions were no better there:

[T]he last opportunity I had [to work in a footwear firm] was one and a half years ago. They contacted me through a common acquaintance. They wanted a competent, skilled person [...]. So, I went. They said, 'Yes, yes! Come, work with us!' I worked for one and a half months. After this month and a half, I asked them: 'Sorry, when is payday here?' They replied: 'We don't have a day; we will pay whenever we can'. 'Ok', I told them, 'and how much are you going to pay me?' [They replied:] 'Look, I cannot give you more than €4 per hour'. It felt like my whole world was crumbling. I told them, 'Ok, you want the worker to be skilled, prepared, that know how to do the job, and you pay this misery?!' I don't think this is normal! I think if you ask certain things, then you should pay for them [...] If they just wanted a girl who knows nothing about this work, then with €3 per hour, they are good to go. (Interview with worker, I-15)

Another informal garment worker with experience working in total informality and under pacing regimes recalled her attempts to find better, formalized employment by moving from one firm to another, without success:

I don't even know anymore [how many firms I changed]. It has been going on for years. One tries to seek the best for oneself to find a more solid solution but [...] I have tried up until today, and still, I cannot find a solution because nobody wants to hire you [formally]; they underpay you. So you move from one firm to another and in 25 years of work you get certain skills and experience, but it is not recognized.

[…]

In all these years, have you ever worked with a contract?

Yes, I had some contracts. But they were part-time contracts for two or three hours [per day]. I mean, it was just to keep them [the employers] safe in case of an inspection. But for you, for your pension, it is hell.

So these contracts were not legitimate?

They were just a cover! (Interview with worker, I-81)

In Albania, the situation is even bleaker. According to the survey with garment-footwear workers carried out in Vlore (Qendra Aulona, 2019), 62.5% of the respondents stated that they work in the garment-footwear industry because they cannot find any other job, while the rest respond either that with their level of education they cannot find better opportunities (16.3%) or that that the job is appropriate to their educational attainment (13%). Other NGOs (I-106; I-50) and a licensed OSH doctor dealing with garment-footwear firms and workers (I-63) confirmed such views are prevalent among workers. As an NGO worker put it:

> These families are very poor; otherwise, the women would not accept to work [in this sector]. So the ones who are working really need that amount of money which is actually ridiculous—at the end of the day—given the hard work they are doing. (Interview with NGO representative, I-50)

The workers I interviewed confirmed they would immediately change their job if they could, but they also had little time and resources to look for and seize other job opportunities (focus group with workers, I-64/67; I-107/111). As the members of a Tirana-based grassroots union pointed out:

> Many of these women that work in Tirana come from outside Tirana. They have rent to pay. If they miss even one month of work—or even one week—they have no resources to pay their rent. They would be ruined. And salaries are so low that they are barely enough to make ends meet. (Interview with social movement unionists, I-45)

Or, as an NGO member put it, these workers would likely emigrate if they could but:

> They don't have money to pay for the trip [...]. They don't know the language; they don't have anybody in Italy or Greece. They get €200 [per month] to keep a family of four people, you know? (Interview with NGO representative, I-106)

Thus, informal workers move from local factory to local factory (focus group with workers I-64/67), and from low-wage job to low-wage job (focus group with workers, I-107/118) and yet such mobility, in most cases, does not shelter them from partial or total employment informalization.

Gender segmentation, informality and labour devaluation

Workforce feminization and informalization are intertwined, mutually reinforcing and both crucial to devalue women's work in the sector. For an Apulian local unionist:

> The process of [local] outsourcing started exactly on the idea that a woman's salary was a supplement and not a means to the woman's development. It was seen as supplementary labour and as a supplementary income. (Interview with unionist I-30; quoted also in Bagnardi et al. 2022, p. 47)

In Apulia, the association between feminization and substandard work has become well entrenched in the industry since the years of its economic take-off in the early 1980s. As one trade unionist put it:

> [The gender dimension] counts. A lot! It counts a lot because you need to consider that you have both an economic-structural dimension as well as a problem of social context that is unable to see illegality in this dynamic [of informalization] because, you know, *they are just girls*. There is a sort of collective complacency because at the end of the day, my dear girl [...] what else should she do? You have to work to make savings, to get some money so that when you get married, you have some savings. The exploitation of women is not seen as bad as the exploitation of men because an underpaid man is a breadwinner who is unable to bring any bread home. This profoundly affects our capacity to organize collective struggles [...]. Nowadays, it is certainly not like in the Seventies. There is a whole story of struggle in between. But [...] there is always a difference. You don't find anybody saying it openly, but if you get a women's factory or a men's factory in crisis, the public always shows more solidarity with the latter than the former. Nobody says it openly anymore.

> Before, they would say it explicitly [...]. Nevertheless, it is no longer the case that you have widespread discrimination, a wage gap, and blocked careers for women. (Interview with unionist, I-80)

Women's average hourly pay in the textile-clothing sector is lower than the economy-wide average, and the wage gap is higher in Apulia (especially in the BAT province) than the national average.[6]

Workforce feminization, vulnerability and informalization are clearly intertwined in the Albanian garment-footwear sector as well. Garment-footwear workers, as mentioned, are associated with low levels of education, the low prospect of mobility, the lowest average salary in the country, and high levels of in-work poverty (interviews with NGOs, I-41; I-50; I-106; social movement union, I-45; trade unions confederations, I-51; I-71; labour inspector, I-49 and OSH doctor, I-63). On top of this, a substantial gender wage gap persists in the sector as in the whole economy (Arqimandriti et al., 2016; Clean Clothes Campaign, 2016) with male workers in garment-footwear generally hired as 'technicians and engineers to oversee machine maintenance and production processes' or in managerial positions and women deployed in low-skilled, labour-intensive tasks (Kacani and Shehi, 2023, p. 22). Furthermore, women are discursively represented, even by trade unions, as a generally docile workforce that can be easily adapted to respond to the hurdles of working in the garment-footwear industry (interview with trade unionists, I-51; I-71). As the representative of one of the two main Albanian trade union confederations revealed, the absence of strikes in the garment-footwear sector is due to the fact that the 'workers are mostly women, so it is impossible to mobilize them' (interview with trade unionist, I-51). Patriarchal power relations remain generally widespread (Vullnetari, 2012), penalizing Albanian women in terms of income and poverty distribution (Betti et al., 2020). Women tend to be segregated into low-wage professions (that are framed as 'feminine') and, even in such sectors, are rarely in leading positions (Vullnetari, 2012). Moreover, women in rural areas are often responsible for subsistence farming, and household and care work on top of factory hours (Vullnetari, 2012). As an NGO representative (I-50) explains, women working in this sector are usually responsible for all household-related activities, such as the care of children and the elderly. In fact, one of the main difficulties of reaching Albanian workers during the fieldwork was the little free time they had

6 In 2016, according to ISTAT data, hourly pay was €7.60 in textiles and clothing against €7.84 on average across the economy as a whole.

as they generally have to work long hours both in and outside the home. Moreover, in more than one case, I had to conclude the interview right away because the worker was called back home by children or a family member.

Here is an excerpt from my fieldnotes written after a series of interviews I carried out in a small town not far from Tirana. While these notes alone offer no generalizability, they provide an additional piece of information about the hardships that some Albanian garment-footwear workers face.

> Doctor Samira lives in Tirana and works two afternoons per week in Skander, a small village not far from the capital. She spends her days in Skander in a public clinic housed in a crumbling one-store building. She agreed to connect me with workers that pass by her clinic. She asks women she knows work in the sector, if they want to reply to a few questions. With those who accept she helps me with translation.
>
> Sonila is one of the women who accepts to talk to me. Doctor Samira translates and adds some pieces of information while we chat.
>
> Sonila lives in the periphery of Skander. She is the mother of five. The youngest child has been ill for some months already. He needs medication and periodical treatments that Sonila struggles to afford. Although her husband emigrated to Greece to find a job, he comes back every six months bringing roughly €200 each time; the rest is spent during his immigrant life.
>
> In the countryside where Sonila lives, for three days now there has been no electricity. They installed water pipes in houses only a few years ago. Tap water still comes from the wells through a system of electric pumps. When the power is off, there is no running water either.
>
> Sonila works at the assembly line sewing undergarments. Her employer works for a brand I have already encountered in my research. She works in the last tier of a long chain. The head is in Italy, with a brand that designs and retails; the intermediaries are in Southern Italy and in Tirana. They buy Turkish or Chinese cotton, dye and treat it, and cut it into pieces that are put together here by Sonila and her other 50 or so colleagues who take care of the sewing and the final trimming of excess threads and imperfections. Most of the times, her pay is less than the legal minimum wage. Every month or so, Sonila has to skip some working days to take care of her child or because of a strong back pain she has experienced for some time. Half an hour into our conversation, in the dark of the poorly lit clinic in the countryside of a peripheral town not far from Tirana, Sonila receives a mobile call. She has to return home to attend to her children. The interview ends.

7.4. *Not just a matter of costs, but control*

Besides different informal practices and the multiple facilitating factors of the local context, it is crucial to analyse the functions that employment informalization serve within production chains. Research on informality generally considers informal practices to be a matter of cutting the costs of production or an individual choice to abide by the scripts of informal institutions against formal ones (see Chapter 1). In both cases, the multiple functions that informal employment perform for firms in coping with structural pressures are overlooked. Reframing informalization *as a tool of labour control*, instead, allows us to address this complexity. Informalization implies not only curbing labour costs and avoiding taxes but also enables firms to cope with the need for enhanced flexibility and responsiveness imposed by the restructuring of production chains. I distinguish three main functions of employment informalization—*cost-squeezing, flexibility, and disposability*—and I detail them with fieldwork data.

Cost-squeezing

Informal labour is cheaper not only because it avoids or reduces the costs of social insurance, pensions, and other taxes but also because it can impose lower remuneration than the minima established by laws and collective agreements. Also, it can redistribute fiscal, production and other bonuses in favour of firms, and it can evade automatic seniority pay increases, paid leave, and other pay increases related to work in public holidays, night shifts and the like. As an informal worker in Apulia illustrated:

> Currently, my hourly pay is €3.80. A misery.
>
> *Is it the same for your colleagues also? Or does it depend on the fact that you just started in this sector?*
>
> Well, among the ladies I work with, nobody gets more than €4.30 per hour, even the ladies that have worked in the sector all their lives[7]. (Interview with worker, I-15)

7 Consider that the 2017–2019 collective agreement signed by the most representative trade unions and employers' organizations fixed the basic, entry-level hourly rate slightly higher than €7.

However, cutting cost through informalization is also about accessing and monetizing fiscal incentives that are supposed to benefit the employees. The pacting regime allows exactly this, as a trade unionist explained:

> The pacting means that you give me €5 per hour, but you [the employer] give only that. All my rights […] you do not pay for those, and you cash them for yourself. (Interview with unionist, I-8)

In Albania, instead, cost-squeezing takes the form of arbitrary payment systems through which workers often do not even get the minimum wage if they refuse to engage in extensive overtime work and work at the weekend (interview with workers, I-107/111; I-112/118; interview with social movement unionists I-41; interview with NGO representative, I-50).

Multiple flexibilities

Informal employees are often highly flexible in terms of tasks and responsibility, as in the example of one sewing-machine operator in Apulia:

> [W]hen you grow expert, you learn to do the cutting, then you learn to draw the models. Also, as I told you, I used to work with a tailor before; I was born with needle and thread in my hands. My first game as a child was to learn embroidery and to sew and to draw paper samples and all that stuff. If somebody could not come to work, there were no problems; we, the older ones, would just take over the task of the girl that could not come. (Interview with worker, I-4)

Informalized employment arrangements rarely include formal training, and are flexible in the allocation of tasks: workers move from one to another if required, they bank on the skills previously acquired, they train or are trained by their peers.

Being *functionally flexibility* and learning-by-doing are common requests, even though it might depend on the actual labour process. For example, if Apulian small sweatshops require workers' versatility (interview with workers, I-4; I-81), Albanian operators report rigid assembly-line work in which the working pace is set by the machines, or the task is repeated with little variation all day long.

In both cases, however, *external flexibility* is equally pivotal. Periods of work and non-work are intermingled, scattered or patterned, and cyclical. As a worker in Apulia explained:

> We, everyone, used to work a lot—always. Only those who did not want to work did not work. Now, of course, there are *periods* of production [...]. I still have friends that work. But it is 6 months, or 3 months [blocks of time] when the employer wants them. Then, once he needs [workers] again, he calls them. So it is on and off. (Interview with worker, I-4)

The risk of not having orders to deliver to clients is fully on workers' shoulder since they just stay home if there is no work to carry out and to be paid for. As one trade unionist put it:

> If tomorrow there is no work to do, you stay at home, and you don't get any payday. So, it is a bit like they are on a piecework [system]. Whatever you complete, that makes your pay. (Interview with unionist, I-8)

Informal work can de-facto be on call/on demand: one works until there is an order, then stays home, and returns to work again when the employer gets a new order. As an informal garment worker (I-81) put it:

> This sector is based on periods. You never manage to work for 12 months. If you work 12 months, it is like winning the lottery. (Interview with worker, I-81).

Classic piece-rate pay systems—which are illegal—persist in the pacting regime or in total informality. As a trade unionist describing working conditions in one specific local factory reported:

> [T]hese workers are basically in a piecework [system...]. They assemble one piece of the sole, and they get four cents for each pair of shoes [soles]. To get €40, they have to assemble 1,000 shoes. Then they get a formal paycheck that states they have received everything: the thirteenth-month-pay, the Renzi bonus,[8] and all the other entitlements they are supposed to receive; but they don't; they receive four cents per piece and [return the rest]. (Interview with unionist, I-8)

In Albania, working on Saturdays, when needed on Sunday mornings and very often having more than two hours overtime per day is very common (focus groups with workers, I-64/65; I-107/111). Workers report that they can ask for free days if needed, but without pay even though they are lawfully entitled to a certain number of paid leave days per year (focus

8 The so-called Renzi bonus was a tax rebate for low-income earners introduced with Decree 66 (24 April 2014).

group and interviews with workers, I-107/111; I-112/118). In general, workers are not sure about the payment system either. Some interviewees reported that their payment rules were opaque and unclear and that they were never sure what wage to expect. As the seamstresses of an underwear factory (interviews with workers, I-112/118) explained, they were paid according to a mix of production quota and hourly pay. They were assigned a given number of pieces to sew that would ideally correspond to eight hours of work. Until they did not fulfil the quota, however, they had to keep working, and regardless of the additional hours needed, they still got paid for an 8-hour shift. As they reported, the production quota assigned was rarely completed within an 8-hour shift. This allowed the firm to have free overtime work at its disposal to respond to the contingent (or patterned) production peaks.

The forms of flexibility required of workers are not necessarily despotic. Stretched working schedules and envelope wages might coexist with benevolent, *paternalistic* or reciprocal relations. In this case, tasks and working time remain flexible but are set on a more equal footing, as two employees of Apulian first-tier suppliers recounted:

> Worker 1: Well, we do not really do *overtime*. Let's say that if we need to stay longer at work, we stay. If you need to deliver an order, you don't really count your working hours.
>
> Worker 2: You know, the workers in production, when they finish their working hours, they leave. For us, it is more flexible. After the working hours, we use that calmer time to plan the future work.
>
> […]
>
> Worker 2: But then, you know, with the employer […], I am his right-hand man and even a safety valve for him. He knows he can count on me, especially if he is out of town for work, meeting clients. We are constantly in touch; he will call to say, 'Oh, there is one more thing to do here! Do this other thing there'. (Interview with workers, I-17/18)

Disposability

Not having a contract, or instead having a contract that one has verbally agreed not to comply with, is associated with all sorts of violations of collective and individual agreement and labour laws. This puts the worker under the pressure of having to be constantly ready to respond to production demands. If one wants to keep the job, one has to be at the firm's disposal, ready to stay home in idle periods and work overtime right before deliveries. The uncertainty of future production periods is a disciplinary tool that produces and maintains workers' disposability. This interview excerpt well illustrates the dynamic:

> *When there was little work to do, which criteria were used to choose the ones that would work and the ones that would stay home?*
>
> Sympathy.
>
> *What do you mean? Was there no criteria of experience or efficiency?*
>
> Well, they [employers] save whenever they can, so they call the ones that are ready to work for less [money]. I mean, they would call you if you would accept to go and work for €3, and they would leave somebody else at home if he were to ask for €6 [per hour]. (Interview with worker, I-15)

The same worker also recalled that she had to cut her maternity leave short because she was working under a pacting regime and the employer needed all workers to deliver some important orders. Thus, she went back to work in violation of the labour law and her contract. She got paid an extra envelope wage but, in any case, she felt she could not refuse to work if she wanted to keep the job.

In Albania, instead, where overtime is the norm, refusing it might lead to dismissal. As an NGO operator reported:

> For example, in one factory, there were women who did not want to work after 8 hours because they were paid only 100 leks more for this. They were not interested, but they still had to do it. (Interview with NGO representative, I-106)

Informalized precarious employment compresses labour costs and guarantees continuous workforce discipline. Informalized labour is a labour without regulatory strings attached. It resembles the 'labour without overhead' of the gig economy (Shapiro, 2018, p. 2967) or the 'canned labour' (Ehrenreich, 2001, p. 28) of low-end services. It is constantly available but activated only when needed. Informalization, in fact, is a tool to offload the responsibility of their income continuity in periods of non-work onto workers and a way to pressure them to remain always at the disposal of the production process. Like for the flexible time arrangements in retail chain jobs described by Wood (2020), (informalized) unilateral managerial control over work schedules is both a way to cope with production volatility and a powerful disciplinary tool that can critically impair a worker's private life (conflicting with childcare or elderly care responsibilities for example) or even her very livelihood (if there is not enough work).

Furthermore, informalization enhances workers' disposability by crucially impairing their *access to justice* for the redress of violations of their rights. In Albania, for example, not withholding a copy of the contract increases the opaqueness of workers' duties and the difficulties of making claims and start a litigation.[9] As an NGO activist pointed out:

> [Employers withhold the contract] because they are not interested in workers seeing their rights. Usually, workers are only informed about their duties and responsibilities, not their rights. (Interview with NGO representative, I-50)

Alternatively, as another NGO's worker explained:

> [The workers] don't know about social security. They are not sure how many years of social security they have [paid], even though some of them are now at the age of retirement. They want to know how many years the employer has paid for them, and they [the employers] are just kidding [lying to] the workers. And if [the employers are] asked by the labour inspectorate, 'Why do you pay [your employees] less than the minimum wage?', they reply that workers missed some days at work, which is not true. (Interview with NGO representative, I-106)

Finally, informalization enhances disposability by impairing workers' ability to unionize and promoting individualized and often non-adversarial patterns of agency.

7.5. *Informalization, unions, and workers' agency*

The main Italian trade union federations active in the garment-footwear sector—namely, CGIL-FILCTEM, CISL-FEMCA and UIL-TEC—account for around 30% of the union density rate at the national level. This data, however, needs to be considered with caution since it includes other

9 This practice recalls what the employment relations literature refers to as 'pay stub violations'—situations where the employer refuses to provide documentation detailing hours worked, deductions, remuneration criteria and the like (see, for example, Bernhardt et al., 2013).

(usually more unionized) sectors. Moreover, in Apulia, unionization occurs almost exclusively in *bigger* and *older* garment-footwear firms rather than in small workshops for a few specific reasons. Firstly, older firms still retain workers that unionized in the past when unions and unionization activities were stronger (interview with worker I-14; interview with unionists, I-1; I-7; I-8; I-77; I-78; I-80); or because unionization occurred during restructuring periods in which firms' management, in order to access temporary layoff funds, sought unions' cooperation; or in case of organizing activities against downsizing and collective dismissals (focus group with managers and one worker I-35/38; focus group with workers I-87/93; I-94). Secondly, firms with more than 15 employees, in Italy, benefit from enhanced protections for plant-level collective rights and trade unions' activities.

In Albania, the membership rate of the two main confederations—KSSh (Konfederata e Sindikatave të Shqipërisë [Confederation of Trade Unions of Albania]) and BSPSH (Bashkimi I Sindikatave të Pavarura të Shqipërisë [Union of the Independent Trade Unions of Albania])—is around 20% of the non-agricultural sector workforce (Doci, 2018, p. 14). Unions count higher membership rates 'in the public sector and in private enterprises that were former state enterprises' (Doci, 2018, p. 6) and with their collective agreements cover 28,000 workers (24.7% of the total workforce), mostly in the public sector (Doci, 2018; confirmed by interviews with trade unionists I-51; I-71). In the garment-footwear, the Trade Union Federation of Textiles, Fashion and Craftsmanship (Federata e Sindikatave të Punonjësve të Tekstilit, Konfeksioneve dhe Shërbimeve Artizanale) affiliated with the KSSH, and the Independent Trade Union of Light and Textile Industry (Sindikata e Pavarur e Industrisë së Lehtë dhe Tekstile) affiliated with the BSPSH count around 8,000 members each (Doci, 2018). In 2017, they reported 110 enterprise-level collective agreements in the garment-footwear industry (written communication with KSSh representative, 2018).

Effective trade unions are often a bulwark against informality. As Packard et al. (2012, p. 113) point out:

> In the parts of the European Union where governments' enforcement capacity is limited, where households and firms have fewer institutional channels to make their voices heard or to seek redress when the law is violated, labor unions (and indeed other nongovernment organized pressure groups) may be acting as default monitors and enforcers of the labor code.

In fact, fieldwork data shows that, in Apulia, the presence of unions thwarts informalization practices and can be a crucial tool for workers' collective mobilization or access to legal pathways for redress. Firstly, union workplace delegates cannot turn a blind eye to informalization, even when they are aware of the market pressures that supplier firms might face. As a unionist stressed:

> When [informalization practices] were reported to us, we intervened, and employers tried to justify themselves, saying they needed to cut labour costs. So then, even though it is hard to say it, we have to say: 'If you are able to make a profit, abide by the rules and stay in the market; otherwise just close down'. It is hard to say it, but, as a unionist, I have to say it because I cannot allow firms to do what they want. There are two main reasons for this. Firstly, because of what I just said. Secondly, these [informalization] strategies are always counterproductive because it is like allowing unfair competition against the other firms close to them that pay all the contributions and salaries. So, it would just produce a backlash, and we cannot allow it. (Interview with unionist, I-24)

As another unionist pointed out referring to employers' attempts of informalization, unions are seen as 'a problem for firms because [we] stop all those *inventive plans* [to skirt the rules] that employers would like to adopt' (I-26, interviewee's emphasis). Even when undeclared work might be attractive to workers to monetize taxes and circumvent working-time regulations, unions resist informalization. As a shoe factory shop steward recalls:

> Women [employees] revolted in my factory. Why, you ask? It is counterproductive to be in a trade union, they told me. One day, a worker came and told me: 'Go upstairs [to the manager] and bargain for some envelope overtime for us'. I told her: 'You know I have a family and a three-year-old daughter, don't you?!' I have no plan to end up in jail or commit an offence. (Interview with worker and shop steward, I-86)

Irregularities might persist where accommodating unions prevail or where informalization compensates for low pay. It was pointed out by workers, for example, that in some cases, the employees benefitting from the temporary layoff fund would keep working informally for an envelope wage. Yet, such cases were then rebuffed with the arrival in the factory of a competitive union or a new delegate (focus group with workers, I-87/93). Confederal trade unions are a guarantee that informal practices will generally be contested and rebuffed because the internal democratic organization and union pluralism within the firms reduce the risk of collusion between worker representatives and management.

Outside the few already unionized factories, however, informality makes organizing workers a daunting task. When workers attempt to unionize, they come under pressure (interview with unionist, I-30). As a trade unionist explains (interview with unionist, I-26; interviewee's emphasis), they had 'to propose to some workers to become delegates informally, without letting the employer know it' because of fear of retaliation. Additionally, '[s]ome workers have been *advised* against their enrolment [to the trade union]' (interview with unionist, I-26). Organizing is difficult also because of the grim prospects for employment alternatives. Even with a widespread presence at the local level, as another trade unionist (I-8) explained, getting in touch with informal workers is only the first step:

> ...but what do you do if a worker loses his job? I don't force them [to unionize] because I don't really want them to lose their job in a place where there are not many alternatives. But, step by step, I organize them. Firstly, I explain the violations and their rights to them [...]. So they tell the employer that they need the union. We frame it as a matter of services in the first instance; we offer bureaucratic assistance and the like so we can enter the firm. [...]. In this way, we avoid open conflicts. (Interview with unionist, I-8)

In contrast, fieldwork data revealed that Albanian unions provide no guarantees against informalization. The two main confederations present most of the features of post-socialist *legacy unions* (see: Sil, 2017; Varga, 2014; Bagnardi and Petrović, 2020): they are de-facto affiliated with one of the two main political parties, maintain good relations with employers' associations, but are unable to mobilize workers (Dragoshi and Pappa, 2015). Unions, in fact, are not generally considered independent from political power and are seen as ineffective in representing workers' interests by the public (Lleshaj and Cela, 2014). They are not democratically organized either. Roles and responsibilities are assigned through top-down appointment, union members seldom vote at all for anything, and often workers are not even aware that they are union members. Even local representatives perceive confederations as non-transparent and distant (Dragoshi and Pappa, 2015) and only 6% of the garment-footwear workers surveyed by Papa and Kongoli (2016, p. 44) reported being unionized. As the staff of a labour-centred NGO put it:

> Activist 1. [Trade unions] don't have as many members as they say they have. All the trade unions in Albania have this problem. They do not really represent workers [...]. [Unionization] is a mechanism of collective bargaining that is used to recruit more workers and members. But [...] if you go to a garment or a shoe factory and ask the workers, mostly women and girls, if they

know their … [union or even] if there is a trade union within the factory or whether they are members of such-and-such trade union, they don't even know in the first place what a trade union is. So, you know, that's the situation.

[…]

Activist 2. The trade union goes directly to the management and signs a formal [collective] agreement. For this reason, we said before that unionization here is formal; it is not something effective (Interview with NGO representatives, I-41).

Consistently, the workers I interviewed either did not know what a union was (interview with workers, I-112/118) or had never tried to contact unions out of fear of losing their job (focus group with workers, I-107/111). At the same time, a few managers mentioned having decided to cover the workers' fee for union membership in order to comply with social audits of foreign buyers, even though the employees themselves had not requested this (I-54; I-101; I-72).[10] Autonomous grassroots unionization, meanwhile, remains a difficult endeavour. As the activists of the social movement union based in Tirana put it:

Activist 1. The difficulties [in unionizing workers] are multiple. First of all, there is a total lack of mobilization experience. These workers have never been organized; they have never organized themselves; they have never taken part in any protest.

Activist 2. They don't feel they could ever have any power.

Activist 1. When you talk to them, they do not even understand what a union is. Many also are afraid to organize because fear losing their job. (Interview with social movement unionists, I-45).

For these reasons, unions in Albania are not a bulwark against informalization, and informals do not see unionization as a tool for resisting exploitative informalization dynamics. For example, survey data on garment-footwear workers reports that the first action employees take against violations of their rights is to complain directly with the supervisor (54%) or peers (14%), while only 4% resort to unions (Papa and Kongoli,

10 In buyer-driven GVCs, it is not uncommon for buyers to require that suppliers show compliance with minimum labour standards, even though audits seldom check the autonomy and effectiveness of companies' unions (see Anner, 2015b).

2016, p. 72). And as an NGO activist (I-50) points out, 'trade union representatives are part of the entire way of exploiting these people. They agree more with employers than with employees'.

With weak or legacy unions, individual forms of agency prevail among informals. Informal workers, for example, might *exit* the informalized employment relationship altogether. Moving from one firm to another is, in fact, common for informals both in Italy and Albania. In Albania, workers, managers and experts alike consistently reported in interviews that outmigration is a crucial path for exit that is pursued whenever possible. An alternative manifestation of agency is direct confrontation with the employer, even though this often preludes exit. As one worker recalled:

> *Have you ever had a conflict with one of your employers?*
>
> Yes! Yes! There was this one time [...] I will never forget this. It was when I used to work for 'Seven'. Mamma mia! It was awful. You entered that company and immediately started feeling incompetent, inadequate. It was the environment, everything. They were oppressive, even without doing anything. So, one day I get there, and I was changing [into my uniform]. The employer told me something harshly; I don't even remember what. It was early morning. So, I turned, got my clothes, and told her: 'This place makes me nauseous!' I turned my back, and I left. (Interview with worker, I-81)

In other cases, workers might turn to a union for support as long as the union established and maintains a degree of legitimacy among non-members. Interviews in Apulia reveal a common pattern of action: an informal worker decides to consider legal action against her employer due to a major conflict or termination. She turns to the local union office to report the wrongdoing, and the union confirms if violations have occurred. If so, the union officer contacts the employer for redress. An informal negotiation, mediated by the union, starts and usually leads to an informal 'permanent deal' in which the employer provides cash compensation, and the worker commits to raising no further claims. However, such deals usually only return a fraction of the credits the worker has accumulated, as a local unionist put it:

> You never get 100% compensation because in that case, the company would say, 'Let's just go to court and see if you win!' In a small number of cases, we got 50% compensation, and this is already a great success. It always depends on what [proof] we have during the negotiations: [we are in a better position] if we have witnesses who worked there in the same period, who are maybe now

> retired or work somewhere else and can therefore speak up. (Interview with unionist, I-83)

Workers can also reject the deal and start a court case. This, however, seldom happens (interview with unionists I-24; I-77; I-83; interview with HRM consultant, I-9), and informal negotiation is by far the most common remedy sought by informals in cases of major conflict. There are several reasons for this. Firstly, partial informality is hard to prove in court. Often, the worker reports her condition to the trade union only after being fired (interview with unionist, I-26) or after a major conflict with the employer (interview with unionist, I-24)—namely, when she has already left the job. Moreover, proving an informal employment relationship requires the testimony of colleagues who are often unwilling to do so because they risk losing their own job (see also: Filho 2016).[11] A court case is also expensive (and unions are increasingly unable to cover such expenses), unsure in its outcome, and usually takes several years to reach a verdict. Finally, a worker who brings a local employer to court risks being stigmatized by other local firms and might find herself unable to find work in the sector again (interview with unionists, I-77; I-83).

Multiple factors, therefore, undermines workers' access to justice. As one union organizer pointed, agency remains deeply enmeshed into these structural constraints even with the support of a collective actor such as the union:

> We have no fear to start a court case, but I have to put myself in these workers' shoes and this reality. And I am neither the inspectorate, nor the police, nor the Carabinieri. When a 46- or 48-year-old worker, with a husband that has recently lost his job, comes to me in tears [...] you know, what the hell does she care about informality, about compliance with the rules?! [...]. Well, then what can I tell her?! (Interview with unionist, I-77)

In Albania, the absence of autonomous unions makes agency even harder. NGOs (I-107; I-50; I-41) and grassroots union activists (I-45) claim that, besides cases related to major accidents at work, there were no other court cases initiated by workers in the garment-footwear industry at the time of my interviews.

11 As I explained in Chapter 4, firms choose partially informalized employment rather than full informality because it reduces the risks of sanction given the prevailing monitoring practices and regulations.

Therefore, the absence of partial legal support in Albania (which in Italy is provided by local union offices) is crucial. The only form of agency left to informal workers seems to be exit. Quitting one firm for another and emigrating whenever possible are the main avenues through which Albanian garment-footwear workers exercise agency.

The effects of these different forms of agency, the permanent deal and the exit strategies are twofold. On the one hand, they do not disrupt the generalized patterns of informalization. Informal practices, in one way or another, are not being publicly addressed amidst exit strategies and individualized permanent delas, even though they remain well-known locally. Public authorities or the broader public are not exposed to such events, so that there is rarely a collective push to challenge the stability that informal practices acquired. This first effect of informal agency partially explains its persistence.

On the other hand, however, workers' agency shapes informalization dynamics as well. Different forms of agency make informalization impossible where genuine unions exist and make the turnover of informals higher than for formal employees. This, as I will show in the next chapter, makes coercive informalization incompatible with those specific phases of production that rely on a highly skilled and committed workforce and therefore are not viable for firms that, for production purposes, rely on specifically trained workers.

To conclude, a few intertwined aspects of the nature and function of informal employment emerge. Firstly, local contexts–highly segmented labour markets, few alternative employment opportunities and the burdens of social reproduction generally on women–crucially shape informalisation dynamics. Secondly, informal employment emerges not only to avoid taxes but it rather is a crucial means to keep labour cheap, flexible and disposable in order to cope with production needs and structural pressures. By informalizing employment relations, in other words, employers can disentangle labour from the rigidities of formal regulations and embed it fully within informal norms and unfettered power relations. Finally, informal workers maintain agency, and even though individual actions prevail and contribute to the reproduction of informalization, a residual presence of unions, at least in the Italian case, matters and remains a bulwark against exploitative forms of informalization.

Not all the firms and workers embedded in the same social contexts go informal, and not all informalization dynamics are equal as new institutionalist premises would assume. Informalization dynamics are, on the contrary, shaped by economic pressures and powers, contexts and agency. The next chapter will spell out these factors and explain how they determine informalization varieties within the chain and across institutional contexts.

8.
FIRMS' STRATEGIES, WORKERS' AGENCY AND INFORMALIZED EMPLOYMENT
The Persistence of Variegated Informal Labour Control Regimes in Global Production Networks

8.1. *Putting the pieces together*

In the previous chapters, I have argued that informal employment is a dynamic process mediated at the workplace level and shaped by the agency of employers and employees which are embedded in (and constrained by) local institutional contexts and structural economic constraints. Informalized employment relations are qualitatively different than formal ones insofar as they eschew the rigidities of formal regulations and move the employer–employee relationship away from collectively bargained agreements and public laws. Furthermore, informality is not just a cost-cutting device but a labour control mechanism that increases labour flexibility and workers' disposability. Through informalization, firms cope with the increasing pressure they experience within production chains while their upgrading strategies can only but amplify these same pressures on others further down the chain. Yet, while informalization can be seen as a response to chain pressures, not all firms respond in the same way. In other words, not all firms go informal and not all informalized employment relations are equal.

Informality might entail benevolent, paternalistic or fully despotic employment relationships; it might enhance cost compression and flexibility at the expense of workers' rights or promote commitment, flexibility and loyalty through the leverage of informal ties. Thus, how can we explain the differences in the informalization patterns that characterize different workplace relations and labour control regimes? And why do both formal and highly differentiated informalized employment relations persist even within the same socio-institutional contexts?

The persistence of diverse dynamics of informalization within common institutional contexts can be partially explained by looking at the position that firms hold within GPNs and the pressures ensuing from such integration. Yet, firms might cope with similar structural pressures in different ways if they are embedded in different institutional contexts and if they face differentiated forms of worker agency.

To explain the diversification and coexistence of formalized and informalized labour regimes, therefore, I focus on how differentiated structural pressures deriving from each firms' position in the chain interact with the local contexts and the *uneven distribution of workers' resistance* (see: Friedman, 1977). It is the unevenness of workers' resistance and their adaptative responses that ultimately shape labour regimes.

Accordingly, in this chapter, I will analyse the varieties of informalization patterns by combining three dimensions that crucially shape employment and informalization dynamics: the *structural pressures* each firm faces and its core activities, the degree of replaceability of its core workforce, and the local associational power of workers.

8.2. *Opportunities and pressures within production networks: Firms' position, core activities and labour control mechanisms*

The GPNs framework provides a tool to read the structural pressures and opportunities that firms integrated into broader production processes face. It allows us to tease out the main core activities of the firms in each node of the chain, the possibility that these firms have to offload some of the cost and flexibility pressures through outsourcing on other firms, and the financial leeway they have to build a more or less hegemonic labour regime.

Table. 8.1. Core activities and labour control mechanisms within the chain

	Core activities; Specialization/ Value creation	Mechanisms of direct/outsourced labour control
Lead firm	High-quality production; branding; marketing.	Direct control over a core skilled workforce (need for creativity, commitment, and high skills); Subcontracting low added-value phases of production (offloading the responsibility of controlling labour directly by outsourcing to suppliers while keeping indirect control over production specifications, costs, and time.
First-tier supplier	Design; sample-making; responsiveness to buyers; ability to offer of a wide menu of options to buyers in terms of designs, quality and prices; high-quality production in-house and tight control of differentiated supply chains.	Direct control over a small skilled workforce (flexibility of tasks/working time, enhanced commitment + small number of employees and direct employee–employer relationship requires a committed but flexible workforce); Tight market control (through subcontracting and *orchestrated competition*) over differentiated suppliers.
Single-phase supplier (second and third tiers)	Low labour cost; short lead times; very small, quick response production batches on demand (Apulia) or mass production (Albania); ability to squeeze and expand the workforce (or working time) according to buyers' orders.	Cost and time pressures make further outsourcing non-viable. Directly controlled workforce needs to be cheap but highly flexible, activated on-call, and without overhead costs attached.

As I showed in Chapters 5 and 6, each position in the chain entails sets of core activities that the firm specializes in, through which each firm produces and appropriate values, that coincide with specific choices in terms of direct employment and outsourcing (see Table 8.1).

Lead firms specialize in high-quality production, branding, marketing activities or retailing. They face relatively lower competitive pressures compared to their suppliers because of the relatively high entry barriers to their core activities and the possibility of outsourcing lower-margin production phases. For example, the core activities of high-quality producers of fashion garments or manufacturers of safety shoes, are a mix of minimal direct production, technology research, and branding activities. The core activities of retailers include the creation of new collections and samples, the management of supply chains, and branding, marketing and distribution. In these cases, most of the labour-intensive phases of the manufacturing process are outsourced, while the core activities require a skilled, committed, and stable workforce. Retaining a hard-to-replace workforce with specific skills and experience calls for specific in-house training and a consent-based labour regime. Control, in other words, requires more than mere coercion. At the same time, the possibility to outsource labour-intensive production phases and offload fluctuations and cyclicity of production on subcontractors guarantee the financial leeway to sustain a control regime based on generating workers' consent and commitment. The fieldwork revealed that only a few lead firms are located in Apulia, and none are in Albania.

First-tier suppliers, instead, specialize in designing, supply-chain management, and often some phases of production. These firms' core business lies in their ability to serve buyers (i.e., retailers and brand manufacturers). These firms are often intermediaries —that is, small companies that retain only the facilities and workforce to design and produce small batches of samples. They specialize in reaching new buyers and managing different supply chains in Italy and abroad for the buyers. They directly employ a small but skilled group of creative and *functionally flexible* workers who can be responsive to clients' requests and control differentiated supply chains. These are usually creative designers, skilled tailors, supply-chain managers, and a few logistics workers. Employees need to be flexible on working time and intensity and highly responsive to production peaks and lows. They are continuously asked to carry out and master new tasks, and they retain a certain degree of autonomy and initiative.

Other first-tier suppliers might be *pure full-package suppliers* that manufacture entirely in-house the orders for lead firms. In the garment industry, these firms usually focus on high-quality products, and their competitiveness depends on their ability to guarantee certified high-quality production and the capacity to reach different buyers and cover different market segments. Both intermediaries and pure suppliers need a stable labour regime built on a certain level of consent and commitment from their core in-house workers. Other full-package suppliers in the garment industry might also develop their own branded lines of products on the side. These firms usually resemble the organization of brand manufacturers with a stable workforce retained through a consent-based labour regime.

The fieldwork revealed that full-package suppliers are located mainly in Apulia, although a handful of this kind of suppliers exist in Albania as well. These are generally strongly tied to a few clients or might even be firms established through greenfield investment by Italian buyers, that become with time autonomous, mono-client suppliers for those same lead firms. Alternatively, full-package suppliers might be previously single-phase assembly suppliers that have upgraded and have incorporated the cutting and packaging phases. Often these firms specialize in low-quality or standardized massive production. In these cases, their labour control regime resembles that of other Albanian single-phase suppliers, in which the required workers' skills are generally low, the workforce is relatively easily replaceable. Their competitive advantage is the low cost of production rather than its quality.

In other cases, Albanian full package suppliers specialize in high-quality production and work for foreign brands (often through intermediaries). These firms invest in automated cutting machines and have a stronger need to retain a stable and committed workforce to operate and organize production around these machines. As a consequence, they are prone to develop a consent-based labour control regime.

Finally, second-tier subcontractors are single-phase suppliers deal with simple, low-margin production tasks and highly fluctuating demand. Given fluctuating orders, short lead times, and low mark-ups, further subcontracting is not viable for them. Thus, they respond to unstable production by banking directly on a workforce that is activated only when needed. Workers in single-phase suppliers repeatedly perform the same production task, often in an assembly line, and have little space for autonomy and creativity; production tasks can often easily be carried out by newcomers. This makes workers highly replaceable. Their core feature is being cheap and disposable rather than creative, autonomous, and committed. As a result, firms cope with chain pressures by imposing a take-it-or-leave-it labour regime based on coercion.

Based on this analysis which draws on the findings of the previous chapters, it is possible to order firms within the chain according to the level of competitive pressure they face, the complexity of their core activities, and the level of skills and commitment required of their workers. As for any simplification of complex phenomena, such a classification presents several shortcomings. The level of competitive pressure in terms of cost and production flexibility, for instance, is hardly a dichotomous one. Different supplier firms, for example, might carry out different phases of production at the same time and face different degrees of competitive pressure for each of these activities. Moreover, the level of competition a company faces depends also on its ability to shelter its core activities from new competitors. In the garment-footwear industry, as well as in other buyer-driven production chains, competitive pressures need to be understood as actively shaped by managerial strategies that continuously strive to build entry barriers and protect their markets from competitors (Kaplinsky, 2004).

The level of workers' skills and commitment required by specific production phases, also, are both measures that can hardly be defined dichotomously let alone the difficulties of precisely quantifying them. How do we measure the level of commitment required from workers within a given labour process? And how do we quantify and categorize the level of skills in a manufacturing process where formal educational attainment but also (and often more so) experience, work speed, accuracy, autonomy, and ability to carry out different tasks are all important aspects of a worker's profile? Further, can we merge commitment and skills in one ordering dimension, assuming that they grow and decrease simultaneously?

To address these issues, an empirical, case-by-case analysis of the fragmented labour processes within production network is needed. Indeed, the definition of skills, dexterity, professionalism and commitment is always the result of a situated, 'contested and socially constructed process' (Edwards et al., 2009, p. 42), and skills are not just a matter of measurable technical expertise but increasingly concern generic, 'soft', and even emotional capacities (Grugulis and Lloyd, 2010). I defined skills as the expertise, knowledge, and experience workers need in order to deliver the tasks managers have assigned them. As for the commitment, I refer to the level of engagement, creativity, and autonomy required of the workers to fulfil their tasks. The combination of skills and commitment can be understood as a proxy for a more general level of *workers' replaceability*. Direct empirical observation makes it is easier to order different firms in the chain by the level of skills and commitment they require from their workers (or by the ease of replacing a worker with a newcomer). Accordingly, a clearly codified, repetitive production task (for example, what sewing-machine operators do on an assembly line) is considered as low-commitment, while a more creative task requiring a high level of autonomy and problem-solving capacity (such as the activity of sample-makers that connect fashion designers and assembly-line operators), or a task that requires specific training (such as the cutting-machine operator's activity) are considered high-commitment.

Further, while each firm might have a tiered internal production process, with a workforce divided into core and peripheral employees engaged in different tasks, I refer to firms' core activities and the workers carrying them out. A single-phase supplier, for instance, relies mainly on sewing machines and quality-control operators. A full-package supplier needs seamstresses, tailors, designers, and supply managers who can link brands and producers. And finally, lead firms need supply and retail managers (in the case of retailers), marketing specialists or executives that manage outsourced operations (brands-without-factories), and production managers, tailors, and skilled operators (high-quality brand manufacturers).

Production and productive demands, however, do not fully determine employment relations and its informalization path. As I show in the next section, other dimensions such as the local labour market, the local socio-institutional contexts, and ultimately the power of workers, need to be considered.

8.3. *Varieties of formal and informal labour control regimes*

Structural pressures and local contexts remain crucial in determining opportunities and constraints for the actors, but it is the analysis of their agency and their bargaining power that ultimately explains differential informalization dynamics. 'Worker resistance may take on many different forms' and 'is unevenly developed among different groups of workers' (Friedman, 1977, p. 50). It is the unevenness of workers' resistance and adaptation responses that ultimately impinge upon employment informalization dynamics. As I showed in Chapter 7, if resistance exists and is collectively exerted through union mediation, informalization ends up being a non-viable solution for firms to respond to increasing competitive pressures. If workers' agency is rather individualized or expressed mainly through direct confrontation, submissive adaptation and exit, multiple forms of hegemonic or coercive informalization occur. To be clear, workers' resistance patterns and firms' control strategies remain crucially shaped by both the structural pressures they face and the institutional contexts in which they develop. Therefore, all these factors are the frame within which the relevant actors need to be analysed and not the direct explanatory variable of informalization dynamics.

Table 8.2 provides a tool to combine all the relevant elements that lead to uneven control strategies and resistance, and therefore to differentiated labour regimes and informalization dynamics.

Table 8.2. Labour regimes within the chains

	Highly replaceable workers		Scarcely replaceable workers	
	Workers associational power		Workers associational power	
	Low	High	Low	High
High competitive pressure	Informalized despotism	Agile sweatshop	Informalized hegemonic regime	Crisis bureaucratic regime
Low competitive pressure	Unlikely to occur		Informalized hegemonic regime	Bureaucratic regime

Firstly, one needs to account for core features of the main activities of each firm and therefore the requirement in terms of workers' skills and commitment. These requirements, though, need to be matched with a local supply of workers with such profiles. Workers' *replaceability*, in other words, is not just the result of firms' technical demands but also reflects local labour markets and workers' agency. As Smith (2006) highlights, local labour markets and exit options shape workers' bargaining power and their capacity to resist or adapt to the given labour control regime imposed by managers. Tightening labour markets might lead local firms to improve labour conditions and shift from a coercion-based to a consent-based labour regime precisely because they need to retain or attract (scarce) local workers that otherwise would shift to other employers. On the contrary, an increase in local labour supply (for example, following the rise of unemployment due to an economic crisis) reduces workers' bargaining power and can lead to an erosion of hegemonic control regimes.

To situate the replaceability dimension in really-existing contexts, therefore, we need to account for both the requirements of the production process (deriving from the company's position in the production chain) and the features of the local labour market. Replaceability works, in this case, as a proxy of workers' individual market bargaining power that crucially steers employment informalization patterns. As the literature confirms, highly standardized working tasks in the labour process usually coincide with high levels of replaceability and despotic styles of management (Anzovino and Regalia, 2020; Pedaci and Betti, 2020). On the contrary, as Regalia (2020, p. 216) notes,

> the rarer and/or more crucial these skills and competences are, and therefore the greater the firm's dependence on the workers whose active consent is needed, the greater the likelihood that informal types of relationship will be characterised by benevolence and/or a propensity for involvement and negotiation.

In other words, firms that rely on scarcely replaceable workers generally need to actively pursue consent and commitment. Building a control system based on consent generally entails higher costs and managerial rigidities and is achievable only for firms that are partially sheltered from heightened competitive pressures.

This calls on the second dimension of the typology, the level of competitive pressures faced by the firm. As labour process theorists stress, hegemonic forms of control emerge as a result of workers' resistance but are made financially viable as the monopoly power of a firm increases: '[a] narchy in the market leads to despotism in the factory [...]. Subordination of the market leads to hegemony in the factory' (Burawoy, 1979, p. 194; see also: Wood 2020, chap. 2). While lead firms can *afford* hegemonic labour regimes, or can outsource on suppliers all the phases with lower returns and higher uncertainties, suppliers either rely on individualized and often informalized consent-based relationship or resort to coercion.

Finally, workers might have the support of trade unions and enjoy a certain level of associational power. As I showed, effective trade unions prevent informalization and provide an avenue for more effective forms of individualized worker agency. Thus, both individual market power and collective associational power shape the effectiveness of workers' resistance against the most coercive forms of informalization and determine—together with structural constraints and managers' strategies—the emergence of more or less informalized, coercive or hegemonic, labour regimes.

The combination of these three dimensions serves as our analytical guide to making sense of differences in the emerging labour regimes and their informalization dynamics.

Lead firms and the bureaucratic control regime

Lead firms are generally older and bigger. In the sector analysed, a company does not get to the head of the chain when it is created; upgrading requires time, and usually, lead firms go through transformations, restructuring, and perhaps crises. Lead firms are very likely to be unionized (see Chapter 7.6), and thus their labour regime is unlikely to be informalized.

On the one hand, as I showed in the previous chapter, the presence of unionized workers and an effective, pluralistic trade union movement prevents informalization dynamics. On the other, lead firms can outsource low-margin production phases and focus on high-added-value activities only. This entails relatively low competitive pressures but also the need to retain skilled and hard-to-replace workers. Therefore, the labour regime that emerges in lead firms is a consent-based, formalized, *bureaucratic control regime*. In this kind of labour regime, as Edwards (1979, p. 131) points out, control

> grows out of the formal structure of the firm, rather than simply emanating from the personal relationships between workers and bosses [...]. The definition and direction of work tasks, the evaluation of worker performances, and the distribution of rewards and imposition of punishments all came to depend upon established rules and procedures, elaborately and systematically laid out.

Bureaucratic forms of control are clearly inscribed in labour laws, collective agreements, and formal internal regulations. Any job comes with a detailed description of expected tasks and duties. Written rules and roles make conflict procedural, and control inscribed in formal regulations rather than on the arbitrary authority of managers and supervisors. Retaining the right workforce without causing productive disruption due to industrial conflicts is crucial in bureaucratic forms of control (Edwards, 1979, p. 146) and is a viable solution for lead firms that can offload demand fluctuations onto suppliers.

The labour process in these firms is technically organized so that productive periods are planned in detail through scientific organization. Remuneration, rewards, and internal labour markets are designed to retain and foster workers' commitment, while bargaining and grievance mechanisms are regulated by formal procedures and the mediation of trade unionists. Collective bargaining, for example, is mediated at the national level, while grievances are generally expressed through the mediation of unions' representatives. In unionized firms, individual grievances are rarely directly addressed to the managers. Instead, they firstly are filtered by the shop steward who can assert a mediating role, 'educating' workers about their rights and their legitimate claims without causing disruptions. As a shop steward described:

> If you do not provide some kind of *education* to the people [working in the firm]; if you have nobody in the plant that can provide answers [to workers' questions], you are lost [...]. The union is like a network. It starts with me in the firm, and then it grows its branches [...]. If workers have a problem, they come to me. (Interview with worker and shop steward, I-86, interviewee's emphasis).

Fluctuations in production are addressed in compliance with labour laws and collective agreements because non-compliant management will likely encounter unions resistance. On the one hand, production phases carried out in-house are scientifically managed to reduce idle times. On the other hand, when these are highly seasonal, temp-agency workers can be recruited while the core employees maintain regular workloads and schedules. As the worker for a brand manufacturer and full-package supplier reported:

> Production peaks in some periods, and then, later, it falls. We manage this, for example, with temp agencies, which are a bit both a blessing and a curse for workers but are indeed very important to manage production, which peaks only in some specific periods of each season. Otherwise, they [the managers] would not be able to afford to keep these [temp-agency] workers all year long because they would not have sufficient work for them. I mean, they would not know what to make these workers do. Instead, in these peaks, you have to deliver [the orders], and you have lots of work concentrated in a few months, and you need many more workers than your core workforce [...]. Also, thanks to this [temp-agency system], let's say that we have solved the problem of black labour. That is the point. I mean, if we would not hire temp-agency workers, we would have had to hire workers informally. But since the company wants to feel calm and does not want to get in any kind of trouble [with inspections], it solves the [production fluctuations] in this way. (Interview with worker, I-14)

Alternatively, production fluctuations are addressed via outsourcing. As the garment workers in a focus group in Apulia explained:

> Worker 1: Clients' demands have greatly changed. You need to deliver the suit within a certain time frame. The company has little time to deliver the orders. If, in some cases, you don't make it in time, the order gets cancelled.
>
> Worker 2: And the [delivery] timing gets shorter and shorter.

> Worker 1: [Delivery] Times are shorter, so we no longer manage to produce everything in-house. That's why they [the managers] decided to rely on other workshops and outsource [...]. It seems they plan it well. (Focus group with workers, I-87/93)

Time and production constraints are also addressed with other tools allowed by contracts and laws such as paid leave, flexible working-time arrangement, temporary layoff funds, and overtime. But, as the garment workers of the focus group again recalled:

> [During non-production periods w]e get our paid leave. I mean, we take all of our annual paid leave entitlement at once [when there is no production]. (Focus group with workers, I-87/93)

Paid overtime, possibly the most expensive solution because of the increased rate of remuneration, is relatively rare. Instead, time banks and similar flexible work arrangement are preferred, as this excerpt from the workers' focus group shows:

> *Do you do overtime throughout the year?*
>
> Worker 1: Well, in some periods, for deliveries, yes. Right before the deliveries only. And however, it is more likely that you get a rest day so that once you finish the delivery period, you can stay home.[1]
>
> [...].
>
> Worker 1: Anyway, every firm has its own style in its approach with the worker.
>
> Worker 4: Yes. Maybe some [firms] pay overtime because they always work. Others use time banks because there are these 'dead' periods, and so the overtime you worked in the previous period can get you some free hours in the following period.
>
> Worker 1: Yes, but then you don't get paid [the increased percentage of] the overtime, right?

1 The interviewees refer here to flexible working-time arrangements (i.e., a sort of working-time-bank system allowed by the contracts). Working overtime in some periods can provide the worker with some free paid hours to be used in the next months when there are no close deadline and production peaks.

> Worker 4: No. they count it differently
>
> *Me: The overtime should be paid at an increased rate, right?*
>
> Worker 1: Yes, exactly.
>
> Worker 5: For us, it is the same. Sometimes you get the overtime, sometimes the time banks. (Focus group with workers, I-87/93)

Finally, another tool to cope with production fluctuation is to access the temporary layoff fund. As explained in the focus group:

> Now it is like a seasonal job. It is not continuous anymore. Now the full production starts in March. In March, we prepare all the samples. The samples are presented [to the public] in April. And those are the full months. So, you start working in March until November/December when you deliver [to the boutiques]. Before you could work for longer periods because the shops would replenish and make new orders. Now it is no longer the case. Our clients [shops and boutiques] choose what to buy in the fairs, and that's it. So, we work for those orders, and then we stop. There are no more orders afterwards. It is a long period of stoppage. For example, this year, we stopped in November. Since November, we have been idle. We are under the layoff fund because we could not cover the whole [idle] period with our annual paid leave [...]. It is already 4 or 5 years that it has gone on like this. (Focus group with workers, I-87/93)

Workers' associational power expressed through the presence of unions—together with the need to retain a skilled and committed workforce—compels lead firms to rely on a *bureaucratic labour control regime* (see the detail of the labour regimes in Table 8.3). This workplace regime relies on the possibility of outsourcing fluctuating and labour-intensive production phases and distributing increasing returns that derive from the position held by the firm in production networks. Thus, on the one hand, lead firms need to retain their workers; on the other, they can afford to comply with the rigidities of laws and contracts with outsourcing and other legal recruitment strategies. As long as such conditions remain, formalized and bureaucratic employment relations persist.

Intermediaries, paternalistic relationships, and hegemonic informality

Albania's first-tier suppliers are often full-package producers of low/middle-quality items. They resemble single-phase suppliers as far as the competitive pressures they face and the skills they require are concerned. Their labour control regime is generally informalized and despotic, as I explain below. Full-package suppliers of high-quality items, instead, are different. They invest in electronic cutting machines and ironing systems, and they prefer to retain a skilled workforce. These firms comply with labour laws and even introduce their own internal labour market systems to reward core workers with higher salaries. As the managers of a first-tier Albanian supplier put it:

> You know, our workers can get 35–40,000 Leks. It is the same one front desk employee in a bank earns. […]. The company we are and the product we make is at a high level. Thus, today, if you want to work well, you should also pay well [your workers]. (Interview with manager, I-69)

This labour regime is designed to secure crucial workers' loyalty and to avoid high turnover. Yet, the absence of effective unions in Albania means it is unilaterally imposed by managers rather than being the result of a bargaining process with workers' representatives.

As for Apulia's first-tier suppliers, these are of two kinds: suppliers-without-factories (intermediaries) and full-package suppliers. In both cases, these firms maintain a small structure, usually less than 15 employees, typically with non-unionized workers. Fifteen employees is the statutory threshold at which increased protection for workers' rights to information and to organize takes effect. In some cases, first-tier suppliers come from a trajectory of restructuring and downgrading; others produce both for their own branded lines as well as for other buyers. In other cases still, they resemble lead firms for the pressures they face, the unionization of their workforce and the labour control regimes on which they rely.

In general, given the small structure of these firms, their lack of unionization, and their position within the production chain, first-tier suppliers rely on an *informalized but hegemonic* (or *paternalistic*[2]*) labour*

2 I use the term 'paternalistic' loosely to refer to a labour regime based on a clear asymmetry between workers and employers, the use of material benefits beyond wages and a (rhetorically) familial atmosphere that rejects class conflict and ensue workers' loyalty to the company banking on their moral obligations towards a common economic enterprise. Paternalistic regimes are historically characterized by employers offering services beyond the point of production (schools, housing, hospitals), yet the term is also used to refer more generally to a form of labour control based on an unitarist vision of the workplace that justifies power and distributive asymmetries with a rhetoric of a benevolent, enlightened father-entrepreneur that takes care of his children-workers without

control regime. These firms rely on informalized employment relationships rather than a system of formal industrial relations, collective bargaining, and grievance-resolution mechanisms. Yet, informalization dynamics do not lead to massive violations of workers' rights. Instead, they are aimed at reaching flexible and *negotiated consent* with employees.

On the one hand, first-tier suppliers do not benefit from the same entry barriers as lead firms and thus face heightened competition. On the other hand, they can still offload the lowest-added-value production tasks to subcontractors and focus on higher returns activities. The competitive advantage of first-tier suppliers comes from their ability to be responsive to the request of lead firms. Therefore, they have to cope with enhanced cost and flexibility pressures and rely on a skilled core workforce that can ensure high responsiveness to clients' requests in terms of designs, quality, and time and supply management. Great functional flexibility is crucial in such a labour regime. Every employee needs to be able to change his or her tasks according to the production requirements of the moment, especially designers and sample-makers. As the manager of a full-package supplier put it:

> We make apparel for babies and for men and women. So, babies, men and women are typologies [of garments] that might seem similar but are actually completely different. Therefore, these [production types] require a workforce that knows how to do all these different things. It requires flexible and open-minded workers [...]. So it is all about the mind and skills of those employees who prepare the samples for men, women, children and [...] so on; you name it. (Interview with manager, I-13)

Working arrangements generally eschew collective agreements and labour laws, but they are not based on a hostile or despotic command because of the need to foster workers' commitment and autonomy. On the contrary, workers are often tied to the employer through personal or familial relations; they face informalization but this is lived as a negotiated process rather than as an overt imposition. Two employees in two different suppliers-without-factories well illustrated some of the dynamics of a hegemonic informalized control regime:

---

them needing to conflict or organize collectively (Ottosson et al., 2020; Gasparri, 2020). Paternalism, as any other labour regime is a continuously contested and negotiated form of control and disciplining as it mixes elements of coercion and hegemony, unilateral command and negotiation.

> Worker 2: [I usually work] five days per week, Monday to Friday. […]. Well, consider that our firm is a sort of family business. So, the manager and the lady that works in administration are siblings; the sample-maker is his brother-in-law […]. So, on Saturday mornings, basically, two or three people meet—that is, me, the manager and the brother—to study the new collections, check the samples, and sketch some new ideas. I join them if I have to fix some of my things, but only casually and for some hours.
>
> Worker 1: [I work] Just five days [per week]. At the end of the day, in my work, I mean, I have some freedom. If I need to, I can go tomorrow and open the office and work. I manage everything in autonomy. (Interview with workers, I-17/18)

Such relationships are based on mutual trust and a friendly and almost familial relationship rather than on the prescription of the collective contract. Workers get rewarded by the employer for their commitment, even though this is not in compliance with formal contractual mechanisms. Production bonuses and overtime, for example, are compensated (in cash) outside the regulation of the contract, and functional flexibility is expected:

> Worker 2: You know, at the end of the month, I always get some extra. It is never quantified. I mean, it is not like X amount per hour.
>
> Worker 1: Everything is according to the rules. I mean, it could happen [that I get] let's call it a [undeclared] production bonus, but, in general, everything follows the contract.
>
> Worker 2: It is also a matter of trust. I will tell you something that happened recently. It was in the first days of August, and we had to deliver the orders. The worker at the warehouse, you know, does his working hours, and that's it. So, the employer and I went, opened the gates for the trucks with the goods that arrived, and offloaded the truck and loaded our own truck. You know, for that activity I got some extra. He [the employer] recognized my work and paid […].
>
> Worker 1: Yes. It is not like in those big companies where you have a badge that counts when you get in and out. The contract is just a formality—an additional thing, let's say.
>
> Worker 2: And anyway, I cannot complain. I don't have to say: 'Don't forget this day I worked longer' or anything. They already know it.
>
> *Me: So if you work more, you get more?*
>
> Worker 2: Exactly, but maybe it is not written anywhere.

> Worker 1: It is not like in big companies with the badge and everything. It is a personal relationship. (Interview with workers, I-17/18)

As the two workers report, family ties or friendship are fundamental to sustaining this kind of informalized labour regime. In these cases, remuneration, rewards, working time, and promotions are decided informally, yet they are not openly oppressive but rather based on employees' cooptation. The promise of future promotions, or in general the ties of an employee to the firm, make sure the informalization of employment is based on a mutual agreement. As one of the two employees pointed out:

> Worker 1: Really, there is a very friendly relationship [among employees and employer]. Imagine, we even go out together—we make little day trips with colleagues, workers, and employers. You know these things in the countryside, little trips […]. And then my wife is the administrative accountant for the firm. So, often I bring the documents home [for her], and she does the accounting for the company. (Interview with workers, I-17/18)

This kind of workplace regime, in other words, copes with a stable but patterned labour process, in which flexibility and commitment are required from workers who have to adapt to intense working periods during peak production and delivery seasons. Remuneration and rewards for overtime often do not comply with the law and the collective agreements and are usually undeclared and paid off the books, in cash. Yet, these employment relations are based on the managerial attempt to build consent and loyalty. A familial atmosphere, informalized reward mechanisms based on mutual trust, and the promise of promotion and professional growth, make this kind of informalization a form of *negotiated consent* (Ram et al., 2007; Ram, 1994; see also: Marchington et al., 2003; for details on the labour regime, see also Table 8.3).

Second-tier suppliers, agile workshops and informalized despotism

For second- and third-tier suppliers, informalization is the main economically viable solution that is compatible with the specific production phases, and the competitive pressures faced. In general, these firms are cutting laboratories and sewing sweatshops in Apulia, big assembly factories of garments and shoes' uppers in Albania, or producers of soles in both regions.

Timing, quantities, and prices are set unilaterally by the buyer, and often these firms are strongly dependent on one or a very few clients. The entry barriers to their core activities are low. Their main comparative advantage is the ability to activate labour when there are orders and keep production costs (mainly labour) down. Moreover, the impossibility to further outsource impairs their ability to cope with production fluctuation through subcontracting. At the same time, the production phases they carry out require, in general, modest skills and commitment. Workers deal with standardized and repetitive production processes that can be controlled either directly by supervisors or through the technical control mechanisms of the assembly line. Informalization in these factories is crucial to cope with flexibility and cost pressures and needs not be hegemonic in any sense. Rather than consent, control can be asserted through coercion as long as workers are easily replaceable.

However, not all firms holding the same position in the chains (i.e., with the same kind of opportunities and pressures to navigate) resort to the same paths of informalization. Indeed, while informality these cases is despotic, labour control regimes in Apulia and Albania maintain important differences. Again, local contexts—and more importantly, the different patterns of labour agency vis-à-vis informalization that emerge in these different settings—are crucial to explaining such variation.

In Albania, second-tier suppliers are rather big factories with a few tens of employees and coercive and systematically informalized employment relations. Their core business relies on the possibility of reducing labour and overhead costs. In these firms, value is created on quantities since mark-ups per piece are very low. As a manager of a single-phase garment supplier in Albania bluntly put it:

> Basically, my only investment and my only advantage is my workforce. I have to put them to work, however. Otherwise, it is worth nothing. (Interview with manager, I-58)

Production fluctuates greatly between high production peaks and low production periods. Production is usually organized in Tayloristic lines of sewing machines or the so-called *manovie,* the conveyor belts used to assemble the pieces of shoes' uppers. These firms need a disciplined and cheap workforce, ready to work overtime in peak production and stay idle (and unpaid) in non-productive months. Informalization, therefore, takes the form of *informalized despotism*, based on over-exploitation, systematic violations of labour laws and workers' rights, and coercive control through aggressive foremen and unilateral pay systems. Trade unions are either inactive or perhaps complicit in the establishment of an informalized despotic labour regime. Lacking any organization to rely on and given the difficulties of bringing individual grievances before the courts, workers respond to informalization and exploitative working conditions through exit—that is, either emigrating or changing employer. Yet, high worker turnover does not impair the functioning of the firms as long as they can find new unskilled workers to take on simple production tasks. Due to fluctuating orders, the labour process in these firms is unpredictable and on demand. The remuneration, and the system of rewards and bonuses, are unilaterally established by the managers. They include mixes of daily pay, quota bonuses, and unpaid overtime. These remain unclear to workers who do not retain any copy of their labour contract. Also, opportunities for promotion are scarce and established unilaterally, while the bargaining mechanisms, when collective agreements exist at the factory level, are generally circumvented by the unilateral imposition of employment terms (see Table 8.3).

In Apulia, however, the forms and organization that single-phase supplier firms take are quite different. They also face unstable production processes that require on-call labour without overhead costs. At the same time, they have to face the rigidities set by labour laws and collective contracts which are more strictly monitored by inspection agencies and local unions. For these reasons, single-phase suppliers struggle to remain union-free, maintain small production facilities partially or totally unregistered, have very short life cycles, depend on a few local clients found through personal networks, and employ only a few workers through the pacting regime or with no contract. Their labour control system, an *agile sweatshop regime*, is informalized and often coercive (even though there are cases of a more benevolent employee–employer relationship), based on the direct control of the manager, the consistent use of pacting, a volatile labour process and constant violations of laws and contracts. These firms remain very small, with usually less than ten workers and anyway never more than the 15-employee threshold that guarantee enhanced union activity protections. The workshops remain small also to avoid the monitoring activities of the labour inspectorate and tax agencies. Workers in agile sweatshops multi-task and are experienced sewers or cutters. They work on-call when employers have orders and stay home without pay when there are no production tasks to be delivered:

> [The firm where I work now does only] the cutting. It has several clients to supply. Cutting is a very quick operation. In the early morning, they [clients or middlemen] bring the fabric, and in the early afternoon, we worked it out already. So he [the employer] counts a lot on speed. Often, we worked even 11 or 12 hours [...]. And you can't plan, you never know who will come. There are periods when, especially when everyone prepares the samples for the Pitti Firenze [fashion fair], all the work accumulates in one day. And later, like in this period, there are whole days when nobody comes, and we stay idle for weeks. (Focus group with workers, I-87/93)

Such flexibility, however, is unilaterally imposed and based on the pacting regime, as this excerpt from a workers' focus group revealed:

> Worker 6: In my case, it is different. When there was work to do in the previous company, we would work overtime, and we got paid in cash off the books.
>
> [Various workers chuckle]
>
> Worker 5: Yes, well, we did not want to mention that.
>
> Worker 6: Yes, the overtime was paid off the books, while now [in the new company I work for] the contract says I should work six hours per day, but I always work at least nine. Sometimes, when there is a lot of work, I have to skip breaks, and I work from 08:00 to 19:00 with no interruption. Of course, I take note of all the hours I work, and I get paid what we verbally agreed on per hour, but it is all a different story on my paycheck.
>
> Worker 1: Oh my [...]. Those things still exist!? (Focus group with workers, I-87/93)

The surprised comment of Worker 1 (an experienced seamstress working in a local lead firm) signalled the coexistence of different levels and kind of employment informalization. Informalization in agile sweatshops is despotic and unilateral, working environment, and the relationships with the employers are often tough, and agency is usually an exercise in exiting rather than an effort in negotiation, resistance, or confrontation:

> Worker 6: Yes. Yes. I mean, it was *exploitation*. I felt *exploited* [...]. But, you know, when there are these things [informalized despotic relationships] in the workplace, there are also always tensions between workers themselves, between workers and the employer, and between workers and supervisors [...]. So if you make a tiny mistake, it is momentous! A tragedy! I mean, I quit for this reason. (Focus group with workers, I-87/93)

Nonetheless, workers' threats of potential lawsuits (supported by local unions) and the risk of unionization maintain agile sweatshops small, with a personalized employer–employee relationship that works as a direct form of normative labour control. A sense of belonging and respect, sometimes weak family ties, and the understanding that employers are also prey to cut-throat competition and powerful clients, in some cases, might defuse resistance. As a worker in the Apulia garment industry recalled:

> [Managers say they cannot formalize my employment relation because] they can't bear the expenses of formally employing a worker full time.
>
> *So they say it is a matter of costs?*
>
> Yes, exactly.
>
> *And what do you think about that?*
>
> No, no—it is true because anyway they also are underpaid and as a consequence, they underpay us. It is all like a chain. (Interview with worker, I-81)

The story of another garment worker is even more telling on this regard. An employee that claimed all her outstanding wages and contributions was even poorly received by other informal workers who instead felt attached to the employer that was going bankrupt and, like them, was struggling against the chain's asymmetrical power relations:

> [Before leaving the company, this worker] wanted the severance pay, up to the very last cent. I mean, we barely got our last salary; we got no severance. The employer would just tell us he did not have money for food. What severance could he ever pay? When the boat sinks, it sinks. You cannot do much about it [...]. So we told the employer: 'Keep yourself out of trouble—pay her, and then later on when you get back on your feet, you will pay us as well'. (Interview with worker, I-4)

All in all, despite variation in size, employee–employer relationships, and production organization, informalized despotism and agile sweatshops share an unstable and unpredictable labour process, unilateral, despotic and individualized employment relations, no formal mechanisms to express grievances and resolve conflicts, and opaque and unilateral setting of remuneration, working time, rewards and bonuses (see Table 8.3).

Table 8.3. Varieties of labour control regimes within the chain

	Lead firm *Bureaucratic regime*	First-tier supplier *Paternalistic (informalised hegemonic) regime*	Single-phase supplier (second and third tiers) *Agile sweatshop regime and (informalised despotism)*
Labour process	Stable: clear working time and periods (8 or 4 hours per day, five days per week); rare overtime; scientific time-management of working phases; strategic planning to ensure stable work for a core workforce despite seasonality and fluctuations; stable outsourcing of peak production, use of temp agencies or reliance on public temporary layoff funds to secure the income of workers during non-productive periods.	Stable but patterned along production cyclicity and seasonality; higher workload, prolonged working day, work in festive days, multiple tasks required in peak production periods.	Unstable and unpredictable; intensity and tasks are highly fluctuating according to seasonality, orders and managers' needs; changing duration and intensity of the working day according to the orders (work on-call when needed and until the needed output is produced). In *Apulia*: flexible multi-tasking (changing tasks according to the day's needs). In *Albania*: fixed roles in assembly lines; increasing intensity.
Remuneration, rewards and bonuses	In line with the National Collective Agreements: working hour and extra-time remunerated at extra rate; payment through transparent bank transfer. Thirteenth monthly pay; extra-time paid at increased rate or through paid leaves (time banks); paid leaves regulated by the National Collective Agreements.	Mixed: basic salary and thirteen-month-pay paid according to collective contracts; overtime, work in festivities and prolonged shifts remunerated in cash at employers' will.	By hour (and by piece-rate) established unilaterally (by the employer) according to experience, skills and tasks (lower than collective and labour laws); envelope wage; In Albania, deductions are commonly applied when a daily production quota is not reached. Rare and arbitrary bonuses (linked often to personal worker-manager ties); arbitrary paid leave; extra-time remunerated at normal hourly rate (in Apulia) or not remunerated at all (in Albania).
Internal labour market	Seniority pay increases established in National Collective Agreements (NCA); promotions and career advancement related to the personal choice of the employers or manager.	Informal promise of future advancement in tasks, responsibility and employment ranking/remuneration level; promotions and career advancement related to the arbitrary power of the employer.	No career advancement; changing tasks according to the production needs (with stable remuneration); higher levels of workers' turnover.
Bargaining mechanisms	National collective bargaining arena; second-tier/plant-level collective bargaining (rare few cases in Apulia and one in Albania); mediation of union delegates, and firms' HRM consultants.	Mixed: initially *[illegible] regime*. Individualised worker-employer relations; personal ties and affiliation; paternalistic hierarchy.	In Apulia: Individualised [illegible] regime; In Albania: Individualised and despotic worker-employer relations.
Grievance-resolution mechanisms	Individual relation and/or union-mediated practices (with plant or territorial union delegates); Major conflict (and termination) are dealt with through highly formalised procedures (formal communication with appeal rights). Collective and individual dismissals are mediated with unions representatives.	Individual and informal relations only; leveraging personal ties and affiliations.	Individual and informal relations only; Major conflicts and termination are dealt with through the threat of lawsuit (with the support of external union advisors) in Italy; through exit in Albania (turnover/poaching or migration).

Source: Author's elaboration based on the labour control regime framework as stylized in Burawoy (1985, chap. 3)

Besides these different types of employment relations, hybrid labour control regimes might exist when firms change position within chains or when workers increase their associational power. For example, what I labelled a *crisis bureaucratic regime* in Table 8.2 coincides with high workers' market bargaining and associational powers but also highly competitive pressures. This means that informalization is precluded by unionization, mere coercion is not a viable option because of the need to retain skilled workers, and yet competitive pressures are increasing. This represents the condition of a lead firm facing a crisis and perhaps undergoing a downgrading process or a first-tier supplier in which workers are organizing and pushing for full compliance with contracts and laws. In the former case, unions will most probably become co-managers of the crisis yet ensure compliance with minimum standards. As a trade union described, for example:

> We don't have conflicts in this sector with the union I represent. We represent workers and workers' interest decently, but at the same time, we know the territory here, and we tend to be conciliatory [with employers] because we know there are very fragile equilibria. Often, when you talk to firms, they would just show us the copies of the commercial agreements that they have with the big fashion houses in Milan or wherever there are the hearts of the industry, and then, everything is set in stone. The firm shows you, very transparently, their revenues, and how much they get paid [by their clients]...because they get paid per minute or per piece. And then it is just about doing the number, firm and unions together, and you realize that after paying for salaries, social insurance, rent, there is nothing left, sometimes not even what would be the return for the same entrepreneur. [...] So, again, we don't have leeway to go beyond the national collective contract and complying with it; it is already a big win. (Interview with unionist, I-24; quoted in Bagnardi et al., 2022, p. 48)

In other cases, the process of unionization within a first-tier supplier might well incur protracted conflicts and negotiations to secure full compliance with contracts and laws. As an employee within an expanding local footwear supplier recalled, his colleagues and him unionized because of '*force majeure circumstances*' (interview with worker, I-94). The employer, in fact, had funded a new company operating within the premises of the warehouse of the first company. He then fired many employees of the old company just to re-hire them in the new company. He repeated the trick twice in a few years to access fiscal incentives related to new hiring. For workers, nothing really changed but their payrolls: seniority pay increase were zeroed, and the second time even the severance was not paid. Workers asked for unions' support and unionized. This created tension within the factory and a slow negotiation to get the employer to comply with workers' rights. As the employee recalled:

> This time [the employer] just cheated on us. He did not pay the severance, and still, he is not paying.
>
> *What do you plan to do about it?*
>
> We will wait, now.
>
> *And what did the union say when you address them?*
>
> They said they also have tied hands. I mean, we unionized, and we could fight, they said. But if you start a fight with these people [the employers], they are ruthless. You never know how it will end. So, for now, we are cautious and wait. Anyway, I think he will also pay this time in the end. He is just keeping us under pressure. (Interview with worker, I-94)

In such cases, the prevailing labour regime will depend on the parties' relative bargaining powers and the firm's financial leeway.

Finally, the informalized hegemonic regime is a viable solution not only for non-unionized first-tier suppliers that face high competitive pressures but also for lead firms facing low competitive pressures but without effective unions. This is probably a rarer case since lead firms are usually associated with unionized workers with multiple unions, yet it remains a possibility.

8.4. *Making sense of informality variegation*

To conclude, lead firms, intermediaries, and sub-suppliers located in Apulia share a common set of formal and informal institutions and yet develop different labour regimes and resort to a different extent to informal employment relationships. On the contrary, sub-suppliers in Apulia and Albania, while holding the same position within the chains, respond with different informalization dynamics to similar chain pressures. As proposed in Chapter 2, through a fine-grained analysis of GPNs and labour regimes—namely, the differentiated economic structures of pressures and opportunities that firms face—these differences between different informalized labour regimes become clearer. In this perspective, economic structures do not replace institutions as the explicans of informality but instead call for an analysis of how chain pressures, together with local contexts, influence actors' bargaining power and their agency. In so doing, one can explain the different forms of informalization (hegemonic or despotic) that characterize the labour regimes of intermediaries and sub-suppliers. Institutions do not explain differences in informalization in this case, but chain pressures do. By the same token, the variations in informalization patterns and labour regimes found in Italian and Albanian second- and third-tier suppliers can be explained by different workers' associational power rather than by structural constraints. While the peripheral position and the competitive pressures, risks and uncertainty of production of these firms are similar in both contexts, it is the presence of effective trade unions that maintain coercive informalization small and hidden in Apulian workshops, overt and massive in big Albanian firms.

If informalization is an important feature of labour control regimes, then its persistence and differentiation depend on the continuous employees-employer negotiations of their employment relationship. Thus, rather than assuming the persistence of informality resulting from enduring unfavourable structural pressures or institutional fallacies, my framework brings agency into the picture and unpacks how actors impose or resist, disrupt or reproduce informalization dynamics.

Moreover, my findings challenge the dichotomous reading of informality as the realm of downgraded labour or the sphere of harmonious capitalism driven by benevolent informal communities. By drawing on the concept of labour control, this analytical framework can explain the conditions under which informality becomes a tool for unilateral coercion or rather a form of negotiated consent.

Finally, the framework developed offers a perspective that brings informalization back in the broader studies of employment relations and avoids considering informality a *sui generis*, deviant behaviour to be studied for itself. My framework provides an analytical toolbox to analyse the interlinkages between (informalized) labour processes and GPNs in an innovative way. While usually the approaches that combine LPT and GVCs look at the governance of GVCs to explain how the pressures of being integrated end up shaping the emerging labour control regimes in some supplier firms (see: Newsome et al. 2015; Hammer and Plugor 2019; Flecker et al., 2013), *this approach looks at the entire chain simultaneously.* It is not merely a lens to explain how labour regimes in some nodes of the chain can be understood in light of the governance of that chain; it is instead a framework to explain production networks *as networks of fragmented but functionally integrated labour control regimes* (see also López, 2021;

Bagnardi, 2023b). Thus, it analyses how labour regimes in different locales of the network—and the informalization patterns prevailing within—are co-constituted and interdependent. In other words, I show that the emergence of hegemonic regimes in lead firms banks on the emergence of other kind of more or less coercive and informalized regimes that allow enhanced flexibility in other nodes of the chain. As such, hegemonic regimes can only be reproduced as long as other regimes emerge and endure, and the persistence of one regime is guaranteed by and guarantees the persistence of the others. Thus, contrary to other similar approaches, my framework allows for an encompassing analysis of the entire chain and takes seriously the re-interpretation of GVCs/GPNs as chains of 'embodied labour' structured around the imperative of disciplining labour to produce and capture the value it creates.

9.
CONCLUSIONS

The persistence of informal employment, despite widespread costs for all actors involved, makes informality a matter of increasing attention for scholars and policymakers alike. The advanced economies of the European Union are not an exception. In 2016, as a sign of commitment in the fight against informal employment, the European Commission set up the *European Platform tackling undeclared work*. The platform brings together different authorities and actors that are involved in the fight against informal work in the member states. The platform has been integrated within the European Labour Authority as a permanent working group in May 2021, and it represents the highest institutional forum entirely dedicated to the fight informal work in Europe. Its strategic priorities are fostering cooperation, carrying out research, disseminating best practices and promoting joint actions such as capacity building, cross-border cooperation, creating common tools for inspectorates among member states (European Platform tackling undeclared work, 2021; 2022). The platform aims to be not only the forum where national policies are discussed and evaluated by member states but also the specialized powerhouse dedicated to the creation of knowledge on undeclared work in the EU.

The working of the Platform has so far been centred around the so-called 'holistic approach'[1] that focuses on designing a balanced policy mix of deterrence, monitoring, incentives for formalization, and awareness campaigns to increase citizens' trust in institutions. While the approach presents several important novelties, it seems to be well rooted within the new institutionalist perspective. As such, it overlooks completely the role of power relations and structural constraints in informalization dynamics. The emphasis of the Platform documents, in fact, has been so far on

1 As the Platform's official document reports "[a]t the Plenary meeting on 25 October 2019, the Platform decided to set up a working group on 'Holistic approaches to tackling undeclared work and developing national strategies'." (Williams, 2020, p. 1).

raising awareness of rules, reducing bureaucratic hurdles, and enhancing workers' trust in institutions. Little attention is, instead, paid to the crucial preventative and reporting role that workers might play whenever they have the power to resist informalization practices. In the workings of the Platform, informalization is not perceived explicitly as a way to increase workers' disposability, and therefore the possibility to enhance workers' power to resist exploitation as a way to rebut informalization practices is never taken into account. In line with the new institutionalist perspective, informalization is instead seen as a product of institutions and the individual perception of their rightness rather than as a matter of power relations, lack of alternatives, and labour control.

In the wake of the Covid-19 pandemic, informal workers and the social consequences of working conditions in informalized workplaces came to the fore of public debate. It was like, for a short period, the workplace returned to be a crucial matter of discussion and analysis: it could be the place where the virus spreads and, at the same time, the lieu of production of much needed essential goods. Informal workers often emerged as the ones carrying out those productive and reproductive activities that were deemed crucial for everyone's life. At the same time, they turned to be the least protected by the formal institutional responses to the pandemic. On the one hand, informals were less likely to be covered by temporary protection and income support measures amidst lockdowns; on the other hand, their work appeared as crucial as ever, very often falling within the category of essential activities. Seasonal and precarious work, often carried out by migrants in agri-food and care chains emerged as crucial and yet strenuously informalized and greatly exposed to the risk of contagion (Caruso and Lo Cascio, 2020; Cosma et al., 2021; Mostaccio, 2021; Tagliacozzo et al., 2021).

Against this background, for the first time, the European Platform, in its first 2021 plenary session, debated the relation between undeclared work and exploitation, even though with a narrow focus on non-EU migrant labourers (van Nierop et al., 2021). While the Platform's documents generally recognized that informalization impairs workers' rights and protections, this was the first time it explicitly enquired into the relationship between the two phenomena. Nonetheless, even in this case, policy recommendations stressed the need for inspection agencies to build trust with non-EU migrant workers rather than problematizing the asymmetrical power relations that favour informalization dynamics. Best practices and recommendations focused on proactive initiatives taken by inspectors to locate the workers directly where they work and to approach them with the support of cultural mediators. Such practices are explicitly deemed crucial to building workers' trust in institutions. Yet, while these measures are important to establishing the first contact with workers and can be used to inform them about their rights, support them when in need, and provide a channel for reporting the offences received, they are still not really a way to structurally rebalance the power relations that allows and reproduces informalization dynamics. More recent activities of the platform have focussed on undeclared/under-declared non-EU posted workers (European Platform tackling undeclared work, 2024a). Also in this case, recommendations focus on sharing with workers information about rules, rights and duties, simplifying regulations and appealing to employers' compliance with due diligence principles.

Building on the framework and the finding of this book, I contend that anti-informality measures should not only aim to increase workers' trust in institutions but should instead aim to empower these same workers, creating the conditions to resist informalization collectively, or at least to report and perhaps access to justice while not putting them in danger to lose their source of livelihood. Such a trade-off between resisting informalization and impairing your own primary source of income is a burden that cannot be offloaded on informalized workers alone. In other words, building trust is not enough; it needs to be coupled with ways for workers to collectively resist informalization and with effective and substantive access to justice, the possibility to find redress in a reasonable time without unsustainable cost, and the possibility to find an alternative, formal source of income. An encompassing strategy for formalization needs to ensure that such workers are not at risk of deportation or just unemployment after having reported their exploiters. Again, it is not only about trust, as this alone would not do. It is about having the material preconditions and the power to resist or report informalized exploitation.

The platform has recently dedicated a subgroup to the issue of safe reporting and complain mechanisms for workers (European platform tackling undeclared work, 2024b). The subgroup surveyed national best practices to protect workers who report informalization to the authorities and recognized the need and challenges to make reporting safe. Also in this case, however, the main focus is on measures that protect the most vulnerable non-EU workers and most dramatic forms of informalization. And while measures to make reporting mechanisms easier and more accessible abound, protections for workers who denounce remain minimal and selective. There is no discussion, instead, on measures that could facilitate the collective organization of workers so that collective resistance to exploitative forms of informalization becomes easier.

This book warns exactly against the risks of simplification and mono-causal explanations of the persistence of informal employment. If informal employment is predominantly framed as a matter of institutional mismatch, the fight against it lies on the realignment of such mismatch, that is, among other things, in re-establishing workers' trust in (monitoring) institutions. Yet, this risks providing only partial solutions because it does not engage with the role of power of the agents involved and structural economic constraints.

To return to the theoretical debates addressed and the contribution of the book, I showed that informality means different things to different people, it encompasses different phenomena, and respond to a variety of diverse drivers and dynamics. That is why I focused on *one specific slice* of the pie: the informalization of dependent employment. Yet, even with such a restrained object of research, the research showed that explanations that look only at institutions or structural drivers are often ill-equipped.

Thus, starting from a redefinition of informalization as a tool of labour control, I advanced a novel theoretical framework that can analytically keep together institutional contexts, structural drivers, and workers' and firms' agency. Such framework has been the result of a continuous iteration between theoretical and empirical advancement of the research. It relies on an extended structuralist approach that maintains the core postulate of the structuralist perspective on informality intact but provides an analytical expansion to account for agency in informalization dynamics. I applied the extended structural approach to the garment-footwear sector in Italy and Albania. This represented a typical case study and allowed me to tease out and analyse the mechanisms behind informal employment's reproduction along a common GPNs but within two different socio-institutional contexts.

First, I sketched an analysis of the politics behind the policies against informalization in Italy and Albania. Within such perspective, the making of policies against informality and the set up and functioning of monitoring institutions can be re-examined not merely in terms of institutional capacities and failures but rather as processes carried out by political actors, within specific economic and political contexts, that need to navigate economic pressures, distributive consequences of their choices, and the political costs and returns of their actions. Such analysis showed that political actors have different approaches to informalization and that even those political actors committed to tackle informality have to cope with the economic and political costs of eradication or formalization campaigns. Anti-informality policies might well be reversed by political competitors once in power, and even apparently hard measures of deterrence might selectively tackle certain forms of informal employment, the most dramatic ones, while remaining relatively tolerant of others. The role of informalization in crucial sectors of the national and regional economies in Italy and Albania, and the political costs that eradicating informality would entail, shaped anti-informality policies and favoured a low-compliance equilibrium in which entirely unregistered employment decreases but other forms of informalization remain. Consequently, an enquiry into the politics of anti-informality campaigns revealed that formal regulations and monitoring mechanisms might well end up focussing their efforts in tackling dramatic forms of informality while forbearing the persistence of new forms of partial informalization dynamics.

Against this background, the persistent sectoral variations in informalization dynamics across different institutional settings call for an in-depth analysis of mechanisms and patterns of agency that reproduce informality. The garment-footwear sector provided a typical case to investigate the role that informalization plays in complex production processes, the importance of sectoral constraints, and the mechanisms through which local context and actors' agency actively reproduce variegated regimes of informalized employment.

An in-depth analysis of informalization practices within the workplace showed that informalized employment not only cuts production costs but it also enhances workers' disposability and helps firms coping with the structural pressures of fast-changing, buyer-driven value chains. However, informalized employment relations are not all equal, and informality might result from despotic imposition or negotiated consent.

The book detailed how reframing informalization as labour control allows for a more nuanced analysis of its role within GPNs and helps to investigate how informalization intertwines with local dynamics of workers' segmentation. Moreover, a framework rooted in LPT enables us not to overlook how informalization dynamics, even when despotic and unilateral, are always the result of workers' and employers' continuous negotiation.

Such an approach allowed me to trace workers' agency even when collective organization and organized forms of contentiousness were absent. The multiple forms of workers' agency, including their individual actions for redress through the support of unions' offices or their multiple exit strategies, significantly contribute to shape differentiated labour regimes and the informalization dynamics that characterize them. The research finds that effective and plural unions make it very difficult for firms to impose informalization practices on unionized workers. Moreover, trade unions' offices represent a potential resource for those workers who want to resist informalization by confronting their employers through legal action. This prevents massive forms of despotic informalization in Apulia but not in Albania, where legacy unions are ineffective in representing workers' interests. In the former case, despotic informalization remains rooted in small sweatshops, while in Albania informalization prevails in bigger factories with production organized along assembly lines. Yet, other forms of hegemonic informalization emerge when workers are not unionized but they retain some form of individual bargaining power since the firm depends on their skills and commitment. In these cases, informality can serve to cope with the chain's requirements of flexibility, speed and quality but consent rather than coercion drives the informalization path.

The coexistence of formal and variegated informalized labour regimes within the same production networks and across institutional contexts needs therefore to be understood at the crossroad of structural pressures exemplified by the position of a firm within the chain, the replaceability of workers given by the combination of productive specialization and local labour supply, and workers' associational power. These three dimensions led to a labour regime typology of the complex dynamics encountered that works as an explanatory device and a summarizing expedient. In fact, the typology in Chapter 8 (Table 8.2) shows how the role of firms and workers agency, given their situated negotiating powers shape labour regimes. At the same time, it problematizes how workers agency vis-à-vis informalization and firms' informalizing strategies remain deeply embedded within structural constraints (i.e., the governance of and position within the chain) and the specific local contexts (i.e., the local labour markets or the presence of functioning workers' associations and the possibility for workers' individual forms of exit).

The research presents several limitations as well. First, it focuses on garment-footwear in Italy and Albania, a specific sector and two specific countries where informalization practices are common and well-entrenched. While this choice increased the possibility of actually getting in touch with hard-to-reach research participants and provided a typical case study setting to analyse dynamics and mechanisms of the persistence of informality, it also raises questions on the generalizability of the research findings. On the one hand, thinking in terms of labour control and power relations certainly provides a fine-grained analytical toolkit to analyse informalization dynamics in the workplace in different situations. On the other hand, the typology of labour regimes and the crucial dimensions underpinning it would need revision according to different structural constraints and labour process characteristics of other industries. Therefore, while the theoretical framework might be applied easily to fragmented and asymmetrical production chains, it would need partial reworking for other less fragmented and asymmetrical sectors.

Other limitations of the study concern the segments of the GPNs analysed. While I analysed the positioning of local lead firms, those encountered were predominantly medium-sized firms. It will be fruitful to investigate how labour regimes work in global or macro-regional lead firms and assess if the same dynamics encountered in this study are at play in such firms.

Thirdly, combining GPNs and LPT provides a set of analytical tools to overcome the connectivity gap of labour process analysis, yet there are factors that play a crucial role in the control-resistance dynamics that originate outside of the workplace and that could be factored in the analysis in a more comprehensive way and as object of analysis in their own right. In this research, the gendered devaluation of informalized workers clearly signalled the mutually reinforcing relations between exploitation in the workplace and gendered domination within and beyond production. The recent debate on *local labour regimes* (Baglioni et al, 2022) as analytical tools to account for the disciplining factors outside the workplace that shape control dynamics within production represents a promising pathway for the analysis of informalization as well.

Finally, one has to add the multiple limits of the empirical data collection techniques adopted (analysed in detail in Chapter 3) and the simplification in-built in the summarizing typology of labour regimes (in Chapter 8). Nonetheless, the research offers a novel framework that reinforces structuralist approaches and brings capitalism and its power relations back in the scholarly and political debate on employment informalization.

10.
ANNEX
List of Interviews

ID INTERVIEW	ROLE OF THE INTERVIEWEE	LOCATION	DATE
I-1	Trade unionist	BAT	June 2018
I-2	Expert – Local think tank	BAT	June 2018
I-3	Manager (garment firm); President of local garment-footwear Consortium	BAT	June 2018
I-4	Worker (garment)	BAT	June 2018
I-5	Local Councillor	BAT	June 2018
I-6	Former head of the regional labour department; Expert	Foggia	June 2018
I-7	Trade unionist	BAT	July 2018
I-8	Trade unionist	BAT	July 2018
I-9	Firms' HRM consultant (garment and footwear)	BAT	July 2018
I-10	President business organization; vice-president of a local consortium	BAT	July 2018
I-11/12	President and board member business organization	BAT	July 2018
I-13	Manager (garment)	BAT	July 2018

I-14	Worker (garment)	BAT	July 2018
I-15	Worker (footwear, garment)	BAT	July 2018
I-16	President regional business organization	Bari	August 2018
I-17/18	Workers (garment)	BAT	August 2018
I-19	Clean Clothes Campaign expert	Tirana (distance interview)	October 2018
I-20	Labour inspector	Bari	October 2018
I-21	Expert	Tirana (telephone interview)	October 2018
I-22	Manager; President regional business organization (garment)	Bari	October 2018
I-23	Sales manager (footwear)	BAT (telephone interview)	October 2018
I-24	Trade unionist	Bari	October 2018
I-25	Firms' consultant (supporting Italian investors in Albania)	Bari	October 2018
I-26	Trade unionist	Bari	October 2018
I-27/28	Firms' HRM consultant (garment and footwear)	BAT	October 2018
I-29	Manager; president regional business organization (footwear)	BAT	October 2018
I-30	Trade unionist	Bari	October 2018
I-31	Manager (footwear)	BAT	October 2018

I-32	Expert (economist)	Bari	October 2018
I-33	Labour inspector	Bari	October 2018
I-34	Apulia regional government executive (Regional office in Albania)	Bari	October 2018
I-35/38 focus group	Managers, one worker (garment)	Bari	October 2018
I-39	Apulia regional government executive (Regional office in Albania)	Bari	October 2018
I-40	Apulia regional government executive (Regional office in Albania)	Bari	October 2018
I-41	NGO representatives (labour issues)	Tirana	November 2018
I-42	Expert (journalist, Italian Embassy in Albania executive)	Tirana	November 2018
I-43	Expert (investigative journalist)	Tirana	November 2018
I-44	NGO consultant (GIZ)	Tirana	November 2018
I-45	Social movement unionists	Tirana	November 2018
I-46	Expert (law professor)	Tirana	November 2018
I-47	Expert (economist)	Tirana	November 2018
I-48	Former Economy minister; expert (economist)	Tirana	November 2018
I-49	NGO representative (labour and OSH issues)	Tirana	November 2018
I-50	NGO head (labour, women's rights issue)	Tirana	November 2018

I-51	Trade unionist	Tirana	November 2018
I-52	Expert (sociologist)	Tirana	November 2018
I-53	Manager (garment)	Shkoder	December 2018
I-54	Manager (garment)	Shkoder	December 2018
I-55	Manager (footwear)	Shkoder	December 2018
I-56	Manager (garment)	Shkoder	December 2018
I-57	Manager (garment)	Tirana	December 2018
I-58	Manager (garment)	Tirana	December 2018
I-59	Managers (garment)	Tirana	December 2018
I-60	Manager (garment)	Elbasan	December 2018
I-61	Firms consultant; expert (textile/ fashion development)	Tirana	December 2018
I-62	Expert (economics researcher)	Tirana	December 2018
I-63	Firms' doctor specialized in OSH issues	Tirana	December 2018
I-64/67 focus group	Workers (footwear)	Tirana	December 2018
I-68	Manager (footwear)	Tirana	December 2018
I-69	Manager (garment)	Tirana	December 2018

I-70	Manager (footwear)	Krujë	December 2018
I-71	Trade unionist	Krujë	December 2018
I-72	Managers (garment)	Berat	December 2018
I-73	Managers (footwear)	Shkoder	December 2018
I-74	Member of Apulia regional task force against informality; Expert (lawyer)	Bari	January 2019
I-75	Former luxury brand supply manager; writer	BAT	January 2019
I-76	Manager (garment)	BAT	January 2019
I-77	Trade unionist	BAT	January 2019
I-78	Trade unionist	Bari	January 2019
I-79	Trade unionist	Bari	January 2019
I-80	Trade unionist	Bari	January 2019
I-81	Worker (garment)	BAT	February 2019
I-82	Manager (technical garment); former manager (safety footwear)	BAT	February 2019
I-83	Trade unionist	BAT	February 2019
I-84	Manager (footwear, garment)	BAT	February 2019
I-85	Manager (footwear)	BAT (telephone interview)	February 2019
I-86	Worker and shop steward (foowear)	BAT	February 2019

I-87/93 focus group	Workers (garment)	Bari	February 2019
I-94	Worker (footwear)	BAT	February 2019
I-95	Manager (garment)	Bari	February 2019
I-96	Designer, worker (garment)	Bari	February 2019
I-97	Manager (garment)	Bari	February 2019
I-98	Trade unionist	Bari	February 2019
I-99	Regional councillor	BAT	February 2019
I-100	Business Organization's president	Tirana	February 2019
I-101	Manager (footwear)	Shkoder	February 2019
I-102	Former labour inspector; OSH expert	Tirana	February 2019
I-103	Head of the Albanian Investment Council	Tirana	February 2019
I-104	Labour inspector	Tirana	February 2019
I-105	Labour Inspector	Tirana	February 2019
I-106	NGO executive (labour issues and women's rights)	Vlore	February 2019
I-107/111 focus group	Workers (garment)	Elbasan	February 2019
I-112/118	Workers (garment, footwear)	Lezhe	February 2019

11. BIBLIOGRAPHY

Abernathy, F. H., Dunlop, J., Hammond, J., & Weil, D. (1999). *A Stitch in Time: Lean Retailing and the Transformation of Manufacturing. Lessons from the Apparel and Textile Industries*. Oxford University Press.

Abernathy, F. H., Volpe, A., & Weil, D. (2006). The Future of the Apparel and Textile Industries: Prospects and Choices for Public and Private Actors. *Environment and Planning A: Economy and Space*, *38*(12), 2207–2232. https://doi.org/10.1068/a38114

ACIT. (2010). *Social Dimensions of the Global Crisis in Albania- The Fason Industry as a Case Study*. Albanian Center for International Trade. http://acit.al/index.php/en/

Afonso, A. (2019). Migrant Workers or Working Women? Comparing Labour Supply Policies in Post-War Europe. *Journal of Comparative Policy Analysis: Research and Practice*, *21*(3), 251–269. https://doi.org/10.1080/13876988.2018.1527584

Afonso, A., & Bulfone, F. (2019). Electoral Coalitions and Policy Reversals in Portugal and Italy in the Aftermath of the Eurozone Crisis. *South European Society and Politics*, *24*(2), 233–257. https://doi.org/10.1080/13608746.2019.1644809

AIC. (2015). *Informality: A common Government-Business Challenge* [Working Document]. Albanian Investment Council.

AIC. (2019). *Investment Climate 2018, On Inspections* [Technical Note]. Albanian Investment Council.

AIDA. (2014). *Made in Albania—Footwear Industry*. Albanian Investment Development Agency (AIDA) and USAID.

AIDA. (2019). *Textile Sector—Country Stand of Albania. A+A International Trade Fair 2019*. Albanian Investment Development Agenct. http://aida.gov.al/broshura/

Aliyev, H. (2014). The effects of the Saakashvili era reforms on informal practices in the Republic of Georgia. *Studies of Transition States and Societies*, *6*(1), 19–33.

Aliyev, H. (2015). Institutional Transformation and Informality in Azerbaijan and Georgia. In Morris, J. & Polese, A. (eds.) *Informal Economies in Post-Socialist Spaces. Practices, Institutions and Networks* (pp. 51–69). Springer.

Aliyev, H. (2016). End to informality? Examining the impact of institutional reforms on informal institutions in post-Euromaidan Ukraine. *Journal of Contemporary Central and Eastern Europe*, *24*(3), 207–221. https://doi.org/10.1080/0965156X.2016.1260206

Almond, P., & Connolly, H. (2020). A manifesto for 'slow' comparative research on work and employment. *European Journal of Industrial Relations*, *26*(1), 59–74. https://doi.org/10.1177/0959680119834164

Amable, B., & Palombarini, S. (2014). The bloc bourgeois in France and Italy. In H. Magara, *Economic Crises and Policy Regimes: The dynamics of Policy Innovation and Paradigmatic Change* (pp. 177–217). Edward Elgar.

Amengual, M. (2016). *Politicized Enforcement in Argentina: Labor and Environment Regulation*. Cambridge University Press.

Amighini, A., & Rabellotti, R. (2006). How do Italian footwear industrial districts face globalization? *European Planning Studies*, *14*(4), 485–502. https://doi.org/10.1080/09654310500421105

Anamali, A., Zisi, A., & Shosha, B. (2015). Albanian Apparel Industry and Its Characteristics of Development. *Academic Journal of Interdisciplinary Studies*, *4*(3), 585–589.

Andersson, J., Berg, A., Hedrich, S., & Magnus, K.-H. (2018). *Is apparel manufacturing coming home? | McKinsey*. McKinsey Apparel, Fashion & Luxury Group.

Anner, M. (2015a). Labor control regimes and worker resistance in global supply chains. *Labor History*, *56*(3), 292–307. https://doi.org/10.1080/0023656X.2015.1042771

Anner, M. (2015b). Social Downgrading and Worker Resistance in Apparel Global Value Chains. In K. Newsome, P. Taylor, J. Bair, & A. Rainnie, *Putting labour in its place: Labour process analysis and global value chains* (pp. 152–171). Palgrave.

Anner, M. (2020). Squeezing workers' rights in global supply chains: Purchasing practices in the Bangladesh garment export sector in comparative perspective. *Review of International Political Economy*, *27*(2), 320–347. https://doi.org/10.1080/09692290.2019.1625426

Anzovino, M., & Regalia, I. (2020). Employment Relations in Small Italian Firms: An Overview. In I. Regalia (Ed.), *Regulating Work in Small Firms: Perspectives on the Future of Work in Globalised Economies* (pp. 33–94). Palgrave Macmillan.

Arqimandriti, M., Llubani, M., & Ljarja, A. (2016). *Wage and Labour Conditions of Shoe and Garment Workers in Albania*. Gender Alliance for Development Center, Friedrich Ebert Stitfung, Clean Clothes Campaign.

ARTI. (2020). *Filiera TAC in Puglia. Una nota del Tavolo della Statistica Territoriale—Puglia.* Consiglio Regionale della Puglia - Agenzia regionale per la tecnologia e l'innovazione.

ARTI, 2021. TAC – Tessile Abbigliamento Calzature. Outlook Report, n. 4. Agenzia regionale per la Tecnologia e l'Innovazione, Regione Puglia - - Agenzia regionale per la tecnologia e l'innovazione

Assaad, R. (1993). Formal and informal institutions in the labor market, with applications to the construction sector in Egypt. *World Development*, *21*(6), 925–939.

Avola, M. (2007). *Lavoro irregolare e politiche pubbliche. La costruzione sociale del sommerso e le misure di contrasto e di emersione*, Bonanno Editore.

Baccaro, L., & Howell, C. (2017). *Trajectories of neoliberal transformation European industrial relations since the 1970s.* Cambridge University Press.

Baez, A. (2014). *A panel data analysis of FDI and informal labor markets* (Working Paper No. 4). Research Institute of Applied Economics, Universitat de Barcelona.

Baglioni, E. (2018). Labour control and the labour question in global production networks: exploitation and disciplining in Senegalese export horticulture, *Journal of Economic Geography*, Volume 18(1), 111–137. https://doi.org/10.1093/jeg/lbx013

Baglioni, E., Campling, L., Coe, N. M., & Smith, A. (Eds.). (2022). *Labour regimes and global production.* Agenda Publishing.

Bagnardi, F. (2023a). Informal employment and the multiplication of regulatory spaces in the Italian construction sector. *Rassegna Italiana di Sociologia*, 2, 345-374. Doi: 10.1423/107863

Bagnardi, F. (2023b). Manufacturing informality. Global production networks and the reproduction of informalized labour regimes in Europe's peripheries. *European Journal of Industrial Relations*, 29(3), 271-299. https://doi.org/10.1177/09596801231167160

Bagnardi, F., D'Onofrio, G., Greco, L. (2022). The state in chains: public policies against adverse incorporation in Southern Italian production networks. *Globalizations*, 19(1), 34-58. Doi: 10.1080/14747731.2020.1849908

Bagnardi, F. and Maccarrone, V., 2023. Labour process theory: taking stock and looking ahead. *Sociologia del Lavoro*, 167, 33–55. Doi: 10.3280/sl2023-167002

Bagnardi, F., & Petrović, V. (2020). Post-socialist labour and the dual logic of collective action: Workers' unrest and trade union strategy in Fiat Automobiles Serbia. *Transfer: European Review of Labour and Research*, *26*(4), 415–430. https://doi.org/10.1177/1024258919879803

Bair, J. (2009). *Frontiers of commodity chain research*. Stanford University Press.

Bair, J. (2010). On Difference and Capital: Gender and the Globalization of Production. *Signs*, *36*(1), 203–226. https://doi.org/10.1086/652912

Bair, J., & Werner, M. (2011). Commodity Chains and the Uneven Geographies of Global Capitalism: A Disarticulations Perspective. *Environment and Planning A*, *43*(5), 988–997. https://doi.org/10.1068/a43505

Baldassarre, F., Salomone, S., Santovito, S., & Silvestri, R. (2014). Prospettive e criticità nella rilocalizzazione delle produzioni manifatturiere. Il backshoring delle imprese tessili pugliesi. *XXXVI Convegno Annuale Di Sinergie - Manifattura: Quale Futuro?* XXXVI Convegno Annuale di Sinergie - Manifattura: quale futuro?, Università di Cassino e del Lazio Meridionale. https://doi.org/10.7433/SRECP.2014.28

Banca d'Italia. (2010). *Measuring the price elasticity of import demand in the destination markets of Italian exports* (Working Papers 776). Banca d'Italia.

Banca d'Italia. (2017). *Back on track? A macro-micro narrative of Italian exports* (Occasional Papers 399; Questioni Di Economia e Finanza). Banca d'Italia.

Banfield, E., C. (1958). *The Moral Basis of a Backward Society*. The Free Press.

Barbieri, M. (2010). L'intervento comunitario di contrasto al lavoro nero alla luce dell esperienza italiana. *Rivista Italiana Di Diritto Del Lavoro*, *2*, 71–109.

Barbieri, P., & Fratocchi, L. (2017). Le peculiarità del reshoring manufatturiero in Italia: Un'analisi basata su dati secondari. *L'industria*, *38*(3), 317–339.

Barrientos, S. (2002). Mapping codes through the value chain: From researcher to detective. In R. Jenkins, R. Pearson, & G. Seyfang (Eds.), *Corporate Responsibility and Labour Rights: Codes of Conduct in the Global Economy* (pp. 61–78). Earthscan Publications.

Barrientos, S. (2013). 'Labour Chains': Analysing the Role of Labour Contractors in Global Production Networks. *The Journal of Development Studies*, *49*(8), 1058–1071. https://doi.org/10.1080/00220388.2013.780040

Barrientos, S., Gereffi, G., & Rossi, A. (2011). Economic and social upgrading in global production networks: A new paradigm for a changing world. *International Labour Review*, *150*(3–4), 319–340. https://doi.org/10.1111/j.1564-913X.2011.00119.x

Beladi, H., Dutta, M., & Kar, S. (2016). FDI and Business Internationalization of the Unorganized Sector: Evidence from Indian Manufacturing. *World Development*, *83*(Supplement C), 340–349. https://doi.org/10.1016/j.worlddev.2016.01.006

Bellavista, A. (2012). Il lavoro nero e le imprese fantasma. *Rivista Giuridica Del Lavoro e Della Previdenza Sociale*, *63*(2), 249–252.

Bellavista, A., & Garilli, A. (2012). Politiche pubbliche e lavoro sommerso: Realtà e prospettive. *Rivista Giuridica Del Lavoro e Della Previdenza Sociale*, *63*(2), 269–282.

Beltrán, A. (2020). Informal sector competition and firm productivity. *Applied Economics Letters*, *27*(15), 1243–1246. https://doi.org/10.1080/13504851.2019.1676383

Benkovskis, K., Masso, J., Tkacevs, O., Vahter, P., & Yashiro, N. (2020). Export and productivity in global value chains: Comparative evidence from Latvia and Estonia. *Review of World Economics*, *156*(3), 557–577. https://doi.org/10.1007/s10290-019-00371-0

Bentivogli, C., Ferraresi, T., Monti, P., Paniccià, R., & Rosignoli, S. (2018). *Italian regions in global value chains: An input-output approach* (Occasional Papers 462; Questioni Di Economia e Finanza). Banca d'Italia.

Berardino, C. D., Mauro, G., Quaglione, D., & Sarra, A. (2016). Structural change and the sustainability of regional convergence: Evidence from the Italian regions: *Environment and Planning C: Politics and Space*. https://doi.org/10.1177/0263774X16655800

Berdiev, A. N., Saunoris, J. W., & Schneider, F. (2020). Poverty and the shadow economy: The role of governmental institutions. *The World Economy*, *43*(4), 921–947. https://doi.org/10.1111/twec.12917

Bernhardt, A., McGrath, S., & DeFilippis, J. (2007). *Unregulated work in the Global City: Employment and Labor Law Violations in New York City*. Brennan Center for Justice, New York University School of Law.

Bernhardt, A., Spiller, M. W., & Theodore, N. (2013). Employers Gone Rogue: Explaining Industry Variation in Violations of Workplace Laws. *ILR Review*, *66*(4), 808–832. https://doi.org/10.1177/001979391306600404

Betti, E. (2019). *Precari e precarie: Una storia dell'Italia repubblicana* (1a edizione.). Carocci editore.

Betti, G., Mangiavacchi, L., & Piccoli, L. (2020). Women and poverty: Insights from individual consumption in Albania. *Review of Economics of the Household*, *18*(1), 69–91. https://doi.org/10.1007/s11150-019-09452-3

Bezemer, D. J. (2001). Post-socialist financial fragility: The case of Albania. *Cambridge Journal of Economics*, *25*(1), 1–23.

Bianchi, L., Faustini, G., & Padovani, R. (2003). *Il Sommerso nei contesti economici territoriali: Produzione, lavoro, imprese* (Quaderno 22). SVIMEZ.

Bigoni, M., Bortolotti, S., Casari, M., Gambetta, D., & Pancotto, F. (2016). Amoral Familism, Social Capital, or Trust? The Behavioural Foundations of the Italian North–South Divide. *The Economic Journal*, *126*(594), 1318–1341. https://doi.org/10.1111/ecoj.12292

Biscione, A., & Caruso, R. (2020). *Static and dynamic analysis of poverty in Albania (2007-2016)* (CESPIC Working Paper 3). Centro Europeo di Scienza della Pace, Integrazione e Cooperazione.

Bobbio, E. (2016). *Tax evasion, firm dynamics and growth* (Occasional Papers 357; Questioni Di Economia e Finanza). Banca d'Italia.

Bodo, G., & Viesti, G. (1997). *La grande svolta: Il Mezzogiorno nell'Italia degli anni novanta*. Donzelli Editore.

Bogdani, M., & Loughlin, J. (2007). *Albania and the European Union: The tumultous Journey towards Integration and Accession*. I.B.Tauris.

Boka, M., & Torluccio, G. (2013). Informal Economy in Albania. *Academic Journal of Interdisciplinary Studies*, *2*(8), 212.

Breman, J., & van der Linden, M. (2014). Informalizing the Economy: The Return of the Social Question at a Global Level. *Development and Change*, *45*(5), 920–940. https://doi.org/10.1111/dech.12115

Brusco, S., & Paba, S. (1997). Per una storia dei distretti industriali italiani del secondo dopoguerra agli anni Novanta. In F. Barca (Ed.), *Storia del Capitalismo Italiano* (pp. 265–333). Donzelli editore.

Bulfone, F., & Tassinari, A. (2021). Under pressure. Economic constraints, electoral politics and labour market reforms in Southern Europe in the crisis decade. *European Journal of Political Research*, 60(3), 509-538

Burawoy, M. (1979). *Manufacturing consent: Changes in the labor process under monopoly capitalism.* University of Chicago Press.

Burawoy, M. (1985). *The politics of production: Factory regimes under capitalism and socialism.* Verso Books.

Burawoy, M: (1998). The Extended Case Method. *Sociological Theory*, *16*(1), 4–33. https://doi.org/10.1111/0735-2751.00040

Burawoy, M. (1991). Reconstructing Social Theories. In M. Burawoy, A. Burton, A. A. Ferguson, K. J. Fox, J. Gamson, N. Gartrell, L. Hurst, C. Kurzman, L. Salzinger, J. Schiffman, & S. Ui, *Ethnography unbound: Power and resistance in the modern metropolis* (pp. 8–27). University of California Press.

Burawoy, M., Burton, A., Ferguson, A. A., Fox, K. J., Gamson, J., Gartrell, N., Hurst, L., Kurzman, C., Salzinger, L., Schiffman, J., & Ui, S. (1991). *Ethnography unbound: Power and resistance in the modern metropolis.* University of California Press.

Burawoy, M., Krotov, P., & Lytkina, T. (2000). Involution and destitution in capitalist Russia. *Ethnography*, *1*(1), 43–65.

Burroni, L., Crouch, C., Kaminska, M. E., & Valzania, A. (2008). Local economic governance in hard times: The shadow economy and the textile and clothing industries around Łódź and Naples. *Socio-Economic Review*, *6*(3), 473–492. https://doi.org/10.1093/ser/mwn005

Cafiero, S. (1996). *Questione meridionale e unità nazionale: 1861-1995* (1a edizione.). Nuova Italia scientifica.

Capestro, M., & Guido, G. (2014). Il ruolo strategico della media impresa nei distretti industriali manifatturieri. *Atti del XXVI Convegno annuale di Sinergie*, *0*(0).

Carlà, D. (2019). L'Ispettorato del lavoro e l'evoluzione degli assetti organizzativi. *Rivista Giuridica Del Mezzogiorno*, *23*(2), 325–339.

Carswell, G., & De Neve, G. (2013). Labouring for global markets: Conceptualising labour agency in global production networks. *Geoforum*, *44*, 62–70. https://doi.org/10.1016/j.geoforum.2012.06.008

Caruso, F., & Lo Cascio, M. (2020). Invisibili ma indispensabili: L'emersione tra i braccianti nel Sud Italia. In L. Cigna (Ed.), *Forza lavoro! Ripensare il lavoro al tempo della pandemia* (pp. 69–80). Fondazione Giangiacomo Feltrinelli.

Cascioli, P. (2017). *Vademecum per l'ispettore del lavoro*. Fondazione Prof. Massimo D'Antona.

Castells, M., & Portes, A. (1989). World Underneath: The Origins, Dynamics, and Effects of the Informal Economy. In A. Portes, M. Castells, & L. Benton, *The Informal Economy: Studies in Advances and Less Developed Countries* (pp. 11–37). The John Hopkins University Press.

Castree, N., Coe, N. M., Ward, K., & Samers, M. (2004). *Spaces of Work: Global Capitalism and the Geographies of Labour*. Sage.

Ceccagno, A. (2017). *City Making and Global Labor Regimes: Chinese Immigrants and Italy's Fast Fashion Industry*. Palgrave Macmillan UK.

CGIL, CISL and UIL (2006). Piattaforma Contro Il Lavoro Nero. http://www.bollettinoadapt.it/piattaforma-contro-il-lavoro-nero/

CGIL, CISL and UIL. (2019). *Audizione CGIL-CISL-UIL, "Indagine conoscitiva sul riordino del sistema della vigilanza in materia di lavoro, contribuzione e assicurazione obbligatoria*. XI Commissione Lavoro pubblico e privato della Camera dei Deputati. https://www.uil.it/documents/Audizione%20Vigilanza%20Cgil,%20Cisl,%20Uil%2020.2.2019.pdf

Charron, N., & Lapuente, V. (2018). *Quality of Government in EU Regions: Spatial and Temporal Patterns* [Working Paper]. Quality of Government Institute, University of Gothenburg.

Chen, M. A. (2016). Informal Employment: Theory and Reality. In S. Edgell, H. Gottfried, & E. Granter, *The SAGE handbook of the sociology of work and employment* (pp. 407–427). SAGE.

Choi, J., & Minondo, A. (2019). The trade effects of Albania's trade agreements with CEFTA members. *Post-Communist Economies*, *31*(4), 451–463. https://doi.org/10.1080/14631377.2018.1537736

Clark, I., Hunter, J., Pickford, R., & Fearnall-Williams, H. (2020). How do licensing regimes limit worker interests? Evidence from informal employment in Britain. *Economic and Industrial Democracy*, 0143831X20903095. https://doi.org/10.1177/0143831X20903095

Clean Clothes Campaign. (2014). *Stitched Up—Poverty wages in the Eastern European and Turkish garment industry*. https://cleanclothes.org/livingwage/stitched-up

Clean Clothes Campaign. (2016). *Albania factsheet*. Clean Clothes Campaign. https://cleanclothes.org/file-repository/livingwage-europe-country-profiles-albania/view

Coe, N. M. (2012). Geographies of production II A global production network A–Z. *Progress in Human Geography*, *36*(3), 389–402.

Coe, N. M., & Jordhus-Lier, D. C. (2011). Constrained agency? Re-evaluating the geographies of labour. *Progress in Human Geography*, *35*(2), 211–233. https://doi.org/10.1177/0309132510366746

Colucci, M. (2018). Per una storia del governo dell'immigrazione straniera in Italia: Dagli anni sessanta alla crisi delle politiche. *Meridiana*, *91*, 9–36.

Comei, M. (2012). *La fabbrica degli abiti: Cesare Contegiacomo e la sua impresa 1905-1985*. Editori Laterza.

Connolly, P. (1985). The politics of the informal sector: A critique. In E. Mingione & N. Redclift, *Beyond employmen: Household, gender and subsistance* (pp. 55–91). Blackwell.

Corò, G., & Grandinetti, R. (1999). Strategie di delocalizzazione e processi evolutivi nei distretti industriali italiani. *L'industria*, *20*(4), 897–924.

Cosma, V. S., Ban, C., & Gabor, D. (2021). The Human Cost of Fresh Food: Romanian Workers and Germany's Food Supply Chains. *Review of Agrarian Studies*.

Crawford, B., Chiles, T. H., & Elias, S. R. S. T. A. (2020). Long Interviews in Organizational Research: Unleashing the Power of "Show and Tell". *Journal of Management Inquiry*, 1056492620930096. https://doi.org/10.1177/1056492620930096

Crouch, C. (2019). *Will the gig economy prevail?* Polity Press.

Crowhurst, I. (2013). The fallacy of the instrumental gate? Contextualising the process of gaining access through gatekeepers. *International Journal of Social Research Methodology*, *16*(6), 463–475. https://doi.org/10.1080/13645579.2013.823282

Cumbers, A., Nativel, C., & Routledge, P. (2008). Labour agency and union positionalities in global production networks. *Journal of Economic Geography*, *8*(3), 369–387. https://doi.org/10.1093/jeg/lbn008

Cunliffe, A. L., & Alcadipani, R. (2016). The Politics of Access in Fieldwork: Immersion, Backstage Dramas, and Deception. *Organizational Research Methods*, *19*(4), 535–561. https://doi.org/10.1177/1094428116639134

Darbi, W. P. K., Hall, C. M., & Knott, P. (2018). The Informal Sector: A Review and Agenda for Management Research. *International Journal of Management Reviews*, *20*(2), 301–324. https://doi.org/10.1111/ijmr.12131

D'Attoma, J. (2017). Divided Nation: The North-South Cleavage in Italian Tax Compliance. *Polity*, *49*(1), 69–99. https://doi.org/10.1086/689982

D'Attoma, J. (2018). Explaining Italian Tax Compliance: A Historical Analysis. In S. Steinmo, *The leap of faith: The fiscal foundations of successful government in Europe and America* (First edition., pp. 106–130). Oxford University Press.

D'Attoma, J. (2019). What explains the North–South divide in Italian tax compliance? An experimental analysis. *Acta Politica*, *54*(1), 104–123. https://doi.org/10.1057/s41269-018-0077-1

Dávalos, M., & Cancho, C. (2015). *Insights into Key Challenges of the Albanian Labor Market*. The World Bank.

De Castro, J. O., Khavul, S., & Bruton, G. D. (2014). Shades of Grey: How do Informal Firms Navigate Between Macro and Meso Institutional Environments? *Strategic Entrepreneurship Journal*, *8*(1), 75–94. https://doi.org/10.1002/sej.1172

de Martino, C., Lozito, M., & Schiuma, D. (2016). Immigrazione, caporalato e lavoro in agricoltura. *Lavoro e Diritto*, *30*(2), 313–328. https://doi.org/10.1441/83366

De Neve, G. (2014). Fordism, flexible specialization and CSR: How Indian garment workers critique neoliberal labour regimes. *Ethnography*, *15*(2), 184–207. https://doi.org/10.1177/1466138112463801

de Soto, H. (1989). *The other path: The invisible revolution in the Third World*. Tauris.

Deloitte. (2020). *Employment & Labour Law 2020: A practical cross-border insight into employment and labour law*. Deloitte Legal Sh.p.k.

D'Ercole, M. (2000). Il distretto barlettano della calzatura. In G. Viesti (Ed.), *Mezzogiorno dei distretti* (pp. 37–58). Meridiana Libri.

Dewey, M. (2014). *Taxing the Shadow: The Political Economy of Sweatshops in La Salada, Argentina* [Discussion Paper 14/18]. Max Planck Institute for the Study of Societies. https://www.mpifg.de/pu/mpifg_dp/dp14-18.pdf

Dewey, M., & Di Carlo, D. (2021). Governing through non-enforcement: Regulatory forbearance as industrial policy in advanced economies. *Regulation & Governance, online first*(n/a). https://doi.org/10.1111/rego.12382

Di Mauro, C., Fratocchi, L., Orzes, G., & Sartor, M. (2018). Offshoring and backshoring: A multiple case study analysis. *Journal of Purchasing and Supply Management*, *24*(2), 108–134. https://doi.org/10.1016/j.pursup.2017.07.003

Dibben, P., & Williams, C. (2012). Varieties of Capitalism and Employment Relations: Informally Dominated Market Economies. *Industrial Relations: A Journal of Economy and Society*, *51*, 563–582. https://doi.org/10.1111/j.1468-232X.2012.00690.x

Dicken, P. (2015). *Global Shift: Seventh Edition: Mapping the Changing Contours of the World Economy* (Seventh Edition). Guilford.

DIN. (2020). *A brief introduction to standards*. https://www.din.de/en/about-standards/a-brief-introduction-to-standards

Doci, N. (2018). *Annual Review of Labour Relations and Social Dialogue—2018 Albania*. Friedrich Ebert Stiftung.

Dorlach, T. (2019). Retrenchment of Social Policy by Other Means: A Comparison of Agricultural and Housing Policy in Turkey. *Journal of Comparative Policy Analysis: Research and Practice*, *21*(3), 270–286. https://doi.org/10.1080/13876988.2018.1466856

Dragoshi, F., & Pappa, A. (2015). *Long road to social dialogue in Albania. Turning challenges into opportunities*. Friedrich Ebert Stiftung and Institute for Democracy and Mediation.

Drahokoupil, J., & Fabo, B. (2019). Outsourcing, Offshoring and the Deconstruction of Employment: New and Old Challenges. In A. Serrano-Pascual & M. Jepsen (Eds.), *The deconstruction of employment as a political question: 'Employment' as a Floating Signifier* (pp. 33–62). Palgrave Macmillan.

Dundon, T., & Ryan, P. (2010). Interviewing Reluctant Respondents: Strikes, Henchmen, and Gaelic Games. *Organizational Research Methods*, *13*(3), 562–581. https://doi.org/10.1177/1094428109335571

Dunford, M. (2002). Italian Regional Evolutions: *Environment and Planning A*, *34*(4), 657–694. https://doi.org/10.1068/a3489

Dunford, M. (2006). Industrial Districts, Magic Circles, and the Restructuring of the Italian Textiles and Clothing Chain. *Economic Geography*, *82*(1), 27–59. https://doi.org/10.1111/j.1944-8287.2006.tb00287.x

Dunford, M., Dunford, R., Barbu, M., & Liu, W. (2016). Globalisation, cost competitiveness and international trade: The evolution of the Italian textile and clothing industries and the growth of trade with China. *European Urban and Regional Studies*, *23*(2), 111–135. https://doi.org/10.1177/0969776413498763

EC. (2016). *Albania 2016 Report* (Communication on EU Enlargement Policy) [Communication from the Commission to the European Parliament, the Council, the European Economic and Social Committee and the Committee of the Regions]. European Commission.

EC. (2018a). *Albania 2018 Report* (Communication on EU Enlargement Policy) [Communication from the Commission to the European Parliament, the Council, the European Economic and Social Committee and the Committee of the Regions]. European Commission.

EC. (2018b). *Revised Indicative Strategy Paper for Albania (2014-2020)* (Instrument for Pre-Accession Assistance (IPA II)) [Commission Decision C(2014)5770]. European Commission.

EC. (2019). *Albania 2019 Report* (Communication on EU Enlargement Policy) [Communication from the Commission to the European Parliament, the Council, the European Economic and Social Committee and the Committee of the Regions]. European Commission.

EC. (2020a). *Albania 2020 Report* (Communication on EU Enlargement Policy) [Communication from the Commission to the European Parliament, the Council, the European Economic and Social Committee and the Committee of the Regions]. European Commission.

EC. (2020b). *Special Eurobarometer 498 – September 2019 'Undeclared work in the European Union'* [Survey requested by the European Commission, Directorate-General for Employment, Social Affairs and Inclusion and co-ordinated by the Directorate-General for Communication]. European Commission.

Edwards, P. (2010). Developing Labour Process Analysis: Themes from Industrial Sociology and Future Directions. In P. Thompson & C. Smith,

Working life: Renewing labour process analysis (pp. 29–46). Palgrave Macmillan.

Edwards, P., Sengupta, S., & Tsai, C.-J. (2009). Managing low-skill workers: A study of small UK food manufacturing firms. *Human Resource Management Journal, 19*(1), 40–58. https://doi.org/10.1111/j.1748-8583.2008.00085.x

Edwards, R. (1979). *Contested Terrain.* Basic Books, Inc.

Edwards, R., & Holland, J. (2013). *What is qualitative interviewing?* Bloomsbury.

Ehrenreich, B. (2001). *Nickel and dimed: Undercover in low-wage USA.* Granta.

Erebara, G. (2015, January 9). Albania PM Declares 'War' on Fiscal Evasion. *Balkan Insight.* https://balkaninsight.com/2015/09/01/albania-government-starts-major-crackdown-against-fiscal-evasion-09-01-2015/

EU & OECD. (2015). *Policy Brief on Informal Entrepreneurship.* European Union/OECD.

Eurofound. (2009). *Regulations to promote regular employment, Italy.* Eurofound. https://www.eurofound.europa.eu/data/tackling-undeclared-work-in-europe/database/regulations-to-promote-regular-employment-italy

Eurofound. (2018). *OVS | European Reshoring Monitor.* https://reshoring.eurofound.europa.eu/reshoring-cases/ovs

European Platform tackling undeclared work (2021). *Biennal Report 2019-2020: Key results and achievements.* European Platform tackling undeclared work.

European Platform Tackling Undeclared Work (2022). *Work Plan 2023 and proposals for 2024-2025.* European Labour Authority.

European Platform Tackling Undeclared Work (2024a). *Tackling undeclared work among third country nationals working in supply chains, including via temporary work agencies.* European Labour Authority.

European Platform tackling undeclared work (2024b). *Platform subgroup on safe reporting and complaint mechanisms for workers to denounce abuse and seek support, Output paper.* European Labour Authority.

Fana, M., & Fana, S. (2019). *Basta salari da fame!* Laterza.

Fasani, M. (2011). *Labour Inspection in Italy* (Working Document 11). International Labour Organization.

Feierherd, G. (2020). Courting Informal Workers: Exclusion, Forbearance, and the Left. *American Journal of Political Science*, *00*(00), 1–16. https://doi.org/10.1111/ajps.12576

Feige, E. L. (1990). Defining and estimating underground and informal economies: The new institutional economics approach. *World Development*, *18*(7), 989–1002. https://doi.org/10.1016/0305-750X(90)90081-8

Feige, E. L. (1997). Underground activity and institutional change: Productive, protective and predatory behavior in transition economies. *Transforming Post-Communist Political Economies*, *21*, 34.

Felice, E. (2010). Regional development: Reviewing the Italian mosaic. *Journal of Modern Italian Studies*, *15*(1), 64–80. https://doi.org/10.1080/13545710903465556

Felice, E., & Lepore, A. (2016). State intervention and economic growth in Southern Italy: The rise and fall of the «Cassa per il Mezzogiorno» (1950-1986). *Munich Personal RePEc Archive*, *Working Paper No. 69466*. https://mpra.ub.uni-muenchen.de/69466/

Fernandez-Kelly, P., & Garcia, A. (1989). Informalization at the Core: Hispanic Women, Homework, and the Advanced Capitalist State. In A. Portes, M. Castells, & L. Benton, *The Informal Economy: Studies in Advanced and Less Developed Countries* (pp. 247–264). The John Hopkins University Press.

Ferragina, E., & Arrigoni, A. (2021). Selective Neoliberalism: How Italy Went from Dualization to Liberalisation in Labour Market and Pension Reforms. *New Political Economy*, *0*(0), 1–21. https://doi.org/10.1080/13563467.2020.1865898

Ferragina, E., Arrigoni, A., & Spreckelsen, T. F. (2020). The rising invisible majority. *Review of International Political Economy*, *0*(0), 1–38. https://doi.org/10.1080/09692290.2020.1797853

FIAA. (2015). *Business Environment Survey*. Foreign Investors Association of Albania. http://fiaalbania.al/business-environment-2015-survey/

FIAA. (2019). *Business Environment Survey*. Foreign Investors Association of Albania. http://fiaalbania.al/fiaa-presents-the-outcomes-of-the-business-environment-survey-in-albania-2018-2019/

Fiengo, G. (2012). Azioni di contrasto al lavoro sommerso e vigilanza. *Rivista Giuridica Del Lavoro e Della Previdenza Sociale*, *63*(2), 313–334.

Filho, R. F. (2016). When informal work becomes litigious in a labour courtroom. In S. Routh & V. Borghi (eds), *Workers and the global informal economy: Interdisciplinary perspectives* (pp. 108–120). Routledge.

Filipi, G., & Balla, B. (2011). *Decent Work: The Albanian Fason Industry* (Briefing #39). AGENDA Instituite, Olof Palme International Center, SOLIDAR.

Fine, J., Gordon, J. (2010). Strengthening Labor Standards Enforcement through Partnerships with Workers' Organizations. *Politics and Society*, 38(4), 552–585. https://doi.org/10.1177/0032329210381240

Flecker, J., Haidinger, B., & Schönauer, A. (2013). Divide and Serve: The Labour Process in Service Value Chains and Networks. *Competition & Change*, *17*(1), 6–23. https://doi.org/10.1179/1024529412Z.00000000022

Flecker, J., & Meil, P. (2010). Organisational restructuring and emerging service value chains: Implications for work and employment. *Work, Employment and Society*, *24*(4), 680–698. https://doi.org/10.1177/0950017010380635

Foerstl, K., Kirchoff, J., & Bals, L. (2016). Reshoring and Insourcing: Drivers and Future Research Directions. *International Journal of Physical Distribution & Logistics Management*, *46*(5), 492–515.

Forges-Davanzati, G. (2008). Le Basi teoriche delle politiche di contrasto al lavoro irregolare nel pensiero economico italiano (1960-2000). *Rassegna Economica*, 105–121.

Forlani, N. (2013). Le procedure per l'emersione del lavoro sommerso degli immigrati e i potenziali effetti dell'Art. 3 del D. lgs 109/2012. *Studi Di Sociologia*, *51*(2), 185–194.

Foschi, P., & Gabanelli, M. (2018, October 7). *Lavoro nero dipendente: Ogni anno evasi 11 miliardi di contributi*. Corriere della Sera. https://www.corriere.it/dataroom-milena-gabanelli/evasione-contributi-pensione-lavoro-nero-controlli-inps-inail-mef/aba36c6c-c8bb-11e8-81ab-863c582a99f0-va.shtml

Frade, C., & Darmon, I. (2005). New modes of business organization and precarious employment: Towards the recommodification of labour? *Journal of European Social Policy*, *15*(2), 107–121. https://doi.org/10.1177/0958928705051509

Frey, L. (1975). *Lavoro a domicilio e decentramento dell'attività produttiva nei settori tessile e dell'abbigliamento in Italia*. Franco Angeli Editore.

Friedman, A. (1977). *Industry & Labour: Class struggle at work and monopoly capitalism.* The Macmillan Press.

Galetto, M. (2007). *Efforts to combat illegal work intensified.* Eurofound. https://www.eurofound.europa.eu/publications/article/2007/efforts-to-combat-illegal-work-intensified

Gallin, D. (2001). Propositions on Trade Unions and Informal Employment in Times of Globalisation. *Antipode*, *33*(3), 531–549. https://doi.org/10.1111/1467-8330.00197

Gasparri, S. (2020). Employee Benefits and Paternalistic Work Regimes. Historical and Contemporary Perspectives on Company Welfare in Italy. *Management Revue*, *31*(4), 465–488. http://dx.doi.org/10.5771/0935-9915-2020-4-465

Gatti, F. (2006, January 9). *Io schiavo in Puglia.* L'Espresso. https://espresso.repubblica.it/dossier/2006/09/01/news/io-schiavo-in-puglia-1.1306

Gereffi, G. (1994). The organization of buyer-driven global commodity chains: How U.S. retailers shape overseas production networks. In G. Gereffi & M. Korzeniewicz (Eds.), *Commodity chains and global capitalism* (pp. 95–122). Praeger.

Gereffi, G. (1999). International trade and industrial upgrading in the apparel commodity chain. *Journal of International Economics*, *48*(1), 37–70. https://doi.org/10.1016/S0022-1996(98)00075-0

Gereffi, G., & Frederick, S. (2010). The Global Apparel Value Chain, and the Crisis: Challenges and opportunities for developing countries. In O. Cattaneo, G. Gereffi, & C. Staritz (Eds.), *Global Value Chains in a postcrisis world: A development perspective* (pp. 157–208). The World Bank.

Gereffi, G., & Memedovic, O. (2003). *The Global Apparel Value Chain: What Prospects for Upgrading by Developing Countries?* UNIDO Sectoral Studies Series Working Paper.

Gërxhani, K. (2004a). The Informal Sector in Developed and Less Developed Countries: A Literature Survey. *Public Choice*, *120*(3–4), 267–300. https://doi.org/10.1023/B:PUCH.0000044287.88147.5e

Gërxhani, K. (2004b). Tax evasion in transition: Outcome of an institutional clash? Testing Feige's conjecture in Albania. *European Economic Review*, *48*(4), 729–745. https://doi.org/10.1016/j.euroecorev.2003.08.014

Gërxhani, K. (2007). Explaining gender differences in tax evasion: The case of Tirana, Albania. *Feminist Economics*, *13*(2), 119–155. https://doi.org/10.1080/13545700601184856

Gërxhani, K., & Wintrobe, R. (2021). Understanding Tax Evasion: Combining the Public Choice and New Institutionalist Perspectives. In E. Douarin & O. Havrylyshyn (Eds.), *The Palgrave Handbook of Comparative Economics* (pp. 785–810). Springer International Publishing. https://doi.org/10.1007/978-3-030-50888-3_30

Ghezzi, S. (2003). Local discourse and global competition: Production experiences in family workshops of the Brianza. *International Journal of Urban and Regional Research*, *27*(4), 781–792. https://doi.org/10.1111/j.0309-1317.2003.00483.x

Ghezzi, S. (2010). The fallacy of the formal and informal divide: Lessons from a Post-Fordist regional economy. In E. Marcelli, C. Williams, & P. Joassart, *Informal work in developed nations* (pp. 114–132). Routledge.

Gibson-Graham, J.-K. (2008). Diverse economies: Performative practices for other worlds. *Progress in Human Geography*, *32*(5), 613–632.

Gifawosen, M. M. (2019). *Labor Rights, Working Conditions, and Workers' Power in the Emerging Textile and Apparel Industries in Ethiopia: The Case of Hawassa Industrial Park* (Working Paper 01/2019; New Research in Global Political Economy). University of Kassel.

Gigio, L.A., Camussi, & S., Maccarrone, V. (2021). *Changes in the employment structure and in job quality in Italy: a national and regional analysis*. Questioni di Economia e Finanza (Occasional Papers), Banca d'Italia.

Giunta, A., Nifo, A., & Scalera, D. (2012). Subcontracting in Italian Industry: Labour Division, Firm Growth and the North–South Divide. *Regional Studies*, *46*(8), 1067–1083. https://doi.org/10.1080/00343404.2011.552492

Gjika, I., & Pano, N. (2017). Recent challenges for apparel companies in Albania. *Book Proceedings*, 169–176.

GoA. (2007). *National Strategy for Development and Integration 2007-2013*. Republic of Albania Council of Ministers.

GoA. (2013). *National Strategy for Development and Integration 2014-2020*. Republic of Albania Council of Ministers.

Godfrey, P. C. (2011). Toward a Theory of the Informal Economy. *The Academy of Management Annals*, *5*(1), 231–277. https://doi.org/10.1080/19416520.2011.585818

Godfrey, P. C., & Schulze, W. (2015). Organization and Contract in the Informal Economy. In P. C. Godfrey, *Management, Society, and the*

Informal Economy (pp. 21–41). Taylor & Francis Group. https://doi.org/10.4324/9781315757445-7

Graziani, A. (1978). The Mezzogiorno in the Italian economy. *Cambridge Journal of Economics*, *2*(4), 355–372.

Greco, L. (2016). *Capitalismo e sviluppo nelle catene globali del valore*, Carocci.

Greskovits, B. (1998). *The political economy of protest and patience: East European and Latin American transformations compared*. Central European University Press.

Grimshaw, D., & Rubery, J. (2005). Inter-capital relations and the network organisation: Redefining the work and employment nexus. *Cambridge Journal of Economics*, *29*(6), 1027–1051. https://doi.org/10.1093/cje/bei088

Grugulis, I., & Lloyd, C. (2010). Skill and the Labour Process: The Conditions and Consequences of Change. In P. Thompson & C. Smith, *Working life: Renewing labour process analysis* (pp. 91–112). Palgrave Macmillan.

Guillemin, M., & Gillam, L. (2004). Ethics, Reflexivity, and "Ethically Important Moments" in Research. *Qualitative Inquiry*, *10*(2), 261–280. https://doi.org/10.1177/1077800403262360

Hadjimichalis, C., & Vaiou, D. (1990). Whose flexibility? The politics of informalisation in Southern Europe. *Capital & Class*, *14*(3), 79–106. https://doi.org/10.1177/030981689004200105

Hale, A., & Burns, M. (2005). The Phase-Out of the Multi-Fibre Arrangement from the Perspective of Workers. In A. Hale & J. Willis, *Threads of Labour: Garment Industry Supply Chains from the Workers' Perspective* (pp. 210–133). Blackwell Publishing.

Hammer, N., & Plugor, R. (2016). Near-sourcing UK apparel: Value chain restructuring, productivity and the informal economy. *Industrial Relations Journal*, *47*(5–6), 402–416. https://doi.org/10.1111/irj.12146

Hammer, N., & Plugor, R. (2019). Disconnecting Labour? The Labour Process in the UK Fast Fashion Value Chain. *Work, Employment and Society*, 0950017019847942. https://doi.org/10.1177/0950017019847942

Hancké, B. (2009). *Intelligent research design: A guide for beginning researchers in the social sciences*. Oxford University Press.

Harrison, B. (1994). *Lean and Mean: The Changing Landscape of Corporate Power in the Age of Flexibility*. Basic Books.

Harrison,J.,MacGibbon,L.,&Morton,M.(2001).RegimesofTrustworthiness in Qualitative Research: The Rigors of Reciprocity. *Qualitative Inquiry*, *7*(3), 323–345. https://doi.org/10.1177/107780040100700305

Harriss-White, B. (2003). Inequality at work in the informal economy: Key issues and illustrations. *International Labour Review*, *142*(4), 459–469.

Hart, C. (2017). *The Albania Delivery Unit: A case study on accountability in action*. Albania Growth Lab, Harvard University. https://albania.growthlab.cid.harvard.edu/overview

Hart, K. (1973). Informal Income Opportunities and Urban Employment in Ghana. *The Journal of Modern African Studies*, *11*(1), 61–89.

Harvey, D. (1990). *The Condition of Postmodernity: An Enquire into the origins of Cultural Change*. Blackwell Publishers.

Hauptmeier, M., & Vidal, M. (Eds.). (2014). *Comparative Political Economy of Work*. Palgrave. http://https://he.palgrave.com/page/detail/?sf1=barcode&st1=9781137322272

Henderson, J., Dicken, P., Hess, M., Coe, N., & Yeung, H. W.-C. (2002). Global production networks and the analysis of economic development. *Review of International Political Economy*, *9*(3), 436–464. https://doi.org/10.1080/09692290210150842

Holland, A. (2017). *Forbearance as redistribution: The politics of Informal Welfare in Latin America*. Cambridge University Press.

Hudson, R. (2005). *Economic geographies: Circuits, flows and spaces*. SAGE.

Hurley, J., & Miller, D. (2005). The Changing Face of the Global Garment Industry. In *Threads of Labour: Garment Industry Supply Chains from the Workers' Perspective* (pp. 16–39). Blackwell Publishing.

Hussmans, R. (2004). *Statistical definition of informal employment: Guidelines endorsed by the Seventeenth International Conference of Labour Statisticians (2003)* [7th Meeting of the Expert Group on Informal Sector Statistics (Delhi Group)]. International Labour Office.

Huws, U. (2011). Passing the buck: Corporate restructuring and the casualisationofemployment. *WorkOrganisation,Labour&Globalisation*, *5*(1), 1–9. https://doi.org/10.13169/workorgalaboglob.5.1.0001

Hylli, M,m Kazani, I., Shehi, E. & Guxho, G. (2021). Leather and footwear industry in Albania - history, tradition and its challenges. *Journal of Leather & Footwear*, 70 (1-2), 4-7. DOI: 10.34187/ko.70.1-2.1

Iannuzzi, F., E., & Sacchetto, D. (2020). Italian Labour Inspectors Facing Posted Workers Phenomena. In J. Arnholtz & N. Lillie (Eds.), *Posted*

Work in the European Union: The political economy of free movement (pp. 109–127). Routledge.

Il Corriere del Mezzogiorno. (2009, June 7). *Vendola dà il via al rimpasto: Cinque nuovi assessori. Ci sono Capone e Viesti—Corriere del Mezzogiorno*. Il Corriere Del Mezzogiorno Online. https://corrieredelmezzogiorno.corriere.it/napoli/notizie/politica/2009/6-luglio-2009/vendola-da-via-rimpasto-cinque-nuovi-assessori-ci-sono-capone-viesti-1601538248191.shtml

Il Tempo. (2009, May 7). Vendola fa saltare la giunta. *Il Tempo.it*. https://www.iltempo.it/politica/2009/07/01/news/vendola-fa-saltare-la-giunta-692847/

ILO. (2008). *Addressing the Problem of Undeclared Work in the Construction Sector through Social Partnership in Albania*. International Labour Organization.

ILO. (2009). *Albanaia labour inspection audit: Joint outcome on labour inspection* (Dialogue Safe Work). International Labour Office.

ILO. (2018). *Women and men in the informal economy: A statistical picture. Third edition* [Report]. International Labour Office.

Imami, D., Pugh, G. & Lami, E. (2024). Fiscal Enforcement and Elections in the Context of High Corruption. Public Finance Review, 52(5), 679-714. https://doi.org/10.1177/10911421241234116

IMF. (2016). *Albania Country Report* (IMF Country Report No. 16/143). International Monetary Fund.

IMF. (2017). *Albania Country Report* (IMF Country Report No. 17/64). International Monetary Fund.

IndustriAll. (2019, April 1). *Ending poverty pay for Albanian workers making big brand clothes*. IndustriAll Europe, European Trade Union. https://news.industriall-europe.eu/Article/319

Invest in Albania. (2018). *Cloth Manufacturing—The Textile Industry in Albania*. https://invest-in-albania.org/industries/clothing-manufacturing/

ISFOL. (2011). *Le Politiche Regionali di contrasto del Lavoro Sommerso*. Istituto per lo sviluppo della formazione professionale dei lavoratori. http://isfoloa.isfol.it/handle/123456789/121

ISFOL. (2014). *Il lavoro sommerso e irregolare degli stranieri in Italia—Sintesi dei principali risultati*. Istituto per lo sviluppo della formazione professionale dei lavoratori. https://www.isfol.it/attivita/indaginie-ricerche/indagini-campionarie/indagine-sul-lavoro-sommerso-e-irregolare-degli-stranieri-in-italia

ISTAT. (2019). *L' economia non osservata nei conti nazionali nel 2017*. Instat. https://www.istat.it/it/files/2019/10/Economia-non-osservata-nei-conti-nazionali-2017.pdf

ISTAT. (2021). *Glossario ISTAT*. http://www4.istat.it/it/files/2011/03/glossario_retribuzioni.pdf?title=Informazioni+e+dati+sulle+retribuzioni+-+23%2Fset%2F2006+-+Glossario+retribuzioni.pdf

Jaehrling, K., & Méhaut, P. (2013). 'Varieties of institutional avoidance': Employers' strategies in low-waged service sector occupations in France and Germany. *Socio-Economic Review*, *11*(4), 687–710. https://doi.org/10.1093/ser/mws016

Jonas, A. E. G. (1996). Local Labour Control Regimes: Uneven Development and the Social Regulation of Production. *Regional Studies*, *30*(4), 323–338. https://doi.org/10.1080/00343409612331349688

Kacani, J. (2017). *Same industry, same host territory, different evolution paths. Breaking the FDI trap in the clothing industry: A case study from clothing manufacturing enterprises in Albania* [PhD Thesis]. Universitat Politècnica de Catalunya Barcelonatech.

Kacani, J. & Shehi, E. (2023). SDG principles and positive practices adopted by the textile, clothing, leather, and footwear sector in Albania. International Labour Organization.

Kaplinsky, R. (2004). *Sustaining income growth in a globalising world: The search for the Nth rent*. Centre for Research in Innovation Management, University of Brighton.

Karini, A. (2019). *International Aid, Administrative Reform and the Politics of EU Accession: The Case of Albania*. Palgrave Macmillan.

Karma, E. (2019). Undeclared work in Albania: Dimension and consequences. *Euro-Balkan Law and Economic Review*, *2*, 15–40.

King, R., & Gëdeshi, I. (2020). New trends in potential migration from Albania: The migration transition postponed? *Migration and Development*, *9*(2), 131–151. https://doi.org/10.1080/21632324.2019.1608099

Kosta, B. (2018a). Emerging from the Darkness: Albania's Informal Economy. *PROSPER - Notes on the Future of Development from CSIS*.

Kosta, B. (2018b). *Problems of Employment Aspects in the Active Processing Regime (Façon) in Albania through the lens of Employees and Employers* (pp. 1–11). Employment and Social Affairs Platform.

Kosta, B., & Williams, C. (2018). *Diagnostic Report on undeclared work in Albania*. Regional Cooperation Council.

Kvale, S. (2006). Dominance Through Interviews and Dialogues. *Qualitative Inquiry*, *12*(3), 480–500. https://doi.org/10.1177/1077800406286235

Kvale, S. (2007). *Doing Interviews*. SAGE.

La Gazzetta del Mezzogiorno. (2009, June 7). Barbieri: Vendola dica se sono un delinquente. *La Gazzetta del Mezzogiorno online*. https://www.lagazzettadelmezzogiorno.it/news/notizie-nascoste/113629/barbieri-vendola-dica-se-sono-un-delinquente.html

La Hovary, C. (2016). A new international labour standard for formalising the informal economy? A discussion of its desirability. In S. Routh & V. Borghi, *Workers and the global informal economy: Interdisciplinary perspectives* (pp. 91–107). Routledge.

La Porta, R., & Shleifer, A. (2014). Informality and Development. *Journal of Economic Perspectives*, *28*(3), 109–126. https://doi.org/10.1257/jep.28.3.109

La Repubblica. (2009, July 7). *Nuova giunta, il presidente tira dritto—La Repubblica.it*. Archivio - la Repubblica.it. https://ricerca.repubblica.it/repubblica/archivio/repubblica/2009/07/07/nuova-giunta-il-presidente-tira-dritto.html

La Repubblica. (2019, February 8). *I sindacati uniti in piazza: Sabato a Roma la manifestazione*. Repubblica.it. https://www.repubblica.it/economia/2019/02/08/news/i_sindacati_tornano_uniti_in_piazza_sabato_a_roma_la_manifesazione-218636591/

Laera, R., Tresca, F. A., & Veshi, A. (2018). *L'internazionalizzazione dell'impresa. Le caratteristiche degli investimenti in Albania*. Ad Maiora Editrice.

Lakhani, T., Kuruvilla, S., & Avgar, A. (2013). From the Firm to the Network: Global Value Chains and Employment Relations Theory. *British Journal of Industrial Relations*, *51*(3), 440–472. https://doi.org/10.1111/bjir.12015

Lane, C., & Probert, J. (2009). *National Capitalisms, Global Production Networks: Fashioning the Value Chain in the UK, US, and Germany*. Oxford University Press.

Ledeneva, A. (2018). Global Informality Project—Mapping informality. *The Global Encyclopaedia of Informality*. https://mag.wcoomd.org/magazine/wco-news-88/mapping-informality/

Lekovic, V. R. (2011). Interaction of formal and informal institutions–impact on economic success. *Facta Universitatis–Economics & Organizations*, *8*(4), 357–370.

Leogrande, A. (2016). *Uomini e caporali: Viaggio tra i nuovi schiavi nelle campagne del Sud*. Feltrinelli Editore.

Leonard, M. (2000). Coping strategies in developed and developing societies: The workings of the informal economy. *Journal of International Development*, *12*(8), 1069–1085. https://doi.org/10.1002/jid.696

Lewis, W. A. (1954). Economic Development with Unlimited Supplies of Labour. *The Manchester School*, *22*(2), 139–191. https://doi.org/10.1111/j.1467-9957.1954.tb00021.x

Lleshaj, S., & Cela, A. (2014). *Albanians and the European Social Model: Towards a redefinition of the social contract*. Friederich Ebert Stiftung and Albanian Institute for International Studies.

Loayza, N., Oviedo, A. M., & Servén, L. (2005). *The Impact Of Regulation On Growth And Informality. Cross-Country Evidence*. The World Bank. http://elibrary.worldbank.org/doi/abs/10.1596/1813-9450-3623

López, T. (2021). A practice ontology approach to labor control regimes in GPNs: connecting 'sites of labor control' in the Bangalore export garment cluster, *Environment and Planning A: Economy and Space*, 53(5), 1012–30. doi:10.1177/0308518x20987563

Lombardi, A. (2015). *Italy: New law streamlines labour inspection*. Eurofound. https://www.eurofound.europa.eu/it/publications/article/2015/italy-new-law-streamlines-labour-inspection

López-Cariboni, S. (2019). Informal Service Access in Pro-Cyclical Welfare States: A Comparison of Electricity Theft in Slums and Regular Residential Areas of Montevideo. *Journal of Comparative Policy Analysis: Research and Practice*, *21*(3), 287–305. https://doi.org/10.1080/13876988.2018.1462604

Luca, M. D., & Rombi, S. (2016). The regional primary elections in Italy: A general overview. *Contemporary Italian Politics*, *8*(1), 24–41. https://doi.org/10.1080/23248823.2016.1153827

Lüttge, J. (2014). Missing an opportunity: The Italian Mezzogiorno's trading troubles during European integration. *Journal of Modern Italian Studies*, *19*(2), 145–168. https://doi.org/10.1080/1354571X.2014.871143

MacKenzie, R., & Martínez Lucio, M. (2005). The Realities of Regulatory Change: Beyond the Fetish of Deregulation. *Sociology*, *39*(3), 499–517. https://doi.org/10.1177/0038038505052491

Macnaghten, P., & Myers, G. (2004). Focus group: The moderator's view and the analyst's view. In G. Gobo, J. Gubrium, C. Seale, & D. Silverman (Eds.), *Qualitative Research Practice* (pp. 65–79). SAGE Publications.

Maloney, W. F. (2003). Informal self-employment: Poverty trap or decent alternative? In Fields, G & Pfeffermann, G. (eds.) *Pathways out of poverty. Private Firms and Economic Mobility in Developing Countries* (pp. 65–82). Springer.

Mara, I., & Narazani, E. (2011). *The effects of Flat Tax on Inequality and Informal Employment: The Case of Albania* (Working Paper 094). The wiiw Balkan Observatory.

Marchington, M., Carroll, M., & Boxall, P. (2003). Labour scarcity and the survival of small firms: A resource-based view of the road haulage industry. *Human Resource Management Journal*, *13*(4), 5–22. https://doi.org/10.1111/j.1748-8583.2003.tb00102.x

Marcus, G. E. (1995). Ethnography in/of the World System: The Emergence of Multi-Sited Ethnography. *Annual Review of Anthropology*, *24*, 95–117. JSTOR.

Martínez Lucio, M., & MacKenzie, R. (2017). The state and the regulation of work and employment: Theoretical contributions, forgotten lessons and new forms of engagement. *The International Journal of Human Resource Management*, *28*(21), 2983–3002. https://doi.org/10.1080/09585192.2017.1363796

Martínez-Mora, C., & Merino, F. (2014). Offshoring in the Spanish footwear industry: A return journey? *Journal of Purchasing and Supply Management*, *20*(4), 225–237. https://doi.org/10.1016/j.pursup.2014.07.001

Mastromarco, C., Peragine, V., Russo, F., & Serlenga, L. (2014). Poverty, inequality and growth in Albania. *Economics of Transition and Institutional Change*, *22*(4), 635–682. https://doi.org/10.1111/ecot.12048

Mazzucato, V., & Wagner, L. (2018). Multi-sited fieldwork in a connected world. In R. Kloosterman C., V. Mamadouh, & P. Terhorst, *Handbook no the Geographies of Globalization* (pp. 412–421). Edward Elgar.

McKay, S., Jefferys, S., Paraksevopoulou, A., & Keles, J. (2012). *Study on Precarious work and social rights* [Report carried out for the European Commission]. Working Lives Research Institute, Faculty of Social Sciences and Humanities, London Metropolitan University.

Meardi, G. (2000). *Trade Union Activists, East and West: Comparisons in Multinational Companies*. Gower.

Medarov, G., Tsoneva, J., & Nikolova, M. (2019). *Exploitation & Resistance: Labour in three Subcontracting Industries*. Collective for Social Interventions.

MEF. (2020). *Relazione sull'economia non osservata e sull'evasione fiscale e contributiva—Anno 2019* [Nota di Aggiornamento del documento di economia e finanza 2019]. Ministero dell'Economia e delle Finanze.

Megale, A., & Tartaglione, C. (2006). *Emersione dal lavoro nero: Diritti e sviluppo. Le principali esperienze di policy in Italia e nei Paesi dell'Unione Europea*. Ediesse.

Menegotto, M., Seghezzi, F., & Spattini, S. (2018). *Misure per il contrasto al precariato: Primo commento al decreto-legge n. 87/2018 (c.d. Decreto dignità)*. Adapt University Press.

Messori, M. (1989). Sistemi di imprese e sviluppo meridionale. Un confronto tra aree industriali. In G. Becattini, *Modelli locali di sviluppo* (pp. 91–130). Il Mulino.

Mezzadri, A. (2010). Globalisation, informalisation and the state in the Indian garment industry. *International Review of Sociology*, *20*(3), 491–511. https://doi.org/10.1080/03906701.2010.511910

Mezzadri, A. (2016). Class, gender and the sweatshop: On the nexus between labour commodification and exploitation. *Third World Quarterly*, *37*(10), 1877–1900. https://doi.org/10.1080/01436597.2016.1180239

Mezzadri, A. (2017). *The sweatshop regime: Labouring bodies, exploitation, and garments made in India*. Cambridge University Press.

Mezzadri, A. (2020). The Informal Labours of Social Reproduction. *Global Labour Journal*, *11*(1), 156–163.

Mezzadri, A., & Fan, L. (2018). 'Classes of Labour' at the Margins of Global Commodity Chains in India and China. *Development and Change*, *49*(4), 1034–1063. https://doi.org/10.1111/dech.12412

Morgan, D., L. (2012). Focus group and social interaction. In J. Gubrium, J. Holstein, A. Marvasti, & K. McKinney (Eds.), *The SAGE Handbook of Interview Research: The Complexity of the Craft* (pp. 161–176). SAGE Publications.

Morris, J. (2012). Unruly Entrepreneurs: Russian Worker Responses to Insecure Formal Employment. *Global Labour Journal*, *3*(2). https://doi.org/10.15173/glj.v3i2.1120

Morris, J. (2013). Beyond coping? Alternatives to consumption within a social network of Russian workers. *Ethnography*, *14*(1), 85–103. https://doi.org/10.1177/1466138112448021

Morris, J., & Polese, A. (2014). *The informal post-socialist economy: Embedded practices and livelihoods*. Routledge.

Morris, J., & Polese, A. (2015). *Informal Economies in Post-Socialist Spaces: Practices, Institutions and Networks*. Springer.

Morrison, C., Croucher, R., & Cretu, O. (2012). Legacies, Conflict and 'Path Dependence' in the Former Soviet Union. *British Journal of Industrial Relations*, *50*(2), 329–351. https://doi.org/10.1111/j.1467-8543.2010.00840.x

Morrison, C., & Sacchetto, D. (2018). Research Ethics in an Unethical World: The Politics and Morality of Engaged Research. *Work, Employment and Society*, *32*(6), 1118–1129. https://doi.org/10.1177/0950017017726947

Mostaccio, F. (2021). Le conseguenze della pandemia sui lavoratori immigrati in agricoltura, tra decisioni politiche e interessi economici. *Cambio. Rivista Sulle Trasformazioni Sociali, OpenLab on Covid-19*. https://doi.org/10.13128/cambio-10293

Muceku, H. (2016). Fiscal Amnesty and its role in the formalization of the Albanian economy. *European Academic Research*, *4*(3), 2997–3012.

Murphy, R. (2019). *The European Tax Gap* [A report developed for the Socialists and Democrats Group in the European Parliament]. Tax Research LLP, University of London.

Murray, F. (1983). The decentralisation of production—The decline of the mass-collective worker?: *Capital & Class*, *7*(1), 74–99. https://doi.org/10.1177/030981688301900104

MVO. (2016). *CSR Roadmap Albania: A guide through Albania's garment and footwear industry*. MVO Nederland and AIDA.

Naz, F., & Bögenhold, D. (2020). Understanding labour processes in global production networks: A case study of the football industry in Pakistan. *Globalizations*, *0*(0), 1–18. https://doi.org/10.1080/14747731.2019.1708658

NBF. (2016). *Perpsectives on the issue of informality in Albania* [Policy Paper]. National Business Forum.

Newsome, K., Taylor, P., Bair, J., & Rainnie, A. (2015). *Putting labour in its place: Labour process analysis and global value chains*. Palgrave.

North, D. C. (1990). *Institutions, institutional change, and economic performance*. Cambridge University Press.

OECD. (2004). *The informal economy in Albania: Analysis and policy Recommendations* [Report prepared by the OECD - Investment Compact for the Mininstry of Economy of Albania]. OECD.

OECD/ILO. (2019). *Tackling Vulnerability in the Informal Economy*. Development Centre Studies, OECD.

Ottosson, M., Jebsen, S., & Matiaske, W. (2020). Paternalistic Work Regimes. *Management Revue*, *31*(4), 395–401. http://dx.doi.org/10.5771/0935-9915-2020-4-395

Packard, T., Koettl, J., & Montenegro, C. E. (2012). *In From the Shadow: Integrating Europe's Informal Labour*. The World Bank.

Papa, A., & Kongoli, Z. (2016). *Labour Standards in Albania* [Research Report]. Institute for Democracy and Mediation.

Pattenden, J. (2016). Working at the margins of global production networks: Local labour control regimes and rural-based labourers in South India. *Third World Quarterly*, *37*(10), 1809–1833. https://doi.org/10.1080/01436597.2016.1191939

Peck, J. A. (1996). *Work-place: The Social Regulation of Labor Markets*. Guilford Press.

Pedaci, M., & Betti, M. (2020). The Regulation of Employment Relationships at the Enterprise. In I. Regalia (Ed.), *Regulating Work in Small Firms: Perspectives on the Future of Work in Globalised Economies* (pp. 131–164). Palgrave Macmillan.

Pejovich, S. (2012). The Effects of the Interaction of Formal and Informal Institutions on Social Stability and Economic Development. *Journal of Markets & Morality*, *2*(2). http://www.marketsandmorality.com/index.php/mandm/article/view/624

Pepe, N. (2014, March 18). *Indici congruità agricoltura parte un nuovo ricorso al Tar*. La Gazzetta Del Mezzogiorno Online. https://www.lagazzettadelmezzogiorno.it/news/home/538599/indici-congruita-agricoltura-parte-un-nuovo-ricorso-al-tar.html

Pere, E., & Bartlett, W. (2019). On the Way to Europe: Economic and Social Developments in Albania. In R. Osbild & W. Bartlett (Eds.), *Western Balkan Economies in Transition: Recent Economic and Social Developments* (pp. 73–88). Springer.

Perry, G. E., Maloney, W. F., Omar, A. S., Fajnzylber, P., Mason, A. D., & Saavedra-Chanduvi, J. (2007). *Informality: Exit and Esclusion*. The International Bank for Reconstruction and Development / The World Bank.

Peticca-Harris, A., de Gama, N., & Elias, S. (2016). A Dynamic Process Model for Finding Informants and Gaining Access in Qualitative Research. *Organizational Research Methods*, *19*(3), 376–401. https://doi.org/10.1177/1094428116629218

Pfau-Effinger, B. (2009). Varieties of Undeclared Work in European Societies. *British Journal of Industrial Relations*, *47*(1), 79–99. https://doi.org/10.1111/j.1467-8543.2008.00711.x

Pfau-Effinger, B. (2017). Informal employment in the poor European periphery. *International Journal of Sociology and Social Policy*, *37*(7/8), 387–399. https://doi.org/10.1108/IJSSP-07-2016-0080

Phillips, N. (2011). Informality, global production networks and the dynamics of 'adverse incorporation'. *Global Networks*, *11*(3), 380–397. https://doi.org/10.1111/j.1471-0374.2011.00331.x

Pici, E. (2016). *Economic Upgrading in Global Value Chains Case of textile and footwear industries in Albania*. Friedrich Ebert Stiftung.

Pickles, J., & Smith, A. (2011). Delocalization and Persistence in the European Clothing Industry: The Reconfiguration of Trade and Production Networks. *Regional Studies*, *45*(2), 167–185. https://doi.org/10.1080/00343401003601933

Pickles, J., & Smith, A. (2016). *Articulations of Capital: Global Production Networks and regional transformations*. Wiley Blackwell.

Pinto, V. (2008). Sanzioni promozionali e indici di congruità nelle politiche di contrasto al lavoro irregolare. *Rivista Giuridica Del Lavoro e Della Previdenza Sociale*, *59*(1), 25–58.

Pinto, V. (2012). Gli interventi legislativi regionali di contrasto al lavoro nero e di sostegno all'emersione. *Rivista Giuridica Del Lavoro e Della Previdenza Sociale*, *63*(2), 291–312.

Polese, A., & Rodgers, P. (2011). Surviving post-socialism: The role of informal economic practices. *International Journal of Sociology and Social Policy*, *31*(11/12), 612–618. https://doi.org/10.1108/01443331111177896

Portelli, A. (1990). *The Death of Luigi Trastulli and Other Stories. Form and Meaning in Oral History*. State University of New York Press.

Portes, A. (1978). The Informal Sector and the World Economy: Notes on the Structure of Subsidised Labour. *The IDS Bulletin*, *9*(4), 35–40. https://doi.org/10.1111/j.1759-5436.1978.mp9004009.x

Portes, A., Castells, M., & Benton, L. (1989). *The Informal Economy: Studies in Advanced and Less Developed Countries*. The John Hopkins University Press.

Portes, A., & Sassen-Koob, S. (1987). Making it underground: Comparative material on the informal sector in Western market economies. *American Journal of Sociology*, 30–61.

Portes, A., & Walton, J. (1981). *Labor, class, and the international system.* Academic Press.

Prometeia. (2019). *Fighting tax evasion: Options for Italy* (Prometeia Discussion Note 11). Prometeia Associazione.

Prota, F., & Viesti, G. (2010). International delocalisation in the Italian fashion industry. *European Review of Industrial Economics and Policy, 1*.

Prota, F., & Viesti, G. (2012). *Senza Cassa: Le politiche di sviluppo del Mezzogiorno dopo l'intervento straordinario*. Il Mulino.

Pugliese, E. (2009). Indagine su 'Il lavoro nero'. In *Il Lavoro che cambia: Contributi tematici e Raccomandazioni*. CNEL. http://www.portalecnel.it/Portale/IndLavrapportiFinali.nsf/vwCapitoli?OpenView&Count=40

Pugliese, E. (2015). Introduzione. Quaranta anni di cambiamenti del lavoro in Italia. *Sociologia del Lavoro*, *138*, 9–34. https://doi.org/10.3280/SL2015-138002

Putnam, R., D. (1993). *Making Democracy Work: Civic Traditions in Modern Italy*. Princeton University Press.

Qendra Aulona. (2019). *Women in the Textile and Footwear Sector: Lots of responsibility but very few rights*. https://www.youtube.com/watch?v=Fdn1fS9zUnc&feature=youtu.be

Rainnie, A. (1985). Is Small Beautiful? Industrial Relations in Small Clothing Firms: *Sociology*, *19*(2), 213–224. https://doi.org/10.1177/0038038585019002005

Rainnie, A., Herod, A., & McGrath-Champ, S. (2013). Global production networks, labour and small firms. *Capital & Class*, *37*(2), 177–195. https://doi.org/10.1177/0309816813481337

Rainnie, A., McGrath-Champ, S., & Herod, A. (2010). Making Space for Geography in Labour Process Theory. In P. Thompson & C. Smith, *Working life: Renewing labour process analysis* (pp. 297–315). Palgrave Macmillan.

Raitano, M., & Fantozzi, R. (2015). Political cycle and reported labour incomes in Italy: Quasi-experimental evidence on tax evasion. *European*

Journal of Political Economy, *39*, 269–280. https://doi.org/10.1016/j.ejpoleco.2015.07.001

Ram, M. (1994). *Managing to Survive: Working Lives in Small Firms*. Blackwell Business.

Ram, M., Edwards, P., & Jones, T. (2007). Staying Underground: Informal Work, Small Firms, and Employment Regulation in the United Kingdom: *Work and Occupations*, *34*(3), 318–344. https://doi.org/10.1177/0730888407303223

Ram, M., Edwards, P., Jones, T., & Villares-Varela, M. (2017). From the informal economy to the meaning of informality: Developing theory on firms and their workers. *International Journal of Sociology and Social Policy*, *37*(7/8), 361–373. https://doi.org/10.1108/IJSSP-06-2016-0075

Ram, M., Edwards, P., Meardi, G., Jones, T., & Doldor, S. (2019). The Roots of Informal Responses to Regulatory Change: Non-compliant Small Firms and the National Living Wage. *British Journal of Management*, *n/a*(n/a). https://doi.org/10.1111/1467-8551.12363

Rama, E. (2016). *'The second stage of the fight against informality has begun'. Speech of Prime Minister Edi Rama at the ceremony for the presentation of the second stage of the fight against informality*. Prime Minister's Office. https://kryeministria.al/en/newsroom/nis-faza-e-dyte-e-betejes-kunder-informalitetit/

Rama, L., & Cabiri, Y. (2018). *Skills Need Albania in 2017*. United Nations Development Programme (UNDP) and Swiss Agency for Development and Cooperation (SDC).

Rangone, M., & Solari, S. (2012). From the Southern-European model to nowhere: The evolution of Italian capitalism, 1976–2011. *Journal of European Public Policy*, *19*(8), 1188–1206. https://doi.org/10.1080/13501763.2012.709014

Rassegna. (2019, April 12). *L'Ispettorato nazionale del lavoro sta naufragando*. Collettiva.it. https://www.collettiva.it/rassegna/2019/12/04/news/l_ispettorato_nazionale_del_lavoro_sta_naufragando-472602/

Regalia, I. (Ed.). (2020). *Regulating Work in Small Firms: Perspectives on the Future of Work in Globalised Economies*. Palgrave Macmillan.

Rekhviashvili, L. (2016). Counterbalancing marketization informally: Georgia's new-institutionalist reform and its discontents. *Journal of Contemporary Central and Eastern Europe*, *24*(3), 255–272. https://doi.org/10.1080/0965156X.2016.1260657

Rizzuto, G., & Tomassetti, P. (Eds.). (2019). *Il dumping contrattuale nel settore Moda: Cause, conseguenze, rimedi*. Edizioni Lavoro.

Roberts, A. (2013). Peripheral accumulation in the world economy: A cross-national analysis of the informal economy. *International Journal of Comparative Sociology*, *54*(5–6), 420–444. https://doi.org/10.1177/0020715213519458

Robinson, P. K., & Hsieh, L. (2016). Reshoring: A strategic renewal of luxury clothing supply chains. *Operations Management Research*, *9*(3), 89–101. https://doi.org/10.1007/s12063-016-0116-x

Rogaly, B. (2009). Spaces of Work and Everyday Life: Labour Geographies and the Agency of Unorganised Temporary Migrant Workers. *Geography Compass*, *3*(6), 1975–1987. https://doi.org/10.1111/j.1749-8198.2009.00290.x

Rosato, P. (2015). Il distretto delle calzature di Barletta: Origini, evoluzione e prospettive. *Meridiana*, *84*, 119–141.

Rotunno, R. (2018, February 14). Lavoro, controlli crollati del 34% in cinque anni e giù del 31% i contributi recuperati. Gli ispettori? Girano in bus. *Il Fatto Quotidiano*. https://www.ilfattoquotidiano.it/in-edicola/articoli/2018/02/14/troppi-morti-e-lavoro-nero-controlli-ridotti-al-lumicino-e-fatti-girando-con-lautobus/4158721/

Routh, S. (2011). Building Informal Workers Agenda: Imagining 'Informal Employment' in Conceptual Resolution of 'Informality'. *Global Labour Journal*, *2*(3). https://doi.org/10.15173/glj.v2i3.1106

Santoro, A. (2012). Il lavoro non regolare: Un quadro statistico e alcune valutazioni di policy. *Rivista Giuridica Del Lavoro e Della Previdenza Sociale*, *63*(2), 253–268.

Scarpelli, F. (2008). Il contrasto al lavoro irregolare, tra sanzioni e regole di responsabilità. *Rivista Giuridica Del Lavoro e Della Previdenza Sociale*, *59*(1), 59–80.

Schneider, F., & Medina, L. (2018). *Shadow Economies Around the World: What Did We Learn Over the Last 20 Years?* [IMF Working Paper]. International Monetary Fund.

Schrank, A. (2004). Ready-to-Wear Development? Foreign Investment, Technology Transfer, and Learning by Watching in the Apparel Trade. *Social Forces*, *83*(1), 123–156. JSTOR.

Schwartz, H. (2019). *Global Secular Stagnation: Keynes, Schumpeter, or Veblen?* [Paper presented at workshop at the European University Institute].

Scott, J. C. (1998). *Seeing like a state: How certain schemes to improve the human condition have failed.* Yale University Press.

Seawright, J., & Gerring, J. (2008). Case Selection Techniques in Case Study Research: A Menu of Qualitative and Quantitative Options. *Political Research Quarterly*, *61*(2), 294–308. https://doi.org/10.1177/1065912907313077

Seelkopf, L., & Starke, P. (2019). Social Policy by Other Means: Theorizing Unconventional Forms of Welfare Production. *Journal of Comparative Policy Analysis: Research and Practice*, *21*(3), 219–234. https://doi.org/10.1080/13876988.2019.1574089

SELDI. (2016). *Hidden Economy and Good Governance in Southeast Europe* [Regional Assessment Report]. Southeast Europe Leadership for Development and Integrity.

Selwyn, B. (2019). Poverty chains and global capitalism. *Competition & Change*, *23*(1), 71–97. https://doi.org/10.1177/1024529418809067

Shapiro, A. (2018). Between autonomy and control: Strategies of arbitrage in the "on-demand" economy. *New Media & Society*, *20*(8), 2954–2971. https://doi.org/10.1177/1461444817738236

Shehi, E. (2017). *Textile and garment: Final report.* Skills for Jobs (S4J).

Shehi, E. (2023). *Mapping and assessment of "Footwear & Apparel" sector in Albania.* USAID and NOA, Tirana.

Siegmann, K. A., & Schiphorst, F. (2016). Understanding the globalizing precariat: From informal sector to precarious work. *Progress in Development Studies*, *16*(2), 111–123. https://doi.org/10.1177/1464993415623118

Sil, R. (2017). The battle over flexibilization in post-communist transitions: Labor politics in Poland and the Czech Republic, 1989–2010. *Journal of Industrial Relations*, *59*(4), 420–443. https://doi.org/10.1177/0022185617705684

Simonelli, M. (2016). *La razionalizzazione dell'attività ispettiva nel jobs act: Problemi e prospettive* (Rivista Di Ateneo 'Tutela e Sicurezza Del Lavoro' 1). Università degli Studi di Milano Bicocca.

Sin, C. H. (2005). Seeking Informed Consent: Reflections on Research Practice. *Sociology*, *39*(2), 277–294. https://doi.org/10.1177/0038038505050539

Slavnic, Z. (2010). Political economy of informalization. *European Societies*, *12*(1), 3–23.

Small, M. L. (2009). 'How many cases do I need?': On science and the logic of case selection in field-based research. *Ethnography*, *10*(1), 5–38. https://doi.org/10.1177/1466138108099586

Smith, A., & Rochovská, A. (2007). Domesticating neo-liberalism: Everyday lives and the geographies of post-socialist transformations. *Geoforum*, *38*(6), 1163–1178. https://doi.org/10.1016/j.geoforum.2007.03.003

Smith, C. (2006). The double indeterminacy of labour power: Labour effort and labour mobility. *Work, Employment and Society*, *20*(2), 389–402. https://doi.org/10.1177/0950017006065109

Smith, V. (2016). Employment Uncertainty and Risk. In S. Edgell, H. Gottfried, & E. Granter, *The SAGE handbook of the sociology of work and employment* (pp. 367–384). Sage.

Snyder, K. A. (2004). Routes to the Informal Economy in New York's East Village: Crisis, Economics, and Identity. *Sociological Perspectives*, *47*(2), 215–240. https://doi.org/10.1525/sop.2004.47.2.215

SPI-CGIL. (2018). *'68 e dintorni. Lotte e protagonisti in terra di Bari*. Edizioni Radici Future.

SRM. (2015). *Un Sud che Innova—La filiera abbigliamento—Moda*. Studi e Ricerche per il Mezzogiorno.

Standing, G. (1989). The 'British Experiment': Structural Adjustment or Accelerated Decline? In A. Portes, M. Castells, & L. Benton, *The Informal Economy: Studies in Advanced and Less Developed Countries* (pp. 279–296). The John Hopkins University Press.

Stark, D. (1986). Rethinking internal labor markets: New insights from a comparative perspective. *American Sociological Review*, 492–504.

Stark, D. (1996). Recombinant property in East European capitalism. *American Journal of Sociology*, 993–1027.

Steinmo, S. (Ed.). (2018). *The Leap of Faith: The Fiscal Foundations of Successful Government in Europe and America* (First edition). Oxford University Press.

Stenning, A., Smith, A., Rochovská, A., & Świątek, D. (2011). *Domesticating Neo-Liberalism: Spaces of Economic Practice and Social Reproduction in Post-Socialist Cities*. John Wiley & Sons.

Szelenyi, I. (1988). *Socialist entrepreneurs: Embourgeoisement in rural Hungary*. http://agris.fao.org/agris-search/search.do?recordID=US8922109

Tagliacozzo, S., Pisacane, L., & Kilkey, M. (2021). The interplay between structural and systemic vulnerability during the COVID-19 pandemic:

Migrant agricultural workers in informal settlements in Southern Italy. *Journal of Ethnic and Migration Studies*, *47*(9), 1903–1921. https://doi.org/10.1080/1369183X.2020.1857230

Taplin, I. M. (1996). Rethinking Flexibility: The Case of the Apparel Industry. *Review of Social Economy*, *54*(2), 191–220. https://doi.org/10.1080/00346769600000036

Taylor, P. (2010). The Globalization of Service Work: Analysing the Transnational Call Centre Value Chain. In P. Thompson & C. Smith, *Working life: Renewing labour process analysis* (pp. 244–268). Palgrave Macmillan.

Taylor, P., Newsome, K., Bair, J., & Rainnie, A. (2015). Putting Labour in its Place: Labour Process Analysis and Global Value Chains. In K. Newsome, P. Taylor, J. Bair, & A. Rainnie, *Putting labour in its place: Labour process analysis and global value chains* (pp. 1–28). Palgrave.

Theron, J. (2010). Informalization from Above, Informalization from Below: The Options for Organization. *African Studies Quarterly*, *11*(2 & 3), 87–105.

Thompson, P. (1990). Crawling from the wreckage: The labour process and the politics of production. In D. Knights & H. Willmott, *Labour Process Theory* (pp. 95–124). Palgrave Macmillan UK.

Thompson, P., & Smith, C. (2000). Follow the Redbrick Road. *International Studies of Management & Organization*, *30*(4), 40–67. https://doi.org/10.1080/00208825.2000.11656799

Thompson, P., & Smith, C. (2009). Labour Power and Labour Process: Contesting the Marginality of the Sociology of Work. *Sociology*, *43*(5), 913–930. https://doi.org/10.1177/0038038509340728

Thompson, P., & Vincent, S. (2010). Labour Process Theory and Critical Realism. In P. Thompson & C. Smith, *Working life: Renewing labour process analysis* (pp. 47–69). Palgrave Macmillan.

Tilly, C., Agarwala, R., Mosoetsa, S., Ngai, P., Salas, C., & Sheikh, H. (2013). *Final Report: Informal Worker Organizing as a Strategy for Improving Subcontracted Work in the Textile and Apparel Industries of Brazil, South Africa, India and China.* Institute for research on labor and employment.

Toffanin, T. (2016). *Fabbriche invisibili: Sorie di donne, lavoranti a domicilio*. Ombre Corte.

Tokatli, N. (2008). Global sourcing: Insights from the global clothing industry—the case of Zara, a fast fashion retailer. *Journal of Economic Geography*, *8*(1), 21–38. https://doi.org/10.1093/jeg/lbm035

Tokatli, N. (2013). Toward a better understanding of the apparel industry: A critique of the upgrading literature. *Journal of Economic Geography*, *13*(6), 993–1011. https://doi.org/10.1093/jeg/lbs043

Tokatli, N., & Kızılgün, Ö. (2009). From Manufacturing Garments for Ready-to-Wear to Designing Collections for Fast Fashion: Evidence from Turkey. *Environment and Planning A: Economy and Space*, *41*(1), 146–162. https://doi.org/10.1068/a4081

Trebicka, B. (2014). The size of Underground Economy in Albania. *Acedemic Journal of Interdisciplinary Studies*, *3*(4), 503–508. https://doi.org/10.5901/ajis.2014.v3n4p503

Trigilia, C. (1992). *Sviluppo senza Autonomia: Effetti perversi delle politiche nel Mezzogiorno*. Il Mulino.

Trigilia, C. (2011). Perché non si è sciolto il nodo del Mezzogiorno? Un problema di sociologia economica. *Stato e Mercato*, *91*(1), 41–75.

Tsing, A. (2009). Supply Chains and the Human Condition. *Rethinking Marxism*, *21*(2), 148–176. https://doi.org/10.1080/08935690902743088

Urbact. (2008, November 20). *Congratulations to the European Regional Champions Awards 2008 winners*. URBACT - Driving Change for Better Lives - European Regional Development Fund. https://urbact.eu/congratulations-european-regional-champions-awards-2008-winners

van der Linden, M., & Breman, J. (2020). The Return of Merchant Capital | Global Labour Journal. *Global Labour Journal*, *11*(2), 178–182.

Van Nierop, P., Schönenberg, L., Terziev, P., Jakubowska, K., Rose, N., Stefanov, R., & Mineva, D. (2021). *Counteracting undeclared work and labour exploitation of third-country national workers*. European Platform Tackling Undeclared Work.

Vanek, J., Chen, M. A., Carré, F., Heintz, J., & Hussmans, R. (2014). *Statistics on the Informal Economy: Definitions, Regional Estimates & Challenges* (Working Paper (Statistics) No. 2). WIEGO. http://www.wiego.org/publications/statistics-informal-economy-definitions-regional-estimates-challenges

Varga, M. (2014). *Worker protests in post-communist Romania and Ukraine: Striking with tied hands*. Manchester University Press.

Verdery, K., & Burawoy, M. (1999). *Uncertain transition: Ethnographies of change in the postsocialist world*. Rowman & Littlefield.

Vesan, P., & Ronchi, S. (2019). The Puzzle of Expansionary Welfare Reforms under Harsh Austerity: Explaining the Italian Case. *South European Society and Politics*, *24*(3), 371–395. https://doi.org/10.1080/13608746.2019.1644811

Viesti, G. (1998). Sommerso ed emersione nell'industria dell'abbigliamento e delle calzature nel Mezzogiorno. *Meridiana*, *33*, 37–81.

Viesti, G. (2000a). L'abbigliamento nella Puglia Centrale. In G. Viesti (Ed.), *Mezzogiorno dei distretti* (pp. 59–96). Meridiana Libri.

Viesti, G. (2000b). Perché le regioni crescono? Sviluppo locale e distretti industriali nel Mezzogiorno. *Stato e Mercato*, *2/2000*, 239–270. https://doi.org/10.1425/448

Viesti, G. (2007). Dinamiche e trasformazioni strutturali nei sistemi produttivi del Mezzogiorno, 2001-2006: Dai beni di consumo all'alta tecnologia. In *Le sfide del cambiamento: I sistemi produttivi nell'Italia e nel Mezzogiorno d'oggi* (Meridiana Libri, pp. 87–120). Donzelli editore.

Viesti, G., & Luongo, P. (2014). Distretti industriali e imprese nel Mezzogiorno. In M. Salvati & L. Sciolla (Eds.), *L'Italia e le sue regioni (1945-2011): Vol. II*. Treccani.

Vosko, L. F., Grundy, J., Tucker, E., Thomas, M. P., Noack, A. M., Casey, R., Gellatly, M., & Mussell, J. (2017). The compliance model of employment standards enforcement: An evidence-based assessment of its efficacy in instances of wage theft. *Industrial Relations Journal*, *48*(3), 256–273. https://doi.org/10.1111/irj.12178

Vullnetari, J. (2012). Women and Migration in Albania: A View from the Village. *International Migration*, *50*(5), 169–188. https://doi.org/10.1111/j.1468-2435.2009.00569.x

Webb, J. W., Bruton, G. D., Tihanyi, L., & Ireland, R. D. (2013). Research on entrepreneurship in the informal economy: Framing a research agenda. *Journal of Business Venturing*, *28*(5), 598–614. https://doi.org/10.1016/j.jbusvent.2012.05.003

Webb, J. W., & Ireland, R. D. (2015). Laying the Foundation for a Theory of Informal Adjustments. In P. C. Godfrey, *Management, Society, and the Informal Economy* (pp. 60–76). Taylor & Francis Group. https://doi.org/10.4324/9781315757445-7

Webb, J. W., Ireland, R. D., & Ketchen, D. J. (2014). Toward a Greater Understanding of Entrepreneurship and Strategy in the Informal Economy. *Strategic Entrepreneurship Journal*, *8*(1), 1–15. https://doi.org/10.1002/sej.1176

Webb, J. W., Tihanyi, L., Ireland, R. D., & Sirmon, D. G. (2009). You Say Illegal, I Say Legitimate: Entrepreneurship in the Informal Economy. *Academy of Management Review*, *34*(3), 492–510. https://doi.org/10.5465/amr.2009.40632826

Weil, D. (2014). *The fissured workplace: Why work became so bad for so many and what can be done to improve it.* Harvard University Press.

Weiss, L. (1984). The Italian state and small business. *European Journal of Sociology / Archives Européennes de Sociologie / Europäisches Archiv Für Soziologie*, *25*(2), 214–241. JSTOR.

Weiss, L. (1987). Explaining the Underground Economy: State and Social Structure. *The British Journal of Sociology*, *38*(2), 216–234. https://doi.org/10.2307/590533

Werner, M. (2016). *Global Displacements: The Making of Uneven Development in the Caribbean.* Wiley.

White, R., & Williams, C. (2016). Beyond capitalocentricism: Are non-capitalist work practices 'alternatives'? *Area*, 48(3), 325–331. https://doi.org/10.1111/area.12264

Williams, C. (2010). The changing conceptualizations of informal work in developed economies. In E. Marcelli, C. Williams, & P. Joassart (eds), *Informal work in developed nations* (pp. 11–33). Routledge.

Williams, C. (2014). *The informal economy and poverty: Evidence and policy review*. Joseph Rowntree Foundation.

Williams, C. (2015). Explaining Cross-National Variations in the Informalisation of Employment. *European Societies*, *17*(4), 492–512. https://doi.org/10.1080/14616696.2015.1051073

Williams, C. (2017). Tackling employment in the informal economy: A critical evaluation of the neoliberal policy approach. *Economic and Industrial Democracy*, *38*(1), 145–169. https://doi.org/10.1177/0143831X14557961

Williams, C. (2020). *Holistic approach to tackling undeclared work and developing national strategies*. European Platform tackling undeclared work.

Williams, C., Bejakovic, P., Mikulic, D., Franic, J., Kedir, A., & Horodnic, I. A. (2017). *An evaluation of the scale of undeclared work in the European Union and is structural determinants: Estimates using the Labour Input Method.* European Commission.

Williams, C., & Franic, J. (2017). Tackling the illegitimate under-reporting of salaries in Southeast Europe: Some lessons from a 2015 survey in

Bulgaria, Croatia and FYR Macedonia. *Eastern Journal of European Studies*, *8*(1), 5–28.

Williams, C., Franic, J., & Dzhekova, R. (2015). Explaining the Undeclared Economy in Bulgaria: An Institutional Asymmetry Perspective. *South East European Journal of Economics and Business*, *9*(2), 33–45. https://doi.org/10.2478/jeb-2014-0008

Williams, C., Gurtoo, A., & Nadin, S. (2012). Evaluating Competing Theorisations of Informal Entrepreneurship: A Study of India's Street Hawkers. *Academy of Management Proceedings*, *2012*(1), 10093. https://doi.org/10.5465/AMBPP.2012.10093abstract

Williams, C., & Horodnic, I. A. (2015). Explaining the Prevalence of Illegitimate Wage Practices in Southern Europe: An Institutional Analysis. *South European Society and Politics*, *20*(2), 203–221. https://doi.org/10.1080/13608746.2015.1013518

Williams, C., & Horodnic, I. A. (2017). Evaluating the Illegal Employer Practice of Under-Reporting Employees' Salaries. *British Journal of Industrial Relations*, *55*(1), 83–111. https://doi.org/10.1111/bjir.12179

Williams, C., & Horodnic, I. A. (2019). *Institutional Asymmetry and the Acceptability of Undeclared Work* (Synthesis Report 01–2019; SHADOWS Working Paper). Sheffield University.

Williams, C., Horodnic, I. A., & Windebank, J. (2017). Evaluating the internal dualism of the informal sector: Evidence from the European Union. *Journal of Economic Studies*, *44*(4), 605–616. https://doi.org/10.1108/JES-07-2016-0144

Williams, C., & Marcelli, E. (2010). Conclusions. In E. Marcelli, C. Williams, & P. Joassart (eds.), *Informal work in developed nations* (pp. 220–232). Routledge.

Williams, C., & Martinez, A. (2016). Tackling the informal economy: A critical evaluation of the neo-liberal policy deregulatory perspective. In S. Routh & V. Borghi, *Workers and the global informal economy: Interdisciplinary perspectives*. Routledge.

Williams, C., & Onoshchenko, O. (2015). Evaluating the Validity of the Contrasting Theoretical Perspectives towards the Informal Economy in Ukraine. In *Informal Economies in Post-Socialist Spaces* (pp. 25–50). Springer. http://link.springer.com/chapter/10.1057/9781137483072_2

Williams, C., & Renooy, P. (2013). *Tackling undeclared work in 27 European Union Member States and Norway: Approaches and measures since 2008*. Eurofound.

Williams, C., & Round, J. (2008). Retheorizing the Nature of Informal Employment: Some Lessons from Ukraine. *International Sociology*, *23*(3), 367–388. https://doi.org/10.1177/0268580908088896

Williams, C., & Shahid, M. S. (2016). Informal entrepreneurship and institutional theory: Explaining the varying degrees of (in)formalization of entrepreneurs in Pakistan. *Entrepreneurship & Regional Development*, *28*(1–2), 1–25. https://doi.org/10.1080/08985626.2014.963889

Williams, C., & Windebank, J. (1998). *Informal employment in the advanced economies: Implications for work and welfare*. Routledge.

Wills, J. (2008). Subcontracted Employment and its Challenge to Labor. *Labor Studies Journal*, *34*(4), 441–460. https://doi.org/10.1177/0160449X08324740

Wood, A. (2020). *Despotism on Demand: How Power Operates in the Flexible Workplace*. Cornell University Press.

Woolfson, C. (2007). Pushing the envelope: The 'informalization' of labour in post-communist new EU member states. *Work, Employment and Society*, *21*(3), 551–564. https://doi.org/DOI: 10.1177/0950017007080016

World Bank. (2009). *Albania: Building Competitiveness in Albania Vloume II. Sector Case Studies: Apparel and Footwear, Tourism, Mining* (Report No. 47866-AL). World Bank Group.

World Bank. (2015). *Next Generation Albania: A Systematic Country Diagnostic*. World Bank Group.

World Bank. (2019). *Enterprise Surveys: Albania 2019* [Enterprise Analysis Unit]. IBRD/The World Bank.

Yin, R. (2003). *Case study research: Design and methods*. Sage.

Ymeri, S., Hoxha, A., Agolli, M., & Jorgoni, E. (2010). *Rapid assessment of the impact of the global economic crisis on the apparel and footwear industry in Albania*. Institute of Contemporary Studies (ISB).

Zahariadis, Y. (2007). *The Effects of the Albania-EU Stabilization and Association Agreement: Economic Impact and Social Implications* (ESAU Working Paper 17). Economic and Statistics Analysis Unit - Overseas Development Institute (ODI).

Zoppoli, L. (2008). Unione europea e lavoro sommerso: Nuove attenzioni e vecchie contraddizioni. *Rivista Giuridica Del Lavoro e Della Previdenza Sociale*, *59*(1), 81–106.

MIMESIS GROUP
www.mimesis-group.com

MIMESIS INTERNATIONAL
www.mimesisinternational.com
info@mimesisinternational.com

MIMESIS EDIZIONI
www.mimesisedizioni.it
mimesis@mimesisedizioni.it

ÉDITIONS MIMÉSIS
www.editionsmimesis.fr
info@editionsmimesis.fr

MIMESIS COMMUNICATION
www.mim-c.net

MIMESIS EU
www.mim-eu.com

Printed by
Rotomail S.p.A.
in October 2024

www.ingramcontent.com/pod-product-compliance
Lightning Source LLC
LaVergne TN
LVHW091258150826
845673LV00006B/1465

9788869774874